Literary Tourism and Nineteenth-Century Culture

Also by Nicola J. Watson

At the Limits of Romanticism: Essays in Cultural, Materialist, and Feminist Criticism (co-edited with Mary Favret)

England's Elizabeth: an Afterlife in Fame and Fantasy (co-authored with Michael Dobson)

Revolution and the Form of the British Novel, 1790–1825: Intercepted Letters, Interrupted Seductions

The Literary Tourist: Readers and Places in Romantic and Victorian Britain

Literary Tourism and Nineteenth-Century Culture

Edited by
Nicola J. Watson

First published 2009 by
PALGRAVE MACMILLAN

Palgrave Macmillan in the UK is an imprint of Macmillan Publishers Limited, registered in England, company number 785998, of Houndmills, Basingstoke, Hampshire RG21 6XS.

Palgrave Macmillan in the US is a division of St Martin's Press LLC, 175 Fifth Avenue, New York, NY 10010.

Palgrave Macmillan is the global academic imprint of the above companies and has companies and representatives throughout the world.

Palgrave® and Macmillan® are registered trademarks in the United States, the United Kingdom, Europe and other countries.

ISBN-13: 978-0-230-22281-6 hardback
ISBN-10: 0-230-22281-1 hardback

This book is printed on paper suitable for recycling and made from fully managed and sustained forest sources. Logging, pulping and manufacturing processes are expected to conform to the environmental regulations of the country of origin.

A catalogue record for this book is available from the British Library.

A catalog record for this book is available from the Library of Congress.

10 9 8 7 6 5 4 3 2 1
18 17 16 15 14 13 12 11 10 09

Printed and bound in Great Britain by
CPI Antony Rowe, Chippenham and Eastbourne

Contents

Notes on the Contributors

Polly Atkin is currently researching her doctoral thesis 'A Place Re-Imagined: The Literary, Cultural and Spatial Construction of Dove Cottage, Grasmere' at Lancaster University in collaboration with The Wordsworth Trust under the AHRC's Landscape and Environment Scheme. Her first degree was from Queen Mary, University of London (English Literature, First Class BA hons), followed by a Master's in Creative Writing at Royal Holloway.

Alison Booth is Professor of English at the University of Virginia, and the author of *Greatness Engendered: George Eliot and Virginia Woolf* (Cornell University Press, 1992) and *How to Make It as a Woman: Collective Biographical History from Victoria to the Present* (University of Chicago Press, 2004; winner of the Barbara Penny Kanner prize). Editor of an essay collection, *Famous Last Words: Changes in Gender and Narrative Closure* (University Press of Virginia, 1993) and of the forth-coming Longman Cultural Edition of *Wuthering Heights*, she is also the co-editor, with Paul Hunter and Kelly Mays, of the *Norton Introduction to Literature*. With longstanding interests in the constructions of author-ship, literary history, gender, and narrative – in particular, collective biography, her research and teaching have spanned nineteenth- and twentieth-century British and American literature. Her articles have appeared in *Victorian Studies, Journal of Victorian Culture, Kenyon Review, American Literary History,* and elsewhere. Portions of her current book-length study, 'Homes and Haunts: Transatlantic Author Country,' are published or forthcoming in *The Henry James Review, Nineteenth-Century Contexts,* and *Romanticism and Victorianism on the Net.* She has served as president of the Society for the Study of Narrative Literature (2005), as co-organiser of the 3rd Annual North American Victorian Studies Association Conference (2005), and as judge of both Perkins (Narrative) and Lowell (MLA) book prizes.

Shirley Foster is (semi-retired) Reader in English and American Literature at the University of Sheffield. Her research interests are in Victorian women's fiction, especially Elizabeth Gaskell, and travel writing, both British and American. She has published widely in both areas, including a literary biography of Gaskell, a co-edited (with Sara Mills) anthology of women's travel writing, and articles on nineteenth-century Americans in Britain and Europe. She has also edited two of Gaskell's novels, *Sylvia's Lovers* for Penguin, and *Mary Barton* for World's Classics. She is just starting new research on gardens and literature, a project undertaken with a colleague at the University of Wollongong, Australia.

Sara Haslam is Lecturer in Literature at the Open University. She is the author of *Fragmenting Modernism: Ford Madox Ford, The Novel and the Great War* (2002) and editor of Ford's *England and the English* (2003), as well as of *Ford Madox Ford and the City* (2005), the fourth volume of International Ford Madox Ford Studies. She has published essays on Ford, James, modernism, Chekhov and George Eliot, most recently writing on 'The Good Soldier' in the *Blackwell Companion to Modernist Literature and Culture* (2006), and has produced a CD-ROM, *The Poetry of Thomas Hardy* (2001). Current projects include a book, provisionally entitled '*Victims of Time and Train': from Victorian Invention to Modernist Novel*.

Erin Hazard received her PhD in art history from the University of Chicago in 2007, and is currently teaching in the University of Chicago's Master of Arts Program in the Humanities. Her dissertation, '"Realized Day-dreams": Excursions to Authors' Homes' examines nineteenth-century British and American authors' homes both as architecture and as exhibition sites between 1800 and 1950. An article of the same title is forthcoming in *Nineteenth Century Studies*. Her awards and honours include a Henry Luce/American Council of Learned Societies Dissertation Fellowship in American Art.

Harald Hendrix is Professor of Italian Studies and heads the programme in Renaissance Studies at the University of Utrecht. Within the Utrecht Research Institute for History and Culture he leads the group on Textual Culture. He has published widely on the European reception of Italian Renaissance and Baroque authors (*Traiano Boccalini fra erudizione e polemica;* Olschki, 1995) and on the early modern aesthetics of the non-beautiful. He is the editor of *Writers' Houses and the Making of Memory* (Routledge, 2007) and has co-edited six volumes in the series, Utrecht Renaissance Studies (Amsterdam UP): *De Vrouw in de Renaissance* (1994), *Kunstenaars en opdrachtgevers* (1996), *Oud en lelijk. Ouderdom in de cultuur van de Renaissance* (1996), *Vreemd volk. Beeldvorming over buitenlanders in de vroegmoderne tijd* (1998), *De grenzen van het lichaam. Innerlijk en uiterlijk in de Renaissance* (1999), *Beschaafde burgers. Burgerlijkheid in de vroegmoderne tijd* (2001). He is currently preparing a book on the cultural history of writers' houses in Italy, from Petrarch to the present day.

Gail Marshall is Reader in Nineteenth-century Literature at Oxford Brookes University. She is the author of *Actresses on the Victorian Stage* (Cambridge University Press, 1998) and books on Victorian fiction, as well as articles on subjects including Elizabeth Barrett Browning, Helen Faucit, Ellen Terry, and Victorian sculpture. She has edited volumes on George Eliot, Victorian Shakespeare and is editor of the *Cambridge Companion to the Fin de Siècle* (2007). She is in the process of finishing a monograph on Shakespeare and Victorian Women.

Samantha Matthews is Lecturer in Victorian literature at the University of Sheffield, and has taught at Goldsmiths College and University College, London. She is the author of *Poetical Remains: Poets' Graves, Bodies, and Books in the Nineteenth Century* (Oxford University Press, 2004), and has wide-ranging interests in the nineteenth century, particularly in material culture, the cemetery, literary London, afterlife and reception theory, book history, the culture of albums and autographs, and reading practices.

Julian North is Lecturer in the English Department at the University of Leicester. Her research interests are in Romantic and early-Victorian literature. She is the editor of volume 11 and a co-editor of volume 20 of *The Works of Thomas De Quincey* (Pickering and Chatto, 2000–2003). She has published on De Quincey, nineteenth-century biography and autobiography, Jane Austen adaptations and Victorian opium literature, amongst other subjects. She is currently working on a monograph, 'The Domestication of Genius: Biography and the Romantic Poet', which looks at literary biography as a genre in relation to *Lives* of Byron, Shelley, Wordsworth, Coleridge and Hemans published in the 1820s and 1830s.

Pamela Corpron Parker is Professor of English and Women's Studies and Chair of the Department of English at Whitworth University, Spokane, Washington. President and co-founder of the British Women Writers Association, her articles have appeared in *Victorian Literature and Culture, Victorian Newsletter, Nineteenth-Century Contexts, The Gaskell Society Journal*, and several essay collections focusing on women's literary history. She is currently completing a book manuscript, provisionally entitled *Literary Tourism and the Victorian Woman of Letters*.

Diane Roberts, Professor at the University of Florida, is author of *Dream State* (Simon and Schuster, 2004), a book about Florida, as well as *The Myth of Aunt Jemima: Representations of Race and Region* (Routledge, 1994), *Faulkner and Southern Womanhood* (University of Georgia, 1993), and numerous articles and book chapters. As well as being a scholar, she is a broadcaster and critic, and writes for the *Times*, the *Guardian*, the *Washington Post* and the *New York Times*. In addition, she works as a commentator for the BBC and National Public Radio in America.

Barbara Schaff (University of Munich) teaches British literature and cultural studies and has held visiting professorships at the Universities of Munich, Tübingen, Vienna, and Bochum. Her teaching and research interests include gender studies, authorship, and travel writing. Her publications include *Venetian Blinds, Venetian Views: English Fantasies of Venice* (co-edited with Manfred Pfister, Rodopi, 1999), *Autorschaft um 1800* (with Ina Schabert), *Bi-Textualität* (with Annegret Heitmann et al.) She is presently a Royal Society of Edinburgh Caledonian Research Fellow at the Centre for the History of the Book, where she is working on the history and cultural significance of John Murray's Handbooks to the Continent. She is also herself a writer of guide books for tourists.

Margaret D. Stetz is the Mae and Robert Carter Professor of Women's Studies and Professor of Humanities at the University of Delaware. Her books include *Facing the Late Victorians* (2007), *Gender and the London Theatre, 1880–1920* (2004), and *British Women's Comic Fiction, 1890–1990: Not Drowning, But Laughing* (2001); and, with Mark Samuels Lasner, *The Yellow Book: A Centenary Exhibition* (1994), *England in the 1890s: Literary Publishing at the Bodley Head* (1990), and *England in the 1880s: Old Guard and Avant-Garde* (1989), as well as *Michael Field and Their World*, co-edited with Cheryl A. Wilson, and *Legacies of the Comfort Women of WWII* (2001), co-edited with Bonnie B.C. Oh. She has published more than a hundred essays and reviews related to nineteenth through twenty-first century literary and cultural history and has curated or co-curated seven major exhibitions on Victorian publishing history and art. Her current book project is *Oscar Wilde, New Women, the Bodley Head and Beyond*.

Lindy Stiebel is Professor of English Studies, University of KwaZulu-Natal, South Africa. She has published books on Africa as imagined space in Rider Haggard's fiction (*Imagining Africa: Landscape in H. Rider Haggard's African Romances* Greenwood, CT, 2001), on the nineteenth-century explorer and artist Thomas Baines (*Thomas Baines and the 'Great Map': Route of the Gold Fields Exploration Company's Expedition 1869–1872* CD ROM Campbell Collections, Durban 2001), and most recently on the work of exiled South African writer Lewis Nkosi (*Still Beating the Drum: Critical Perspectives on Lewis Nkosi*, Rodopi and Wits University

Press, 2005/6). She has been project leader of the KZN Literary Tourism research group for the past five years and has published a number of articles on this subject. She is on the editorial board of *Transformation*.

Julia Thomas is Senior Lecturer at the Centre for Editorial and Intertextual Research, Cardiff University. She is the author of *Victorian Narrative Painting* (Tate, 2000) and *Pictorial Victorians: The Inscription of Values in Word and Image* (Ohio University Press, 2004), and director of the AHRC-funded *Database of Mid-Victorian Wood-Engraved Illustration* (www.dmvi.cardiff.ac.uk). She is currently writing a monograph on the Victorians and the cult of Shakespeare's birthplace.

Nicola J. Watson is currently Senior Lecturer in Literature at the Open University, having held posts at Oxford, Harvard, Northwestern and Indiana Universities. Broadly based as a specialist in the early nineteenth century, her publications include *Revolution and the Form of the British Novel 1790–1825* (Oxford University Press, 1994), *At the Limits of Romanticism* (Indiana University Press, 1994, co-edited with Mary Favret), an edition of Sir Walter Scott's *The Antiquary* for World's Classics (2002), *England's Elizabeth: An Afterlife in Fame and Fantasy* (Oxford University Press, 2002 co-authored with Michael Dobson), and most recently *The Literary Tourist: Readers and Places in Romantic and Victorian Britain* (Palgrave 2006), along with many essays, articles, entries, and reviews for academic collections and journals. She is Director of the Research Group in Travel Writing and Literary Geography at the Open University. Her interests and activities extend to radio and broadsheet journalism. Her current research project is entitled *Transatlantic Pilgrims,* a book-length study of the investment of American culture in British literary geography.

Paul Westover received his PhD from Indiana University in 2008, specialising in British Romantic literature, and is now Assistant Professor of English at Brigham Young University, Utah. The working title of his book project is *Traveling to Meet the Dead: Literary Tourism and Necro-Romanticism*, a study of literary tourism and its relation to reading practices and the nineteenth-century cult of the dead.

Karyn Wilson-Costa lives and teaches near Marseilles, France. She is currently finishing her PhD on the French reception of Robert Burns and his poetry and songs.

Introduction

Nicola J. Watson

Should you be travelling in the far north of Vermont, USA, in the vicinity of the town of Brattleboro, you might chance upon a road called Kipling Road. If you were of an inquisitive disposition you might even follow it, and if you did, you'd come upon a grey, shingled house set into the hill, called Naulakha. Although, this being Vermont, you might well assume that this was a name derived from native American language, you would be wrong, because it is derived from a different Indian tongue entirely: it is the Hindi word for 'priceless jewel'. This, in fact, is the house that the newly married Rudyard Kipling designed, built and inhabited from 1893 until 1896, and where he wrote both of the *Jungle Books*, parts of the *Just So Stories*, and parts of *Kim*. It houses a miscellany of Kipling furniture and possessions – his golf clubs, an Indian teakwood sideboard, a couple of plaster statuettes of Bagheera and Grey Brother, and the desk at which he wrote the *Jungle Books*. The nomination which aimed to put Naulakha on the USA's National Register of Historic Places, strikingly, argued not for its literary but for its architectural significance, describing this house – part American vernacular architecture, part allegedly inspired by the Kashmiri boathouse and the Indian bungalow – as 'a dramatic cross-cultural expression, spanning two continents stylistically.'[1] This formulation efficiently elides Britain as the third term implied by a building mainly notable as the place where an Englishman wrote about one former British colony in the hinterlands of another. As it happens, the notion that the *Jungle Books*, which are generally taken to be a meditation upon the Raj from the perspective of the Raj, are in any way 'about' or can be usefully related to this setting in the midst of what would normally be thought of as Robert Frost country is thoroughly incongruous; Naulakha, despite its evident importance in Kipling's early life and career, does

1

not 'mean' enough of anything currently culturally useful either to the Americans or to the British to make promotion to monument status seem plausible. By contrast, Kipling's last house, Bateman's in Sussex, which prominently displays the original illustrations to the *Jungle Books* by Kipling's father and Kipling's desk garnished with all sorts of Indian knick-knacks, seems altogether more appropriate as a place in which to consider the cross-cultural exchange between Britain and India which this writer's works dramatise. It is not surprising, therefore, that, unlike Bateman's (which is now in the care of the National Trust), Naulakha is not open to the public as a literary museum, although, recently restored at lavish expense by the (British) Landmark Trust, it is now available for private rentals by those in search of a recherché Anglo-Indian twist on their New England holidays.

Naulakha, then, is an excellent instance of a bona fide writer's house that does not work properly as a Writer's House: even though it is in reality the place where Kipling wrote his most Kiplingesque works, it apparently does not offer the same imaginary access to the essence of Kipling that may be obtained from a visit to Bateman's. Clearly, the business of literary tourism – the interconnected practices of visiting and marking sites associated with writers and their work – is by no means as uncomplicated as it is often casually taken to be. This volume of essays accordingly sets out to investigate and analyse the entire phenomenon, making a crucial contribution to the study of this topic by bringing into print papers presented at the ground-breaking conference 'Literary Tourism and Nineteenth-Century Culture', held in London at the Institute for English Studies in June 2007. It is intended to provide an introduction for advanced students and scholars to an emergent and vibrant field within literary and cultural studies, whilst also offering a rich collection, centred upon nineteenth-century culture, of some of the most up-to-date research within it.

This volume's focus upon the nineteenth century is to some extent inevitable, since it was this period which first saw the practice of visiting places associated with Anglophone authors in order to savour book, place, and their interrelations achieve wide enough currency to attain commercial significance. It witnessed the rise of Shakespeare's Stratford in the aftermath of David Garrick's Jubilee of 1769, the development of pilgrimage to Robert Burns' birthplace in Alloway from as early as 1799, the building and display of Sir Walter Scott's Abbotsford from 1811 onwards, and the enshrinement of the Brontë sisters' home at Haworth by the end of the century, to pick out only four instances from amongst the many others that developed over the period. As this would suggest, nineteenth-century British travellers developed to an unprecedented extent a taste for visiting a range of places of purely literary interest, associated with dead authors and their writings. Aristocrats and would-be aristocrats on the Grand Tour had long exhibited a sometimes dilettante interest in continental European sites such as Francesco Petrarch's house, and by the end of the eighteenth century some were also seeking out Jean-Jacques Rousseau's old haunts around Lake Geneva. But in the nineteenth century this itinerary expanded both socially and geographically, as both highbrow and middlebrow readers embarked on pilgrimages to literary destinations within Britain and, rather later in the century, in America. Readers were seized en masse by a newly powerful desire to visit the graves, the birthplaces, and the carefully preserved homes of dead poets and men and women of letters; to contemplate the sites that writers had previously visited and written in or about; and eventually to traverse whole imaginary literary territories, such as 'Dickens' London' or 'Hardy's Wessex'. At the same time, entirely new genres sprang up to cater for and to refine this impulse, ranging through the personal travelogue, the topographical essay, the literary guidebook as invented by John Murray, the book of text-themed topographical engravings, the literary map, and the book of practical literary walking and cycling itineraries. This clutter of inter-related modes would eventually mature into the twinned forms of literary atlas and gazette, still flourishing in the form of *The Oxford Literary Guide to the British Isles,* revised and relaunched for an eager readership as recently as 2008. Alongside these new types of publication, new systems of memorialisation developed, ranging from the grand and occasional, such as public celebrations of authors' birthdays, to the official and topographical, such as the setting up of memorials and plaques, down to more intimate and individualised tourist rites of following in the footsteps of writers or their characters, reading (and composing) on significant spots, purloining relics, purchasing souvenirs, pressing flowers for albums, and leaving signatures, whether as graffiti or, more politely, in a visitors' book. This taste, these genres, these practices are still very much alive in today's tourists, and still largely dictate the ways in which nineteenth-century literary culture is being consumed on the ground by moderns.

Yet despite the scope, scale and rapid development of this phenomenon over the nineteenth, twentieth and twenty-first centuries, it has only recently begun to attract critical attention in and of itself. Indeed, it could be said that it has only recently become visible at all to the academy. This invisibility of literary tourism has perhaps been the result of its troubling interrogation of the boundaries between those disciplines and sub-disciplines between which it has to date found itself situated: literary and cultural studies (especially work on travel-writing and the history of the reading experience), history and heritage studies, cultural geography, and tourism studies.

From the point of view of scholars of literature, for example, literary tourism has remained until very recently a blind spot, despite a small but distinguished amount of high theory with an explicit and implicit bearing on tourism and modernity, most notably Walter Benjamin's seminal essay 'The work of art in the age of mechanical reproduction' (1936), Roland Barthes' *Mythologies* (1972), Jean Baudrillard's *Simulations* (1983), Guy Debord's *Society of the Spectacle* (1983), and Pierre Bourdieu's *Distinction* (1984). Researchers with interests in the history of travel, travel-writing, and imaginary national geography have sometimes remarked on the leverage of the literary upon the tourist imagination: notable in this respect is Ian Ousby's pioneering discussion of the making of the Lake District in *The Englishman's England* (1990), and James Buzard's influential discussion of the impact of Byron's poetry via Murray's guidebooks on the nineteenth-century tourist's experience of the Grand Tour in his study *The Beaten Track* (1993). Individual scholars have occasionally touched upon literary pilgrimage to sites associated with live and dead authors as an aspect of reception: in 1988 Graham Holderness revivified a tradition of discussing the production of Stratford as a tourist destination which goes back to Ivor Brown and George Fearon's *Amazing Monument: A Short History of the Shakespeare Industry* (1939), Stephen Bann considered the formation of Abbotsford in relation to romantic historiography in *The Clothing of Clio* (1984), Stephen Gill's *Wordsworth and the Victorians* (1998) suggestively if briefly discussed the practice of visiting Wordsworthian homes and haunts both in the poet's lifetime and after his death, and there has been some scattered publication on early visitors to the site of Milton's birthplace in Bread Street, on the first Brontë readers to have travelled to Haworth, and on Hardy's participation in the development of 'Wessex' as a tourist destination.[2] More pragmatically, committees of literary societies from the Shakespeare Birthplace Trust onwards have regularly concerned themselves with the problems of the preservation and display of literary sites.

But, generally, writers on place and literature have usually been more interested in the effect of place upon an individual author's *oeuvre* (as in Diana Fuss's *The Sense of an Interior: Four Writers and the Rooms that Shaped Them*, 2004) than in how an *oeuvre* might have shaped the subsequent history of a place. Nor have any of these constituencies been interested on the whole in enquiring into how the history and analysis of practices surrounding their own pet author might be slotted into a general understanding of the development of this cultural practice. One of the reasons for this is that literary tourism has been embarrassing – an embarrassment that runs rather deeper than the mere professional hauteur of literature academics trained, even in the era of cultural studies, to give a certain priority to the literary text in relation to competing contexts, intertexts, paratexts, and, especially, to the biographical evocation of the Author. The embarrassment of literary tourism is encapsulated in the very phrase, which yokes 'literature' – with its long-standing claims to high, national culture, and its current aura of highbrow difficulty and professionalism – with 'tourism', trailing its pejorative connotations of mass popular culture, mass travel, unthinking and unrefined consumption of debased consumables, amateurishness, and inauthenticity.[3] As a practice that tries to make the emotional and virtual realities of reading accountable to the literal, material realities of destination, it is bound to make literary specialists uneasy.

Literary tourism has recently become more interesting to the academic eye in part simply because of the astonishing acceleration over the last 20 years of all forms of travel and tourism worldwide and a related desire to develop and memorialise places and localities as unique in a postmodern world in which they may otherwise appear to be becoming so many interchangeable provinces of Planet Global. This has led to an increase in the number of writers' houses on show and a rash of new blue plaques across Britain, plus a steady stream of broadsheet journalism and lavishly illustrated publications designed to cater to the desire for literary travel both virtual and actual.[4] Within the academy, meanwhile, a number of cross-disciplinary strands of investigation have begun to converge suggestively upon literary geography. Within the humanities, specialists in literary reception have attended to the posthumous reputations and evocations of authors and their works. Scholars of British and American travel-writing have shifted towards examining the ways that tourism has constituted national and international subjectivities. A resurgent interest in the history and nature of literary biography, especially collective biography, has brought the production of sites associated with writers' lives into focus as themselves modes of biography. Historians of print culture and the book, meanwhile, have increasingly focussed on readers and reading practices, meaning that forms of reading-experience supplemental to the book proper – such as the desire to remember and re-read particular books at particular significant sites – have become more visible. With the de-differentiation of the literary from other forms of story-telling, scholars of the cross-media migration and adaptation of story in popular culture have become aware of tourism as a form of adaptation. Historians' long-standing critical interest in heritage culture and popular memory, most influentially anatomised in the British context by Raphael Samuel in *Theatres of Memory* (1994), and echoed in continental interest in 'lieux de mémoire' or places of collective memory, has fed into the newly constituted field of heritage studies, which has begun to describe how literary heritage is expressed in place.[5] Within the social sciences, meanwhile, tourist studies have begun to study literary tourism from both theoretical and empirical standpoints, despite the difficulties of quantifying, cueing and managing a tourist experience compounded nebulously of individuals' memories of reading and of numinous space.[6]

There have been and still are significant disciplinary obstacles to cross-fertilisation or convergence between these various vantages and perspectives. Tim Dolin, for instance, has recently remarked on the way that tourist studies, with its interest in systems, images, cultures, and tourist motivations, its theory and language derived from the social sciences, notably cultural geography and anthropology, and its empirical methodologies of surveys and quantitative analysis, is hard to square with the emphasis in literary studies on obliging para-literary practices to reframe and reflect upon the literary text itself – especially given that the discipline of literary studies remains loyal to a generally qualitative and non-instrumental approach. If tourist studies have been inadequately sensitive to reading practices, literary production, and the structural specificity of individual literary locale to individual literary text, literary studies have been comparably uninterested in the motivations and behaviours of real tourists, whether historical or modern, except when those tourists have themselves been major writers.[7] Equally, for historians, the celebration of the collective memory of events that have occurred purely within the shared imagination of writer and reader is suspect and unsettling. Literary scholars, with their investment in the timelessness of the virtual reality provided by the portability and reproducibility of the book, have been potentially worried both by historians' insistence on specificity of time, and geographers' on that of place. That said, scholars from all these disciplines have found a touchstone in John Urry's influential study, *The Tourist Gaze* (1990, 2nd edn, 2002). Setting out a general set of axioms for considering tourism as a mass activity explicitly opposed to, differentiated from, and suspending the quotidian realities of both work and home, and as specifically associated with daydreaming and fantasy, Urry's work has continued to suggest to scholars from both the social sciences and the humanities ways of thinking about literary tourism as travel into the extraordinary realms of the virtual 'for real'.

There have been a number of recent publications and conferences (including the one from which this volume arises) which have derived from this varied critical, theoretical and disciplinary genealogy. The conference 'Tourism and Literature: Travel, Imagination and Myth', convened by Sheffield University's Centre for Tourism and Cultural Change under the auspices of Mike Robinson, showcased some of this work in Harrogate in 2004, while in 2007 Nottingham University ran a conference entitled 'Literary Geographies' which, in its interest in the spaces of literary production and consumption, also began to touch upon tourism. Samantha Matthews' *Poetical Remains: Poets' Graves, Bodies, and Books in the Nineteenth Century* (2004), in drawing attention to the contested meanings of poets' graves from Burns to Tennyson, also considered their significance as tourist destinations. Over the last four years Alison Booth has published a number of essays on the practice of keying biography to travelogue initiated by William Howitt's *Homes and Haunts of the Most Celebrated British Poets* (1847), the frontispiece of which serves as the cover illustration for this volume.[8] My own *The Literary Tourist: Readers and Places in Romantic and Victorian Britain* (2006) developed a history and a taxonomy of literary tourist sites, principally British, from the late eighteenth century through to the late nineteenth, arguing that literary place is (counter-intuitively) produced by writing mediated by acts of readerly tourism, and that it is the internal dynamics of an author's works, buttressed by a particularised series of intertexts and associated publishing practices, which produce literary place, and not the other way around (however strenuously place may subsequently be organised to look like the originating ground for writing). Identifying the ways in which texts solicit readers to locate and re-experience them within the specificities of place, the book also examined how places have been designed to accrete, secrete, and authenticate 'memories' of writers and of works, effecting in aggregate a mapping of national literary heritage onto a national mythic geography. By contrast, Harald Hendrix's edited collection of essays, *Writers' Houses and the Making of Memory* (2007), ranges far further into continental Europe for its case studies, but confines itself to considering writers' houses rather than other forms of literary sites. It divides such houses into two broad categories – houses designed by their authors as a 'self-fashioning' extension of their writing practices and celebrity personae, and houses fashioned by processes of cultural memory after the author's death so as to agree with the dominant version of what the author stands for. Like this collection, it locates the epicentre of the desire to make and preserve writers' houses within nineteenth-century culture, arguing that it resulted from a mixture of local and national pride, romantic interest in personality and genius, and a new desire to get in touch with history where it was made. Hendrix makes a case for the exceptionality of writers' houses (and, by extension, of all literary tourist sites) in that they are not merely places of memorial, nor merely spaces that dramatise and document biography, but emptinesses that supposedly 'enable visitors ... to come into contact with the imaginative world created by the author, and thus to participate in his imagination.' As he points out, they accordingly come complete with rituals of contact such as the signature, the ritual taking of relics, or acts of re-enactment.

These divergent and cross-disciplinary approaches to the subject are reflected in the essays included here, which come at it from varied but generally historicist angles – amongst them, architectural history, book history, and the history of literary biography. Read against one another, they share, however, a number of related concerns: the gendering of the tourist site and experience; the nature and grounding of claims to authenticity and literary authority within tourist sites and the writings associated with visiting them; and the linkage of literary heritage with the invention and elaboration of national identity. They also display a number of shared foci: writing by women; American writers; and genres associated with the inception of literary tourism.

In keeping with the broadly chronological organisation of the volume, the opening essay, Hendrix's comparative study of the modes of early modern and romantic tourism, focuses on tourism associated with Francesco Petrarch (1304–1374) so as to offer a way of framing and defining what is particular to nineteenth-century literary Anglophone tourism. Matthews then moves into the nineteenth century proper to deal with Victorian trips to the graves of poets, specifically the graves of Keats and Shelley in Rome, analysing tourist practices and associated forms of writing as conflicted composites of homage and aggression on the part of the tourist. The following essay by Wilson-Costa describes the evolution of one of the earliest of British literary terrains, 'The Land of Burns', by considering and comparing accounts of British, American, and French literary pilgrimages to Ayrshire. North's essay describes how the emergent genre of literary biography scripted the visit to the writer's house, with special reference to biographies of Byron and

Letitia Landon, and to William Howitt's project of collective biography. It inaugurates a series of related essays tackling the conceptualisation of the writer's house: Hazard's, which examines the contrasting authorial ideas behind the building of two very different 'literary' houses, Scott's Abbotsford and Hawthorne's Wayside; Thomas's, which charts the ways in which Shakespeare's birthplace took on its modern 'authentic' shape through Victorian conservationist committee-work; and Atkin's, which considers the founding ideas that drove the purchase and preservation of Dove Cottage, a project modelled upon the Shakespeare Birthplace. Marshall's essay returns us to Stratford to deal with re-readings of Shakespeare country by three women, Eleanor Marx, Mathilde Blind, and Marie Corelli, considering how their formulations of Shakespeare country served their own personal and political agendas.

North's interest in the relations between genre and literary tourism is picked up again in the next two essays, which consider genres specifically associated with the production and management of tourism. Schaff investigates the phenomenal success of Murray's Handbooks in rendering mass tourism 'romantic' through their extensive citation of Byron, while Stetz describes how *The Bookman* promoted virtual and actual tourism to sites of literary interest in the 1890s. There then follow four essays on urban and provincial tourism associated with individual novelists. Parker's analysis of how Gaskell's writing changed Haworth into Brontë-land, and Knutsford into Cranford, as suitable localities within which to imagine the woman writer, is followed by two essays which deal with Dickens' wide-ranging effect on the tourism and heritage industries: Watson relates the development of the urban literary ramble around London to Dickens' own novelistic aesthetic, and Booth brings the story up to date by considering the recent opening of 'Dickens' World' in terms of the long history of producing Dickens' home and Dickens' country. Haslam brings this series to a close by reconsidering the development of Hardy's 'Wessex'.

The next three essays foreground American tourism both in Britain and back in the States: Foster analyses American strategies for managing, enhancing, and resisting their transatlantic tourist experience, with especial reference to accounts of visiting sites associated with Shakespeare, Burns, and Scott by Irving, Cooper, Stowe, Hawthorne and James, and a number of less well-known women travellers; Westover is similarly preoccupied with American responses, taking as his subject the ways in which American writers constructed themselves and American culture as the legitimate heirs to British literary culture, and the consequences for the development of literary tourism in the United

States; and Roberts tells the unlikely story of how the author of *Uncle Tom's Cabin* herself became a Florida tourist attraction in the aftermath of the Civil War, thus contributing, if temporarily, to the production of a regional identity for Florida and the South more generally. The collection concludes with another account of literary tourism transplanted in the service of national identity, this time to South Africa, in the shape of Stiebel's account of the newly developed Rider Haggard literary trail.

Taken together, these essays tackle the production of nineteenth-century literary culture both as a nineteenth-century tourist phenomenon and as a twenty-first century experience. They raise, although they do not resolve, common questions concerned with the history and genealogy of the practices of literary tourism. One large question they suggest is to do with whether nineteenth-century British literary tourism was merely derivative from earlier European sites and practices, or whether it was distinctive and seminal, providing models for later literary tourist industries in North America and elsewhere and for the forms of cultural nationalism which they typically serve. Another set of questions constellates around how the relative power, authority or even ownership of Author and Reader at literary sites has been calibrated and valued. Is there a spectrum of levels of authorisation and authenticity across types of sites? Or, to put it another way, does the Author's writ run more reliably at the grave than on literary 'trails'? Depending on how the Author is valued in relation to the Reader, literary tourism will be condemned as derivative, parasitic, and decadent, or celebrated as a creative and transformative system of enhancing or extending reading activity. A final question concerns the literary tourism of the future. It is unclear whether the present-day practice of literary tourism simply repeats Victorian strategies, and is thus merely a fossil reading practice, doomed to extinction with the book itself, or whether nineteenth-century literary tourism, with its pervasive penumbra of the performed and enhanced experience, actually pre-figures the multi-media futures of reading.

What is certain is that thinking about the nineteenth-century literary tourist, the tourist site, and the practices and writings associated with them allows us to study that most elusive of things to pin down – how Victorian readers experienced and lived out their reading, and how their successors have experienced and lived out their experience of reading the Victorians. To attend to this history is to construct a materialist history of those amateur reading pleasures that are still available and commercially viable today. It might even enable us to understand why anyone would want to travel all the way from

Britain to Vermont in order temporarily occupy Kipling's beloved and abandoned Naulakha.

Notes

1. www.crjc.org/heritage/V03–3.htm. (accessed on 7 July 2008).
2. Graham Holderness, 'Bardolatry: or, the Cultural Materialist's Guide to Stratford-upon-Avon' in *The Shakespeare Myth* (Manchester: Manchester University Press, 1988). See also Barbara Hodgdon, *The Shakespeare Trade: Performances and Appropriations* (Philadelphia: University of Pennsylvania Press, 1998), 191–240; Péter Dávidházi, *The Romantic Cult of Shakespeare: Literary Reception in Anthropological Perspective* (Basingstoke: Macmillan, 1998). Nicola J. Watson, 'Shakespeare on the Tourist Trail' in Robert Shaughnessy, ed., *The Cambridge Companion to Shakespeare and Popular Culture* (Cambridge: Cambridge University Press, 2007), 199–226. For Milton, the Brontës, Martineau, Dickens, and Hardy respectively, see Aaron Santesso, 'The Birth of the Birthplace: Bread Street and Literary Tourism before Stratford', *ELH* 71, no. 2 (2004 Summer), 377–403; Charles Lemon, ed., *Early Visitors to Haworth* (Haworth: Brontë Society, 1996); Douglas Pocock, 'Haworth: The Experience of a Literary Place' in W. Mallory and P. Simpson-Housley, eds *Geography and Literature: A Meeting of the Disciplines* (Syracuse, NY: Syracuse University Press, 1987), 135–42; Alexis Easley, 'The Woman of Letters at Home: Harriet Martineau and the Lake District', *Victorian Literature and Culture* 34: 1 (2006), 291–310; Murray Baumgarten, 'Urban Labyrinths: Dickens and the Pleasures of Place' in Peter Brown and Michael Irwin, eds *Literature and Place 1800–2000* (Bern: Peter Lang, 2006); Peter Widdowson, *Hardy in History* (London: Routledge, 1989); Jeff Nunokawa, '*Tess*, Tourism, and the Spectacle of the Woman' in *Rewriting the Victorians: Theory, History, and the Politics of Gender,* ed. Linda M. Shires (New York and London: Routledge, 1992), 70–86.
3. Cf. Jean Baudrillard, *Simulations* (New York: Semiotext(e), 1983).
4. For details of this expansion of writer's houses in Europe see Harald Hendrix, ed., *Writers' Houses and the Making of Memory* (London: Routledge, 2007); this volume also supplies a comprehensive bibliography of criticism relating to literary tourism beyond the Anglophone which is the focus here, and a representative list of the many recent books offering coffee-table literary tours.
5. For an influential treatment of 'lieux de mémoire' see Pierre Nora, 'Between Memory and History: Les Lieux de Mémoire', *Representations* 26 (Spring 1989), 7–24. For a representative and influential example of the theorisation of heritage studies in relation to tourism and museums see Barbara Kirschenblatt-Gimblett, *Destination Culture: Tourism, Museums and Heritage* (Berkeley: University of California, 1998); her introductory insight that 'tourists travel to actual destinations to experience virtual places' (9) seems especially pertinent to acts of literary tourism. For an example of an early effort to deal with literary tourism as a 'heritage experience' with regard to the houses of Dylan Thomas and Jane Austen at Langharne and Chawton respectively see David T. Herbert, 'Literary Places, Tourism, and the Heritage Experience', *Annals of Tourism Research*, 28: 2 2001), 312–33.

6. See Peter Newby, 'Literature and the Fashioning of Tourist Taste' in Douglas Pocock, ed., *Humanistic Geography and Literature* (London: Croom Helm, 1980); Pocock, 'Haworth: The Experience of a Literary Place' 135–42; Clara Fawcett and Patricia Cormack, 'Guarding Authenticity at Literary Tourism Sites', *Annals of Tourism Research* 28: 3 (2001), 686–704; and David Herbert's essay cited above.
7. Tim Dolin, Literary Subjectivity and Literary Tourism in Hardy's Wessex, unpublished paper, 30 January 2008, Centre for Nineteenth-Century Studies, Birkbeck College, London University.
8. See Alison Booth, 'The Real Right Place of Henry James: Homes and Haunts', *Henry James Review* 25, no. 3 (2004 Fall), 216–27; 'Rewriting the Homes and Haunts of Mary Russell Mitford', *Nineteenth-Century Contexts* 30: 1 (2008), 39–65; and 'Author Country: Longfellow, the Brontës, and Anglophone Homes and Haunts', *Romanticism and Victorianism on the Net* Special Issue: Victorian Internationalisms, ed. Lauren Goodlad and Julia M. Wright, 48 (November 2007). http://www.erudit.org/revue/ravon/2007/v/n48/017438ar. html. (accessed on 13 July 2008).

1
From Early Modern to Romantic Literary Tourism: A Diachronical Perspective

Harald Hendrix

In nineteenth-century Great Britain, literary tourism develops into a remarkable phenomenon that in many ways transcends and explodes the traditional peculiarities of this ancient cultural practice. Preceding developments in other countries, and even dictating their orientations, British romantic literary tourism, moreover, discloses some of the more essential qualities that govern and help to explain its very existence, from the gradually evolving relationship between readers, authors and texts on the one hand, to the appropriation of essentially elitist and universalist habits into emergent mass cultures susceptible of supporting nationalist ideologies on the other. The invention of specific textual genres like the *Homes and Haunts* books, the construction of writers' houses as literary shrines, and the tourist transformation and development of entire regions according to their supposed literary representation, make the British situation an eminently suitable case study to better understand how in nineteenth-century culture the practice of literary tourism came to be so successful. In order, however, to grasp its specificity, not only in a chronological and international perspective, but also as to its *literary* nature, a comparative approach is called for. This essay therefore sets out to discuss British nineteenth-century literary tourism as part of an ancient tradition, identifying what distinguishes it from earlier manifestations of this cultural practice, not just in Britain but all over Europe, notably in Italy. In fact, while sketching the passage from ancient to early modern and finally romantic literary tourism it also describes a geographical change in cultural hegemony, since in this process the centre of cultural innovation gradually moves from Italy to France and ultimately Britain.[1]

Places associated with writers and their writings have attracted special attention since ancient times, both from fellow writers longing for some kind of intellectual exchange or simply keen on expressing their admiration, and from other persons eager to honour poets, their works, or literature as such. The generally high status of writing in antiquity, considered to guarantee eternal life to what and whom it depicted, was certainly one of the first motives for such reverence; during his siege of Thebes, Alexander the Great is said to have spared Pindar's home from destruction, fearing the consequences such an act of violence might have for his posthumous fame.[2] But the attention to literary sites was part of a more comprehensive memorial practice dedicated to honouring illustrious men whose intellectual heritage was considered particularly present in the places where they had lived, worked and died. 'Our emotions are somehow stirred in those places in which the feet of those whom we love and admire have trodden,' Cicero stated in his *De legibus,* "twas here they dwelt, 'twas here they sat, 'twas here they engaged in their philosophical discussions. And with reverence I contemplate their tombs.'[3] The particular 'genius loci' Cicero describes here results from a yearning to transform the rather passive admiration for a revered predecessor into a much more active intellectual exchange beyond the grave, a 'conversation with the dead' to which literature – given its capacity as a textual medium to be eternally present – in particular invites.[4] This accounts for the fact that most evidence we have for antique cultural tourism is provided by writers and intellectuals visiting sites, notably graves, associated with their predecessors, as is the case with the well established tradition of travelling to Virgil's (alleged) grave near Naples.[5] However, it also shows that this practice originates both in admiration for the author's work and in a desire to go beyond it, and thus essentially in a dissatisfaction with the limits of that very work.

It is precisely this combination of admiration and dissatisfaction that motivates literary tourism as it develops in later times. The combination is not a paradoxical one, since the dissatisfaction is caused by the desire to have more of the same. But it can easily entail uneasiness with the content of literary texts and with the way such content is expressed, indeed textually. This is what we see in the passage from the late medieval to the early modern version of literary tourism, a passage dominated by the figure of Petrarch, first as a literary pilgrim himself, and then as an object of literary tourism. Well aware as he was of the classical version of the visit to literary sites – quoting for example Cicero's lines from *De legibus* at his Roman coronation as poet laureate in 1341[6] – he relates in a letter from 1343 his long-planned trip to the various locations near Baia portrayed in Virgil's *Aeneid* (Book IV), underpinning his enthusiasm with a joyous 'Vidi loca a Virgilio descripta'.[7] Seeing with his own eyes the reality of the locations so powerfully evoked in Virgil's poem is like looking for confirmation of his experience as a reader. But it is at the same time an attempt to go beyond the text, and personally and even physically to immerse himself in that reality, transforming it from a fictional idea into an empirical experience. This first glimpse of dissatisfaction with the fictional nature of literary texts then in the early sixteenth century rather suddenly develops into a much more elaborate practice, precisely in the memorial culture dedicated to Petrarch himself, which I would not hesitate to define the first manifestation of a comprehensive literary tourist industry.[8] Essential to its genesis is the transition from a purely author-oriented perspective, limited to aspects like memory, worship and 'conversation with the dead', to an interest in the literary work and the imaginative world of fiction it suggests.

From his death in 1375 through the late fourteenth and fifteenth centuries, Petrarch's heritage was memorialised in mostly conventional ways reminiscent of ancient practices: in texts; in a few monuments, including an imposing tomb; and in occasional visits to his grave in the small village of Arquà near Padua, echoing habits from antiquity reinstated by Petrarch himself. This radically changed in the 1520s, when his work started to attract a different kind of admiration and thus readership. Instead of his learned Latin works, Petrarch's poetry in Italian became the focus of attention, principally because it was hailed as the model for all modern poetry in the vernacular. In these lyrics, the poet relates his emotions during the various phases of a passionate infatuation for a young woman, Laura, who remains a rather mysterious figure since she is only observed from a distance. It was this mystery and the allegedly autobiographical nature of Petrarch's love poetry that triggered an essentially new kind of readerly interest dominated by curiosity. Petrarch's admirers started to interpret his predominantly fictional emotions as real, and to read his poetry thus in a documentary fashion. This drive then quickly developed into a fundamentally different kind of literary tourism, when fans started to make trips to the South of France where this allegedly real love affair had been situated. They visited not only the house in Fontaine-de-Vaucluse where Petrarch was supposed to have written his love verses, but the many locations in the area surrounding Avignon where the poet had observed the object of his love, Laura. This gave rise to unprecedented expressions of literary tourism: the publication of maps indicating these very locations (the first one is from 1525), the construction of museum-like collections of literary conundrums including trivialia like fragments of Laura's alleged chamber-pot, and the rise of more or less organised tours of these attractions.[9]

The rise of this phenomenon was triggered by a strictly biographical, even documentarist interpretation of Petrarch's poetry. Some of the more fervid readers and fans in fact undertook serious archaeological enterprises in order to prove Laura's historical reality, like the French poet Maurice Scève who in 1533 was certain he had discovered her grave, a sensational claim that provoked the general enthusiasm of contemporaries including the French king, Francis I, who visited the site and composed an epigram in honour of it. As of this moment, a visit to Petrarchan locations in Provence became standard for poets and other literature fans travelling in the South of France, a practice well documented in topographical poetry, travelogues and diaries from the mid sixteenth through the eighteenth centuries.[10]

Almost simultaneously, this newly established habit evolved into an even more material practice at the location traditionally associated with Petrarch, Arquà, where, besides his tomb, his house also now became the focus of an intense memorial culture. In the 1540s the poet's home was transformed into a memorial place by a new owner, Paolo Valdezocco, who decorated it with fresco cycles glorifying Petrarch's vernacular poetry and his alleged love affair with Laura. As such it soon became a place of particular interest, not only to fans of Petrarch but also to travellers in general. It appealed particularly to foreigners, who as of the late sixteenth century started to tour the rich cultural heritage of Italy as part of their education, thus initiating a powerful new cultural habit later called the Grand Tour. In the purposively arranged interior of the house in Arquà – the oldest literary museum still in existence – visitors like the Scottish globetrotter Fynes Morrison who visited in 1595 found frescoes illustrating and exalting Petrarch's works together with various objects associated with his person, from his library and chair to the mummy of his beloved cat. It is especially this remarkable object, which is recorded with insistence in most of the reports on visits to Arquà, which reveals some of the inner drives of this early modern literary tourism. Its objective was still firmly author-oriented, the cat's mummy being a very personal, even domestic kind of memorial object. It in fact reinforces the house's potential as a means to come into personal contact with the poet, and thus serves as a medium for the ancient practice of the 'conversation with the dead'. But it also demonstrates the limits of such practices. From its installation in the 1590s to the present day, the cat's mummy has been an object of jest, attracting ironical, teasing and even outright censorious comments, some of which were even formally inscribed on the marble slab surrounding the relic. Critical reactions towards the new phenomenon of the literary pilgrimage to Petrarchan Provençal locations had already appeared almost as soon as it made its appearance, as of the 1530s.[11] But in the poet's house in Arquà, such attitudes were integrated into the attraction itself. To visitors to Petrarch's house the cat's mummy offered – and indeed still offers today – the opportunity to engage in this profane pilgrimage and yet simultaneously to criticise it.

The literary tourism that was invented in early sixteenth-century Italian culture thus had a complex and actually rather sophisticated nature. It was conditioned by a change in attitudes towards literary texts, which became increasingly interpreted as expressions of an author's biographical condition, and thus as rooted in historical and topographical reality. Obviously, this ultimately presupposes a distrust, or even denial, of fiction. This explains why literary pilgrims to Petrarchan locations did not stop at having a 'conversation with the dead' author – as previous generations had done at poets' graves – but went beyond such intellectual exchange and tried to project onto reality the fictional world of their idol's poetry. Favoured by the contemporary rise of travel for educational and generally cultural motives, this encouraged the invention and construction of a rather elaborate literary memorial cult around places where the author's biographical and fictional realities were supposed to meet. From the outset, however, such practices attracted fierce criticism, being considered inappropriate and even absurd because of the material banalities to which they gave rise. Significantly, though, this critique was somehow integrated in the cult itself, thus becoming fundamentally ambiguous. By turning it into an object of ironic meditation on literary memorial culture, the cat's mummy in Petrarch's house in Arquà was saved, both as a tourist attraction and as a multileveled 'conversation piece' able to mediate between the poet and his readers and to stimulate in them some amusing and yet serious self-reflection.

If in the early modern memorial cult surrounding Petrarch we can detect on the one hand a first articulate effort to go beyond the limits of a text and project its fiction onto reality, we must, on the other hand, be aware that this effort remains still firmly author-oriented. Visitors to the poet's house in Arquà and to the various locations around Avignon were interested in establishing a kind of personal contact with the author, carving for example their names in a fireplace in his bedroom (the oldest of these graffiti dates from 1544, by German students). Or they wanted to reconstruct in reality an episode of the author's life as it is evoked in his poetry: the Petrarch–Laura trail in Provence. It was precisely this combination of (presumed) autobiography and fiction that turned admirers into literary pilgrims, not fiction as such. This is what other evidence on early modern literary tourism confirms. There are no reports of readers trying to locate fictions like Ariosto's *Orlando Furioso* or the novellas from Boccaccio's *Decameron*, although these very texts were esteemed models for contemporary vernacular literature as much as Petrarch's poetry was. We have, however, evidence of travellers paying homage to these great authors by systematically visiting their homes and graves. For example, in his visit to Italy, Fynes Morrison made trips to the tombs and houses of Aretino, Ariosto, Boccaccio, Dante, Michelangelo, Petrarch, Sannazzaro and Virgil.

Outside Italy, where early modern evidence is extremely rare, we also come across this same author-oriented disposition. In Rotterdam, the house where Erasmus was allegedly born became a kind of tourist attraction immediately after his death in 1536, and therefore at exactly the same period in which the Petrarch cult developed in Arquà and Provence. In the year 1540 the extremely modest building was visited by a smart group of courtiers following Charles V on his visit to town, and in 1549 the entourage of his son and heir Philip repeated this experience.[12] By the year 1589, the house was adorned with a trilingual inscription – the first ever of its kind – commemorating the great humanist, as we know from a report by the Utrecht scholar Arnoud van Buchel:

Aedibus his ortus mundum decoravit Erasmus,
artibus inenuis, relligione, fide.
En esta casa es nascido Erasmo Teologo celebrado,
por doctrina senelado la pura fee nos a revelado.
In dit huijs is gebooren Erasmues vermaert,
die ons Gods woort vuijtvercooren wel heeft verclaert.[13]

Together with a statue erected in nearby church square, first in wood and then in stone in 1622, the house became a standard ingredient of a visit to Rotterdam and was marketed as such particularly to foreigners, as a detailed engraving of its facade from 1696 containing elaborate explanations in English attests.[14]

The predominantly author-oriented disposition of early modern memorial culture accounts for these still rather isolated endeavours to turn authors and their works into monuments and museums. It perhaps also explains why another even more ambitious expression of sixteenth-century literary memorial culture totally failed: Anton Francesco Doni's 1563 project to build around Petrarch's grave in Arquà a huge temple of fame, intended as a pantheon of literature as such.[15] Dedicated as this plan was to all major authors, classical and modern, whose statues were to adorn a large theatre centred on the poet's tomb, the project failed to attract the princely sponsorship Doni vigorously tried to obtain, presumably because at that moment the very idea of a pantheon and thus of a collective memorial cult was too far-fetched. It anticipated, though, a tendency that was to produce great memorials as of the early eighteenth century. Poets' Corner in London's Westminster Abbey, although originating in a few late sixteenth-century tombs, assumed its appearance as a pantheon in the 1720s, while the Paris Pantheon and Santa Croce in Florence – in many ways a literary pantheon – were inaugurated as such only in the early nineteenth century.[16] This suggests that literary memorial culture all through the seventeenth and eighteenth centuries maintained and even strengthened its essentially author-centred nature.

The development of the cult surrounding Petrarch may confirm this. On the one hand there is up until the nineteenth century a remarkable continuity in the practice of visiting Arquà and the Vaucluse, on the other there are small but significant indications of change. In Arquà there is first, in 1630, the curious episode of the sensational theft of part of the poet's bones from his tomb, indicating a fetishist interest in the man's remains – perhaps motivated by the prospect of profit that the thriving tourist business promised.[17] Then, as of the late 1780s the owners of the house got impatient with the visitors' habit of carving their names on the walls and furniture, and decided to invite them to sign a visitors' book instead. In both instances, the underlying acts and habits of vandalism seem to indicate an ardent desire to get near to the poet, or to appropriate his remains. Analogously, in the locations near Avignon that traditionally had been visited by readers eager to find evidence for the fictional reality of Petrarch's love affair with Laura, the figure of the poet became more and more the centre of attention. Arquà and Avignon even got mixed up, in testimonies like Casanova's highly emotional memories of his visits to both, Vaucluse in 1760 and Arquà in 1776:

> Arrivé a Vaucluse [1760], je voulus monter jusqu'à la pointe du rocher où Pétrarque avait sa maison. Les larmes aux yeux, j'en contemplai les vestiges, comme Leo Allatius en voyant le tombeau d'Homère. [...]

Seize ans plus tard [= 1776] je pleurai de nouveau à Arquà, lieu où Pétrarque est mort et où la maison qu'il habitait existait encore. La ressemblance était étonnante car de la chambre où Pétrarque écrivait à Arquà, on voit la pointe d'un rocher qui ressemble à celui que l'on voit à Vaucluse et où demeurait madonna Laura. [...] Je me jetai sur ces ruines, les bras étendus comme pour les embrasser; je les baisai, je les mouillai de mes larmes; je cherchais à respirer le souffle divin qui les avait animées.[18]

In his eagerness to get in touch, preferably in a physical manner, with the divine spirit that had animated Petrarch while writing his poetry, Casanova is typical of the late eighteenth-century interest in genius. Remarkably, however, this fascination did not distinguish between living and dead persons, and thus deviates from the more generic patterns oriented towards memorial cults. In mid eighteenth-century France especially, the living seem to have outdone the dead, when a widespread practice of visits to the 'great authors' came into being.[19] Reminiscent of habits introduced in the context of the Grand Tour and its educational programme, these visits arose from the desire to pay homage to a revered intellectual and to learn from his conversation. But visits such as the trips to Voltaire in his Villa Les Délices in Geneva or James Boswell's 1764 visit to Rousseau also entailed a cult of genius and the desire to locate this, not just in a person but also in a place, as Casanova in these same years did with Petrarch. This is particularly what the cases of Rousseau and Goethe suggest; where we can witness the shifting of a cult of genius first directed to the person himself and then to places linked to his person.

As a young man still living in his parental house in Frankfurt, Goethe used himself to entertain the visitors that wanted to pay him their respect.[20] After his departure in 1775, first to Weimar, then to Rome, and finally to Weimar again, this visiting-practice however was transferred from the person to the location, his family home soon becoming an attraction for literary pilgrims. This memorial cult gained particular momentum when the first books of Goethe's autobiographical *Dichtung und Wahrheit* (part I: 1811, part II: 1812, part III: 1814), with their account of the author's Frankfurt years, became available, and when in 1835 Bettina von Arnim published *Goethe's Briefwechsel mit einem Kinde*. In the house a special remembrance installation was arranged in what Von Arnim had incorrectly indicated as the poet's bedroom and study. As we know from a contemporary source, the novel *Casa santa* dedicated in 1853 to the house by its then inhabitant Virginia Wunderlich, the display comprised a few of the poet's autographs under glass, some of the furniture he had used, particularly his desk, and a life-size bust dominating a visitors' book in which visitors could leave their name and a comment. With this simple arrangement both the person of the poet and his work were remembered and evoked. These two elements actually tended to fuse in the perception of the literary pilgrim, who in this case was motivated to visit the place because of his knowledge of the poet's autobiographical account of his life in these very rooms and of the works written here, notably *Die Leiden des jungen Werther* (1774) and *Götz von Berlichingen* (1773).

In Rousseau's case, the publication of his autobiographical *Confessions* in 1782 was the key moment in the development of literary pilgrimages to the most significant of his houses, the villa Les Charmettes in Chambéry where he had lived as a young man from 1736 until 1742. Fifty years after his final departure, his admirer Hérault de Séchelles put up a plaque on the façade of the villa remembering this short but significant stay:

> Réduit par Jean Jacques habité
> tu me rappeles son génie
> sa solitude, sa fierté
> et ses malheurs et sa folie.
> A la gloire, à la verité
> il osa consacrer sa vie,
> et fut toujours persécuté
> ou par lui-meme, ou par l'envie.

While paying tribute to the genius of Rousseau, the text underlines that his was a personality full of contradictions, precisely because the author had depicted himself as such in his *Confessions* while giving a detailed account of his life in Les Charmettes. After the posthumous publication of the autobiography the house in Chambéry quickly became an attraction for literary pilgrims, who clearly wanted to get in touch personally with the places where the genius Rousseau was thought to have lived his finest years. This contact however was no longer merely personal, as it had been in the case of Voltaire. It had become 'practical yet mystical',[21] based as it was not just on the material evidence of the house itself, but also on its imaginative representation given by Rousseau in his *Confessions*. In the following years, this moreover became intertwined with the fictional world the author had evoked in his most popular novel, *Julie ou la Nouvelle Héloise* (1761), a text that contemporary readers tended to interpret in a semi-autobiographical key.

As in the case of Petrarch's poetry, the juxtaposition of biography and fiction triggered a curiosity in Rousseau and his work that was deeply dissatisfied with the limits imposed by textuality. From the 1780s on, readers travelled to Lake Geneva not just in search of Rousseau but of his heroine, echoing a practice invented centuries before in Provence. But unlike its early modern counterpart, romantic literary tourism did not remain firmly author-oriented and did not develop ironic connotations. From the prototype offered by tourism to the various locations around Lake Geneva associated with *Julie* the model of literary pilgrimages inspired by fictions was transplanted to other locations equally evocative, both by their natural allure and by their association with compelling fictions: first the Scottish Highlands as they were depicted in Walter Scott's work, notably *The Lady of the Lake* (1810), and later, following this success, the Italian lakes, particularly Lake Como described in Manzoni's equally successful novel *I Promessi Sposi* (1827).[22] In this process, literary tourism developed as of 1810 into a commercially interesting business uninterested in self-reflective ironies. While becoming a mass phenomenon, supported and enhanced by a newly developed travel industry based on guides and tour operators, it thus changed its orientation. Instead of being dominated by the venerated author and his biography, the tourist perspective came to be dominated by the fictional world of his texts. The reader's desire to go beyond the text and its fictional world evolved into an all-embracing experience, no longer mitigated by ironic self-reflection, but on the contrary even appropriating large portions of reality – from Lake Geneva through Loch Katrine to 'The Land of Burns' – to the domain of literary fiction.

Notes

1. The essay takes its point of departure in two recent, complementary books: Nicola J. Watson, *The Literary Tourist. Readers and Places in Romantic & Victorian Britain* (Houndmills: Palgrave Macmillan, 2006), and Harald Hendrix, ed., *Writers' Houses and the Making of Memory* (New York: Routledge, 2008). For a first bibliographical survey of the field of literary tourism, see Hendrix, 245–62.
2. See Franz Rudolf Zankl, 'Das Personalmuseum. Untersuchung zu einem Museumstypus', *Museumskunde* XLI (1972) 1–132, esp. 39–40.
3. The quotation is from Cicero's *De legibus*, II.2.4. English translation in Ernest Hatch Wilkins, *Studies in the Life and Works of Petrarch* (Cambridge, Mass.: Medieval Academy of America, 1955), 305.
4. See Jürgen Pieters, *Speaking with the Dead. Explorations in Literature and History* (Edinburgh University Press, 2005).

5. For Virgil's tomb see Mario Capasso, *Il sepolcro di Virgilio* (Naples: Giannini, 1983) and Joseph Burney Trapp, 'The Grave of Virgil', *Journal of the Warburg and Courtauld Institutes* 47 (1984): 1–31. See also Capasso and Trapp, 'Ovid's Tomb. The Growth of a Legend from Eusebius to Laurence Sterne, Chateaubriand and George Richmond', *Journal of the Warburg and Courtauld Institutes* 36 (1973): 36–76.

6. *Collatio edita per clarissimum poetam Franciscum Petrarcam florentinum Rome, in Capitolo, tempore laureationis sue*, caption 6.2. See also Wilkins, *Studies in Petrarch*, 305.

7. *Familiares*, V.4.

8. See my 'The Early Modern Invention of Literary Tourism: Petrarch's Houses in France and Italy' in Hendrix, *Writers' Houses*, 15–29.

9. Ibid. 21.

10. Eve Duperray, *L'Or des mots. Une lecture de Pétrarque et du mythe littéraire de Vaucluse des origins à l'orée du XXe siècle. Histoire du pétrarquisme en France* (Paris: Publications de la Sorbonne, 1997), to be complemented by Joseph Burney Trapp, 'Petrarch's Laura: the Portraiture of an Imaginary Beloved', *Journal of the Warburg and Courtauld Institutes* 64 (2001): 55–192.

11. Notably in Niccolò Franco's anti-petrarchistic pamphlet *Il Petrarchista* (Venice: Giovan Giolito de' Ferrari, 1539).

12. René van der Schans, Lucy Schlueter, *De plek waar eens de wieg van Erasmus stond* (Rotterdam: Stichting Erasmushuis Rotterdam, 2007).

13. *Diarium van Arend van Buchell,* ed. L.A. van Langeraard, G. Brom (Amsterdam: Historisch genootschap, 1907); Buchelius also included a pencil sketch from 1583 of the wooden statue of Erasmus on the Rotterdam church square in one of his unpublished manuscripts (Utrecht University Library, Ms. 798, vol. I, 138r).

14. 'The House at Rotterdam where Erasmus was Born; Inscrib'd to the Hon.ble Sr. Charles Nager Knt.one of the Lords of the Admiralty,' engraving by I. De Vou, 1696 (Rotterdam Library, Erasmiana Collection). The first engraving made of Petrarch's house in Arquà dates from 1635 and was published in Jacopo Filippo Tomasini, *Petrarcha redivivus* (Padova: Pasquati and Bortoli, 1635), 137.

15. Sonia Maffei, 'Il progetto del "tempio" o "teatro" della Fama per Petrarca' in Anton Francesco Doni, *Pitture dei Doni,* ed. Sonia Maffei (Napoli: Stanza delle Scritture, 2004), 13–17.

16. See Mona Ozouf, 'Le Panthéon. L'École normale des morts' in *Les lieux de mémoire,* ed. Pierre Nora, 2nd edn (Paris: Gallimard, 1997), vol. I, 155–78; *Il Pantheon di Santa Croce a Firenze,* ed. Luciano Berti (Florence: Cassa di Risparmio di Firenze, 1993).

17. On the history of Petrarch's house in Arquà, see Gianni Floriani, *Francesco Petrarca. Memorie e cronache padovane* (Padua: Antenore, 1993), 111–29.

18. Jean Casanova de Seingalt, *Mémoires* (Paris: La Sirène, 1924–1935), vol. VII, 55–6.

19. Olivier Nora, "La visite au grand écrivain" in *Les lieux de mémoire,* ed. Pierre Nora, 2nd edn (Paris: Gallimard, 1997), vol. II, 2131–55.

20. On the cult surrounding Goethe's houses in Frankfurt, Rome and Weimar, see my 'Philologie, materielle Kultur und Authentizität. Das Dichterhaus zwischen Dokumentation und Imagination', in *Die Herkulesarbeiten der*

Philologie, ed. Sophie Berto and Bodo Plachta (Berlin: Weidler, 2008), 211–31.

21. The definition is taken from Julian Barnes' description of his own literary pilgrimage to Flaubert's house in Croisset. See my 'Epilogue: The Appeal of Writers' Houses' in Hendrix, *Writers' Houses*, 235–43.

22. On Rousseau and Scott see Watson, *The Literary Tourist*, 133–62; on Manzoni see my "Topografia manzoniana: il romanzo storico fra turismo letterario e culto della memoria" in *Manzoni and the Historical Novel*, ed. Salvatore Bancheri et al. (Toronto, LEGAS, 2008).

2
Making Their Mark: Writing the Poet's Grave

Samantha Matthews

Writers' graves are famously contested sites, but my focus in this discussion of Victorian responses to the graves of Romantic poets is not the many historical disagreements between the voracious yet capricious public and interest groups with conflicting affective, psychic and legal claims to control the appearance, upkeep and access to poets' graves.[1] Instead I want to consider the contest for creative and imaginative agency between the literary tourist or 'pilgrim' (the traveller performing a ritual of homage) and the dead poet – a contest traceable through the objects and texts visitors produce to record their experience at the grave. The conventional nineteenth-century figuration of the literary tourist as a secular or sentimental 'pilgrim' and literary tourism as a quasi-religious ritual in an age of religious doubt and division has been discussed by recent cultural anthropologists, literary historians, and sociologists.[2] The pilgrim's typical self-presentation is humbled, grieving, overwhelmed and silenced in the presence of the remains of immortal, transcendent 'genius'. However, he or she is generally 'literary' also in the sense of being a writer (whether by professional vocation or as a correspondent and diarist), and the pose of humility is often qualified or undermined by gestures that assert the visitor's own agency, and inscribe his or her subjectivity onto the grave of 'genius'. Rituals of homage enacted at the grave can appear akin to desecration, and the rhetoric of some tribute poems gives the impression that the writer triumphs over the dead poet who is ostensibly being praised. This essay reads this conflicted encounter with the poet's grave using signature as a model for writing and its complex motivations, drawing illustrations from a few of the many Victorian accounts of pilgrimages to the graves of Keats and Shelley in the Protestant Cemetery, Rome.[3]

My rationale for not discussing memorials and commemorative sites associated with nineteenth-century writers generally, is that the poet's grave focuses with exceptional intensity and symbolic complexity questions of literary authority, posterity and influence. Amongst writers the poet has a unique status as symbol of high culture and aesthetics in its purest form, as distinct from the complicating commercial and professional signification of the novelist or journalist. Victorian accounts of visiting the graves of Romantic and Victorian poets specifically focus questions of literary inheritance, the visitor's 'secondariness' or belatedness. Further, the intimate scale of most poets' graves gives the site a concentrated significance and single focus not shared with the spatial and symbolic diffuseness of writers' houses. The burial place also has a peculiar claim to authenticity as the site most directly connected to the poet, through the physical remains of the corpse: the poet as a biographical entity is in some sense still present, a few feet under the surface of grass or stone.[4] Yet since nineteenth-century culture also privileges the immaterial and transcendent qualities attributed to 'genius' and individual identity, and separates them from the mortal body, the grave is also troublingly inauthentic. The body's presence demonstrates the absence of the vital creative author, and the grave, with its sometimes disappointingly prosaic inscription, stony memorial and fixed place within a landscape of death, defines the writer as dead and finished. The poet's grave and responses to it dramatise the period's bifurcated attitude to poetic genius as both embodied and transcendent.

Barbara Bender's observation that 'the permutations on how people interact with place and landscape are almost unending, and the possibilities for disagreement about, and contest over, landscape are equally so' suggests another approach to the instability and contested nature of the literary grave-site: heritage landscapes are not static and stable, because they are constantly being reshaped by diverse perceptions of them.[5] While graves seldom undergo the material reinvention that literary houses are subject to in their commercial exploitation as heritage sites, it is not unknown: Robert Burns's modest family grave in an obscure corner of St. Michael's churchyard, Dumfries, was replaced in 1815 by a prominent and elaborate neoclassical mausoleum containing an allegorical stone relief of the ploughman poet; a recent *Guardian* campaign led to the restoration of William Hazlitt's tombstone in St. Anne's Churchyard, Soho in 2003.[6] Literary graves are living, in process, reconstructed by the physical interventions of supporters and enthusiasts, but also imaginatively reshaped by the subjective perceptions of literary tourists and armchair travellers alike.

The grave-visitor attempts to reconcile two irreconcilable impulses: on one hand, respect for the dead, which positions the visitor as subordinate and secondary, a mere witness or passive documenter, or more overtly implies the suppression of his or her role as a writer; and on the other, the visitor's awareness of his or her own ongoing imaginative agency, which is heightened by contemplating the burial place of the dead literary mentor, and evidenced by the text(s) that not only record but create the encounter. The occluded act of inscription is central to the negotiation of this problematic site, since the pose of merely describing the grave – dictating, as it were, from objective reality, or from the uniquely inspiring presence of the dead poet's spirit – may also be read as the writer's assertion of his or her subjectivity and creative agency. The name of the author, engraved on the stone of the tomb, is through the diverse texts of literary tourism annotated with or even over-written by the visitor's signature.

The visitor's conflicted relationship with a literary precursor can be traced through the objects and texts that visitors handle and create to record, commemorate and interpret their encounter: the hand that reaches out to make contact with genius through the medium of the material grave is also the writing hand. I propose an analogical relation between the heterogeneous texts of grave-tourism (personal letters and diaries, newspaper reports of anniversary ceremonies or wreath-layings, tribute poems and *tombeaux*, guidebooks of 'homes and haunts'), and the physical interventions visitors make in the site to provide evidence of their visit. These interventions include removing souvenirs (grass, leaves, flowers, stones, even fragments of the memorial), mementoes to stimulate memories of the visit, and leaving other traces of the visitor's presence at the site, notably wreaths, flowers, commemorative inscriptions, even occasionally graffiti. Invested with affect, aura, and signifying power, grave-souvenirs are traces of the absent presence of the dead; like the literature of literary tourism, they are at once physical evidence that 'I was there', records of an intellectual and emotional transaction, and constructed texts, subjective projections of the visitor's fantasy, or urgent rewritings of a disappointing site. Correspondingly, texts of grave-pilgrimage are constructed fictions, and even ostensibly 'documentary' treatments are couched in factual error, myth and fantasy.

Nicola Watson has described '[t]he touristic impulse to take relics' as marking 'the emergence of a new model of tourism driven by a desire on the part of the tourist to construct a more intimate and exclusive relationship with the writer than is supposed to be available through mere reading'.[7] I would add that the more passionate pilgrims tend to be motivated precisely by the 'intimate and exclusive relationship' they have formed with the poet through intense and engaged private reading experiences: this subjective relationship with the author through the works creates expectations that help to account for the visitor's frequent disappointment with the grave, and the desire actively to 'correct' the appearance or atmosphere of the shrine when representing their encounter with it. Taking souvenirs from the grave also implies its inverse – leaving a trace of the visitor's presence, through the often visible absence of what has been taken. Reciprocally, when pilgrims leave flowers, wreaths, and other tributes inscribing their presence, something is also taken away – the capacity of other visitors to fantasise that they are in sole imaginative possession of the grave and the poet. I want to use this presence/absence figure to think through the literally rare but symbolically ubiquitous phenomenon of graffito at the grave, the signing of the visitor's name on or close to the poet's monument. Derrida's account of the 'enigmatic originality' of signature suggests the aura typically attributed to autograph in the nineteenth century:

> [A] written signature implies the actual or empirical nonpresence of the signer. But, it will be said, it also marks and retains his having-been-present in a past now, which will remain a future now, and therefore … in the transcendental form of nowness (*maintenance*).[8]

The signature cannot denote 'I am here', but only 'I was here'. Within landscapes of death such as the poet's grave, where issues of presence and absence are heightened, the 'transcendental … nowness' of the absent signer's assertion of subjectivity through his unique autograph has special force. To make one's mark at the grave once is in some sense to make it permanently.

Isaak Walton wrote and dated his initials on a tomb in Poets' Corner in 1658, as Watson notes, and some nineteenth-century visitors to Stratford signed the bust of Shakespeare on his tomb.[9] But those who were happy to scratch their names on the walls or window at Shakespeare's birthplace did not graffito the graves of Romantic and Victorian writers in the way that in the twentieth century Jim Morrison's fans defied regular coats of whitewash to write repeatedly all over his tomb in Père Lachaise Cemetery, Paris. Self-evidently, writing on the tombs of the recently dead was taboo, as a literal mark of disrespect to the poet, family and survivors, too close to an act of desecration. For the less scrupulous, the growing public visibility, busyness and supervision of many popular sites such as the Protestant Cemetery, was another inhibiting factor.

Yet autographing the literary grave, inscribing a unique marker of individual identity on sites that were increasingly public and communal, is the unacted desire of many Victorian literary tourists. An episode from Mark Twain's *The Innocents Abroad: Or, The New Pilgrims' Progress* (1869) describes the kind of thing I mean. The monument is not literary, but comparable because ancient Christian and sacred, a rock at Nazareth where Jesus' disciples were traditionally believed to have rested:

> Our pilgrims would have liked very well to get out their lampblack and stencil-plates and paint their names on that rock, together with the names of the villages they hail from in America, but the priests permit nothing of that kind. To speak the strict truth, however, our party seldom offend in that way, though we have men in the ship who never lose an opportunity to do it. Our pilgrims' chief sin is their lust for 'specimens'.[10]

Twain affects to invoke the practice of stencilling names and origins on tourist landmarks as a way of discriminating between the comparative self-restraint and decorum of 'our party' and the offensive, destructive tourism of anonymous fellow-travellers. The 'men in the ship...never lose an opportunity', whereas 'Our pilgrims would have liked very well to...' but do not. The fact of whether the names are stencilled or not is down to individual discretion, but in Twain's view the urge is fundamental to the 'pilgrim'.

The nineteenth-century literary tourist's desire to make his or her unique mark is practically evident from the rise of the visitors' book, a device for redirecting questionable writing urges into a more socially acceptable form: that at least seems to have been the rationale for introducing the first visitors' book at Shakespeare's Birthplace in 1812. Visitors' books are usually associated with houses – the Wordsworths kept one at Rydal Mount between 1838 and 1847. (It is characteristic of Wordsworth's attempt to control and distance the flood of unsolicited visitors that the book is not a record of autographs, but all written in Mary Wordsworth's hand.) Yet where they are linked with poets' 'last homes', they provide intriguing evidence of the special character of signature in relation to grave-pilgrimage. William Winter's 'homes and haunts' memoir *Gray Days and Gold* (revised edition, 1896) refers to the first visitors' book kept in Hucknall-Torkard church for visitors to Byron's grave, 'an album given by Sir John Bowring, containing the record of visitations from 1825 to 1834'.[11] The album disappeared in the mid 1830s, and a footnote records that as of 1896 the book is rumoured to 'be in the possession of a resident of one of our Southern cities', whose relative had been given it by the parish clerk in 1834. As a record of the visitors to Byron's grave during the decade after his death, when debates about the poet's controversial literary legacy and his body's exclusion from Westminster Abbey were at their fiercest, the album acquires a peculiar and peculiarly ironic prestige through its absence. William MacDowall, writing in 1876 about Burns's mausoleum, presents the prestigious numbers and status of visitors in terms of their autographs – or rather, the lack of them:

> Since the completion of the Mausoleum many illustrious men, from all parts of the world, have stood beneath its dome, paying homage due to the still more illustrious dead. No album has been kept, in which their names, with those of other visitors, might have been entered; had there been such it would have been perhaps the most precious collection of autographs ever made.[12]

As a local historian, MacDowall's frustration at the non-existence of this unique record is understandable. But the imaginary album of 'illustrious' autographs ('with those of other visitors') foregrounds what was by the 1870s a commonplace – that a fundamental aspect of the cultural activity of literary tourism was writing to testify that 'I was there'. Yet the nature of the autographic gesture differs widely.

My view of the usefulness of signature for theorising the gestures made at poets' graves by all kinds of amateur and professional 'writers' goes against the dominant rhetorical conventions of literary touristic writing. Tribute poems set at the grave, for instance, tend to suppress the act of writing, transforming it metaphorically into something less worldly, tangible or deliberate. Grave-pilgrims present themselves weeping, lamenting, singing; their spirits rise up, words shape themselves in the ether: what they do not acknowledge doing is jotting down notes, or coolly crafting their impressions in retrospect. Emma Blyton's 'To the Memory of Keats' (1858) presents one version of this trope:

> Still o'er that fragrant mound the tear is shed –
> The tear of sympathy for one long dead.
> O, KEATS! for ever hushed is thy mute lyre –
> Unstrung it may no more its bard inspire;
> Yet kindred bards may kindred notes prolong,
> And to thy memory tune a mournful song.

Enough for me to mourn thy once sad state,
And leave to nobler pens to trace thy fate;
Still round thy name the laurel shall entwine,
And in thy words thy monument shall shine! (ll.19–28)[13]

Blyton adapts elegiac conventions to elide the distinction between literal tears shed by visitors grieved by Keats's premature death in exile, and the 'tear[s] of sympathy' and 'mournful song[s]' performed by after-coming poets. Although Blyton has the confidence to directly address the spirit of the dead ('O, KEATS!'), she also adopts the Victorian woman poet's common stance of staking authority in emotional sincerity rather than genius ('Enough for me to mourn thy once sad state'); yet the reference to 'nobler pens' also undermines the musical metaphor of her 'mournful song', reminding the reader that Blyton's consummately literary construct was transmitted to the printed page via a handwritten manuscript, rather than by the unstrung lyre alluding to the carving on Keats's headstone. This is how Alexander Anderson's 'In Rome. A Poem in Sonnets' (1875), a working-through of the mature writer's disillusion with his youthful idol Keats, presents the pilgrim's encounter with the grave:

And as kindred spirits call
Each unto each, my own rose up to crave
A moment's sweet renewal by the dust
Of that high interchange in vanish'd time,
When my young soul was reeling with his prime; (ll.329–33)[14]

Anderson describes a characteristically post-romantic failure, present-ing his experience as comparable to ('as') but falling short of the ideal communion of 'kindred spirits call[ing]/Each unto each' for which the speaker nostalgically yearns. Although this sonnet opens with the speaker's self-reproach that he had almost left Rome without seeing Keats's grave, Keats 'from whom thy soul/Took early draughts of wor-ship and control – /Poet thyself' (324–6), that self-identification as poet is disavowed. Despite the substantial textual evidence to the contrary, tourists are rare who acknowledge the mediating hand and inscribe themselves as writers in their account of the poet's grave.

Joseph Severn's *Atlantic Monthly* essay, 'On the Vicissitudes of Keats's Fame' (1863) both documents the possible negative consequences of intensive grave-tourism and argues for a more constructive reading of such interventions. Severn invokes the grave as a measure of the growth in Keats's critical reputation and popularity between 1821 and 1861:

> That grave, which I can remember as once the object of ridicule, has now become the poetic shrine of the world's pilgrims who care and strive to live in the happy and imaginative region of poetry. The head-stone, having twice sunk, owing to its faulty foundation, has been twice renewed by loving strangers, and each time, as I am informed, these strangers were Americans. Here they do not strew flowers, as was the wont of olden times, but they pluck everything that is green and living on the grave of the poet. The *Custode* tells me, that, notwithstanding all his pains in sowing and planting, he cannot 'meet the great consumption.' Latterly an English lady, alarmed at the rapid disappearance of the verdure on and around the grave, actually left an annual sum to renew it. When the *Custode* complained to me of the continued thefts ... I replied, 'Sow and plant twice as much ...'[15]

Severn's idealised rendering of the grave-visitors as occupying 'the happy and imaginative regions of poetry' seems at odds with the two more practical gestures he cites. On one hand, there is the donation of funds by 'loving strangers' to re-erect the headstone with its famous inscription 'Here lies one whose name was writ in water'; on the other there is the 'great consumption' and 'theft' of 'everything that is green and living on the grave.' The latter behaviour appears less like the tribute of 'loving strangers' than the voracity of a plague of touristic locusts. This is evidently how the *Custode* and 'English lady' perceive the 'alarming' traces of the mass tourism. The organic aesthetic of Keats's grave is not incidental to its prestige: symbolically, a green and living grave affirms the writer's vital afterlife, and implicitly if the taking of violets, daisies and leaves continues on the same scale, the grave's affective and aesthetic integrity will be exhausted or 'consumed'. Yet Severn's determinedly optimistic reading presents these attentions as affirming the priority of Keats's grave as the 'poetic shrine of the world's pilgrims'. It is a subtly autographic gesture, part of Severn's long career as the self-appointed authority on Keats's last days and death.

We might compare Severn's recuperation of apparent desecration with the sometimes intrusive or aggressive presence of the literary pilgrim in tribute poems. Alfred Austin's near-contemporaneous 'At Shelley's Grave', was written after the young author visited the Protestant Cemetery in April 1863, during the French occupation of Rome.[16] The irony of visiting the grave of a great poet of political liberty when '[t]he insolence of a stranger drum,/Vexing the broad blue air,// … Rolls unrebuked around his grave' (17–18, 24) stimulates an apostrophe to Shelley's spirit – 'Oh wake, dead heart! Come back!' (33) – and a fantasy that the extent of oppression is enough to 'reanimate thy dust' in indignation and revenge (40). If the speaker then seems to recognise the inappropriateness (as well as impossibility) of his fantasy, reflecting 'Nay, Poet, rest thou quiet there' (41), the tact of the moment is soon undermined by the speaker's pose as activist-hero: 'I snatch the banner from thy grave,/I wave the torch on high; 'Spite smiling tyrant, crouching slave,/ The Cause shall never die!' (65–8). While the banner and torch that Austin snatches may be purely symbolic, the writing of himself into the tribute poem as Shelley's heroic successor demonstrates an intention to snatch Shelley's pen. Although the mood of exhilaration is quickly punctured by anxieties about his secondariness – 'Alas! You failed, who were so strong: /Shall I succeed, so weak?' (73–4) – the gestures are disingenuous, because they force an association with Shelley that the dead cannot refuse. Similarly, while we may warmly assent to Austin's self-criticism 'You sang – I scarce can speak' (76), the poem itself performs Austin's ability to 'speak' in the present tense, speaking which locates Shelley's song in the past ('You sang'), and hints that the living dog might be better than the dead lion.

A more satisfyingly strong autographic rewriting is the young Oscar Wilde's account of a visit to Keats's grave in 1877, in which he expresses his dissatisfaction with the 'common-looking grave' by radically re-presenting it.[17] Wilde pays lip service to the Romantic convention that a modest, natural grave is most fitting for a poet, but he also grumbles that 'this time-worn stone and these wild flowers are but poor memorials of one so great as Keats': 'For very noble is the site, and worthy of a noble monument'. By rhetorical sleight of hand he even attempts to create the 'noble monument': the nearby first century BCE pyramid of Caius Cestius, a forgotten Roman, 'will be ever dear to the eyes of all English-speaking people, because at evening its shadow falls on the tomb of one who walks with Spenser, and Shakespeare, and Byron, and Shelley, and Elizabeth Barrett Browning, in the great procession of the sweet singers of England.' Through the shadow's insubstantial contact with Keats's grave, the classical pyramid is appropriated as a monumental signpost to the English poet whose mean grave is occluded by a transcendent procession of 'sweet singers'. Wilde also rhetorically refurbishes the grave by citing the texts which came to his mind while looking at 'the violets, and the daisies, and the poppies that overgrow the tomb': evocative celebrations of the Protestant Cemetery and its Keatsian associations from Robert Monckton Milnes, Shelley (in his preface to *Adonais*), and Keats himself in his last words to Severn ('I feel the flowers growing over me'). A footnote reveals that Wilde's determination to aestheticise Keats's grave has a particular environment stimulus, since 'some well-meaning persons' (for which read wrong-headed philistines) had recently erected a memorial slab on a nearby wall, with a medallion-profile representing Keats's face as 'ugly, and rather hatchet-shaped, with thick, sensual lips', accompanied by 'some mediocre lines of poetry'. Wilde replaces the ugly portrait (marginalised to the footnote, where he hopes this 'marble libel' will be removed) and inadequate grave with his own aestheticised symbolic fantasy:

> As I stood beside the mean grave of this divine boy, I thought of him as a Priest of Beauty slain before his time; and the vision of Guido's St. Sebastian came before my eyes as I saw him at Genoa, a lovely brown boy, with crisp, clustering hair and red lips, bound by his evil enemies to a tree, and, though pierced by arrows, raising his eyes with divine, impassioned gaze towards the Eternal Beauty of the opening heavens. (478)

This 'vision' of the consumptive Keats as a martyred Sebastian pierced through with arrows, and the dramatic rewriting of the grave in the image of the pilgrim's eroticised fantasy, bear the unmistakable early Wildean autograph, not least because the grave is presented in terms of the art he has seen while touring Italy. Guido's painting provides a counter-aesthetic to the medallion, while 'a coloured bust, like that of the young Rajah of Koolapoor at Florence', is urged as a replacement, and Wilde's sonnet 'Heu Miserande Puer' ('Alas Wretched Boy'), a substitute for the mediocre poetry. The sonnet is presented not as a written text, but as the involuntary spontaneous growth of inspiration: 'And thus my thoughts shaped themselves to rhyme' (478). Wilde's article concludes with the sonnet, which appears in a heavily revised version as 'The Grave of Keats' in editions of his collected works.

The selected texts of literary grave-tourism I have discussed make partly legible the elusive mindset of the Victorian 'pilgrim' visiting the graves of Keats and Shelley at Rome. Reading literary grave-visitors' behaviour through the terms of literal and metaphorical signature could provide an interpretative model that responds to the extremely variable quality, interest and sophistication of the heterogeneous literature of literary tourism. The signature is the barely legible name of a forgotten person scribbled in a visitors' book; it is also the unique stamp of 'genius', the authenticating and powerful name of the author; and in symbolic terms it is the mark of personality and subjective experience that subtly permeates even the most apparently generic accounts. These scribbling pilgrims position themselves not only as humbled worshippers of genius, but as active, creative beings, empowered at the grave by its evidence of their own creative life.

Notes

1. See Ian Hamilton, *Literary Estates and the Rise of Biography from Shakespeare to Plath* (London: Hutchinson, 1991); Michael Millgate, *Testamentary Acts: Browning, Tennyson, James and Hardy* (Oxford: Clarendon Press, 1992); and my *Poetical Remains: Poets' Graves, Bodies, and Books in the Nineteenth Century* (Oxford: Oxford University Press, 2004).
2. See Péter Dávidházi, *The Romantic Cult of Shakespeare: Literary Reception in Anthropological Perspective* (Basingstoke: Palgrave, 1998); Allison Lockwood, *Passionate Pilgrims: The American Traveler in Great Britain, 1800–1914* (New Jersey: Fairleigh Dickinson University Press, 1981); Chris Rojek, *Leisure and Culture* (New York: St. Martin's Press, 1999).
3. For a detailed case study of the development and representation of Keats and Shelley's 'exile' graves, see my 'Bringing Home Keats and Shelley', *Poetical Remains*, 113–53.
4. The 'authenticity' and aura conferred by corporeal presence is degraded by factors such as missing body parts, cremation, or a memorial or setting at odds with the author's *oeuvre* or wishes. Conversely, aura can be conferred by a minimal corporeal relic. Shelley's charred heart was supposedly buried with Mary Shelley at St. Peter's Churchyard, Bournemouth, in 1852, and Thomas Hardy's heart was interred in the family grave at Stinsford, Dorset. The heart, symbol of both immortal poetry and personal passion, is a powerful synecdoche. See Kirstie Blair, *Victorian Poetry and the Culture of the Heart* (Oxford: Oxford University Press, 2006).
5. Barbara Bender, 'Place and Landscape' in C. Tilley et al., *Handbook of Material Culture* (London: Sage, 2006), 303.
6. See John Ezard, 'William Hazlitt's Near-Derelict Grave Restored', *The Guardian*, 11 April 2003.
7. Nicola J. Watson, *The Literary Tourist: Readers and Places in Romantic & Victorian Britain* (Basingstoke: Palgrave Macmillan, 2006), 34.
8. Jacques Derrida, 'Signature Event Context' (1977) in *A Derrida Reader: Between the Blinds*, ed. Peggy Kamuf (New York: Columbia University Press, 1991), 107.
9. Watson, 25.
10. Mark Twain, *The Innocents Abroad: Or, The New Pilgrims' Progress*, fwd. Shelley Fisher Fishkin, intr. Mordecai Richler, awd. David E.E. Sloane ([1869] Oxford: Oxford University Press, 1996), 529.
11. William Winter, *Gray Days and Gold. Revised, with Illustrations* ([1889] New York: Macmillan, 1896), 134.

12. William MacDowall, *Memorials of St. Michael's, The Old Parish Churchyard of Dumfries* (Edinburgh, 1876), 109.
13. Emma Blyton, 'To the Memory of Keats', *Poetical Tributes to the Memories of British Bards, and Other Poems* (London: A.W. Bennett, 1858), 22.
14. Alexander Anderson, 'In Rome. A Poem in Sonnets', *The Two Angels and Other Poems* (London: Simpkin, Marshall and Co., 1875), 122–39.
15. Joseph Severn, *Atlantic Monthly* 11 (April 1863): 406–7.
16. Alfred Austin, 'At Shelley's Grave. Rome, April 1863', *Interludes* (Edinburgh: William Blackwood, 1872), 15–20.
17. Oscar Wilde, 'The Tomb of Keats', *Irish Monthly* (July 1877), 477.

3
The Land of Burns: between Myth and Heritage

Karyn Wilson-Costa

Writing in 1893, the French poet and scholar Auguste Angellier remarked on the huge numbers of literary pilgrims who came to Britain from the four corners of the world to pay homage to the country's writers.[1] The most visited of these literary shrines, according to him, was the 'clay biggin' where the Scottish poet Robert Burns was born. His birthplace and mausoleum, his favourite haunts and walks in what had become known as the 'Land of Burns', attracted literary tourists from early in the nineteenth century, responding to the Ayrshire bard's creation of a sense of literary place in his poems and songs.

In the verse epistle 'To William Simson of Ochiltree', written in May 1785, Burns had bemoaned the fact that his native Ayrshire had been ignored by previous poets:

Nae *Poet* thought her worth his while,
To set her name in measur'd style;
She lay like some unkend-of isle
      Beside *New Holland.* (11.37–40)

A year later, Burns clearly stated his intention of creating a literary space for Ayrshire through writing and naming in his poem 'The Vision,' published in 1786, in which he celebrates an Ayrshire landscape energised by the power and beauty of its rivers:

Here, DOON pour'd down his far-fetched floods;
There, well-fed IRWINE stately thuds:
Auld hermit AIRE staw thro' his woods,
      On to the shore;

And many a lesser torrent scuds
With seeming roar. (79–84)

These Ayrshire destinations were to become increasingly popular with tourists over the course of the century. Writing a hundred years later, when literary tourism had become a widespread middle-class pursuit, critic Principal Shairp, professor of English literature at Oxford University, remarked in his 1879 biography ‚of Burns, that 'In his ardour to look upon places famous for their natural beauty or their historic associations, or even for their having been mentioned in some old Scottish song, Burns...anticipated the sentiment of the present century.'[2]

Robert Burns was born on 25 January 1759, in Alloway, Ayrshire, a small town in the Scottish Lowlands, and spent his youth in the surrounding area before moving to Edinburgh after the success of the first edition of his poems, published in Kilmarnock in July 1786. He undertook tours to the Borders and to the Highlands during this period, before leasing a farm in Ellisland, near Dumfries, which he was forced to relinquish in 1791 for financial reasons. He then took up a full-time position in the Excise in Dumfries, where he died on 21 July 1796. This region of south-west Scotland was referred to as early as 1818 as 'Burns's Country' by John Keats, one of the first of many poets to make a pilgrimage to the land of the birth of Scotland's national poet.

Keats visited the 'Bard's low cradle-place,'[3] after touring the Ayrshire landscape, which he initially found charming, but his buoyant mood of expectancy vanished on entering the cottage and finding it converted into a common drinking-shop.[4] Evidently outraged at such a betrayal of genius, he dismissed it as a 'flummery of a birthplace!'[5] Before leaving Scotland, he visited Burns's white marble mausoleum in Dumfries, whose 'cold Beauty' (8) inspired his sonnet 'On Visiting the Tomb of Burns.' This poem, together with 'Lines Written in the Highlands after a Visit to Burns's Country', contributed to what Archibald R. Adamson, a future rambler through the 'Land of Burns', in 1879, was to refer to as 'the thought-gemmed literary cairn raised to the memory of the Peasant Poet.'[6] The first stones of that virtual cairn had already been laid by William Wordsworth, when he composed 'At the Grave of Burns' and 'Thoughts Suggested the Day Following, Near the Poet's Residence,' after visiting the birthplace and the original grave of Burns in Alloway churchyard, in 1803. Written on the banks of the Nith, one of Burns's favourite spots, this last poem imagined the Scottish bard finding inspiration in his rural home and haunts, laying down a template for how to enhance an experience of the physical landscape with the imagined figure of the poet:

> How oft inspired must he have trode
> These pathways, yon far-stretching road!
> There lurks his home; in that Abode,
>   With mirth elate,
> Or in his nobly-pensive mood,
> The Rustic sate. (31–6)

The trope of the literary pilgrim treading in the footsteps of the revered author was to become a key feature of nineteenth-century literary reception and literary tourism in general. Minor Scottish poet Hew Ainslie's *A Pilgrimage to the Land of Burns and Poems*, an account of a visit in 1820 published in 1822, is full of admiration for Burns's genius and descriptions of the 'fair land of the Patriot and Bard' that gave him birth, the rivers by which he wandered and the woods that inspired him. For Ainslie, the land in which Burns lived both inspired his songs and faithfully amplifies them for the visitor:

> All around – the mounts, rivers, forests and floods – cry loudly of him, for he spoke of them. There lies the living library that stored his mind, and the pages from which he faithfully copied. His soul gushed forth in the brawl of the Bonny Doon, melted into the melody at the song of these leafy woods, or mounted into Heaven with the wing of the morning lark. Nature, in a word, was his nurse, and while she lives, will be his monument.[7]

Like Ainslie, the American poet Fitz-Greene Halleck also made an early visit to Burns country. He composed 'To a Rose, brought from near Alloway Kirk, in Ayrshire, in the autumn of 1822' on his return to the United States after visiting the land of the 'Bard-peasant'. The poem is a narration of his pilgrimage from Burns's birthplace, 'the cottage-bed/ Where the Bard-peasant first drew breath' (25–6), to the pilgrim shrine of his grave, the poet's tomb in Dumfries and 'his funeral columns, wreaths and urns' (150). This 'flower culled for Burns'[8] was thus added to Adamson's 'posy of other men's flowers' (Preface), to be laid on the poet's grave, a bouquet of responses to his poems, made up of so many echoes of his most cherished lines.[9]

In 1840, with the publication of *The Land of Burns,* David Octavius Hill invented another type of tribute to the poet, a virtual and visual literary pilgrimage. *The Land of Burns* supplied over 30 engravings depicting places celebrated for their connection with the great man's life and works, accompanied by a series of descriptions in prose directing the reader to the relevant topographical references in the poems and songs in essays written by Professor John Wilson (*The Works of Robert Burns and Complete Life of the Poet and an Essay on his Genius and Character*, 1846) and Robert Chambers (*The Life and Works of Robert Burns*, 1856–1857), two of Burns's most influential mid nineteenth-century biographers. The relationship between biography and literary tourism is clearly very close in this guided tour of both Burns's poetical works and private space. Volume 1 of *The Land of Burns* is prefaced with lines by Fitz-Greene Halleck which pay tribute to the places depicted as tourist attractions, and constitute the experience of perusing this drawing-room book as itself a virtual tour and guide to future would-be pilgrims with its direct references to places evoked in some of Burns's best-known songs and poems:

> All ask the cottage of his birth,
>   Gaze on the scenes he loved and sung,
> And gather feelings not of earth
>   His fields and streams among.
> They linger by the Doon's low trees,
>   And pastoral Nith, and wooded Ayr,
>   And round thy sepulchres, Dumfries!

Hill's volumes are notable for newly extending 'The Land of Burns' out of Ayrshire into wider Scotland, and most notably, into the Highlands. Several of Hill's scenes are set in the Highlands and tacitly reflect the widely-held idea that Burns's romantic sensibility made him heir to the third-century Gaelic bard Ossian. During his lifetime, the notion of Burns as an uncultivated 'national' poet was widely propagated in the wake of the success of James Macpherson's Ossianic poems,[10] all of which were warmly received by Edinburgh literary society. Macpherson's poems turned attention to wild nature, Scotland's mythic past and folk culture, playing a crucial role in the creation of the new, romantic Highland identity which was conferred on Scotland principally by the writings of Sir Walter Scott in the decades following Burns's death. In the early years of the nineteenth century, the topography of the Highlands was established as one of the country's prime visual signifiers, and it would-be rendered the height of fashion by Victoria and Albert's purchase of Balmoral Castle in 1848, where the Queen thereafter spent every autumn 'living in a whimsical candyfloss world of "traditional" Scottish culture.'[11] So by providing Burns with Highland credentials, Hill widened the geographical scope of the Land of Burns so the poet was not merely the local Ayrshire bard or the poet of the Lowlands but the national bard of all Scotland, a flexible position he has continued to fill to this day. For Penny Fielding, writing on the act of imagining place through Burns and his poetry, 'Along with all the other paraphernalia of Victorian and contemporary Scotland, not forgetting the practices of the Scottish tourist board, Burns was pressed into service to stand for various divisions: Scotland in general, the Lowlands, and the South-West of the country.'[12] Indeed, since 1840 the geographical borders of the Land of Burns have not been fixed; they have been porous and provisional, with a tendency to shift according to the social, political, artistic and cultural construct of the historical moment.

The practice of providing landscape illustrations to Burns's poems and songs which followed on Hill's pioneering publication reinforced the nineteenth-century and early twentieth-century myth of Burns as a purely pastoral poet of rusticity, created in 1800 by his first biographer, Dr James Currie. Andrew Nash argues that 'by encouraging readers to approach Burns's poetry with an accompanying set of visual references, nineteenth-century editors were giving currency to the understanding of Burns as a poet who laid bare the realities of everyday life in Scotland in the manner of a tourist's guidebook.'[13] In reading Burns, it was widely believed that one was reading about traditional rural, peasant Scotland, so attractive to Victorians caught up in pastoral nostalgia for a vanishing primitive world.

The lure of a sense of past rural life and an agrarian utopia, romantic sentiments that still resonate widely in the heritage industry of today's post-industrial, post-modern society, underpinned to a large extent the Victorians' enthusiasm for the Land of Burns and their desire to conjure up an imagined past. Perhaps the Victorians' favourite poem of all was 'The Cotter's Saturday Night' which freeze-framed Scotland for them as a country of pious, humble, God-fearing peasants, and offered a comforting picture of a pious all-accepting country folk to a literati which felt increasingly threatened by an anarchic urban, industrial crowd. Tourists flocked to the whitewashed cottage in Alloway, described by Archibald Adamson as the 'cottage of the pious father of the "Cotter's Saturday Night"':

After looking around the memorial chamber, I was next conducted to the most hallowed part of the cottage – namely, the kitchen for in it, on a humble pallet, Robert Burns was ushered into the world. Its walls echoed with the first tones of his voice, and its spacious hearth was the altar round which William Burness and his family assembled to hymn the Creator's praise (chapter VI).

There was, it must be said, more than a touch of voyeurism in the Victorians' desire to peep into every corner of Burns's life. They consumed not only his literary life in the numerous biographies that were published in the nineteenth century, but also his private space by visiting all the nooks and crannies associated with him and his poetry. Adamson's *Rambles* are studded with examples of this desire to relive the life of the poet.

For Raymond Williams, the 'Memory Place' depends on appeal to the 'escalator effect' of pastoral nostalgia, which he traces back to Anglo-Saxon times, 'each generation recalling the last as having lived in closer intimacy with our natural surroundings.'[14] Writing about place-attachment, environmental critic Laurence Buell has foregrounded the role of places as 'centres of felt value, defined by physical markers',[15] the retention of which often depends on story and song, as more and more migrants take their places abroad with them. By the middle of the century Robert Burns had reached the peak of his fame, and this in many ways is attributable to a confluence of both these types of nostalgia. The widespread centenary celebrations of 1859 marked 'the point at which the transformation of Burns from controversial literary celebrity into "immortal memory" seems to have been completed.'[16] Burns Clubs had sprung up around the world: the first was founded in Greenock in 1801, and clubs at Paisley, Kilmarnock and Dunfermline followed close on its heels. The idea spread to India in 1812 and thereafter to Canada, the United States of America and Australia. By 1885, there were so many Burns Clubs in existence that an international Federation of clubs was instituted to coordinate this extraordinary network dedicated to the memory not merely of Burns, but also of the Land of Burns, a construct in the collective memory of all those who were part of the huge Scottish Diaspora, large numbers of whom were Lowland Scots. Scotland was, in fact, the emigration capital of Europe for much of the nineteenth century, the number of British emigrants doubling between 1801 and 1851, a large proportion of whom were Scots. With a certain amount of perspicacity, Dr Currie had foreseen the power which Burns's poems and songs would have over exiled Scots: '[...] the idiom of their country unites with the sentiments and the description on which it is employed, to recall to their minds the interesting scenes of infancy and youth – to awaken many pleasing, many tender recollections.'[17] Burns's use of the Scots dialect did indeed facilitate the development of this nostalgia bred by exile; when Scots expatriates wished to remember the vanished rural Scotland of their childhood, they would evoke it through listening to and singing the songs of Burns. In America, three seminal song collections containing ballads of the Anglo-Celtic tradition, products of the European Folk Movement of the late eighteenth and early nineteenth centuries, were extremely popular. Robert Burns had been a primary contributor to one of them, James Johnson's *Scots Musical Museum,*[18] and as a result his songs were widely sung and exerted substantial influence over home-grown American songwriters. These included Stephen Collins Foster (1826–1864), who wrote lilting, nostalgic melodies of home and hearth, love and longing, such as 'Ah! May the Red Rose Live Alway' (1850), inspired by Burns's 'My Love is Like a Red, Red, Rose', and 'Jeanie with the Light Brown Hair' (1854); both owe much to the Scottish folk tradition that Burns sought so tirelessly to preserve. Burns-worship was intrinsically linked to this nostalgic reminiscing for an idealised, long-lost 'Scotland' and Burns himself venerated for having preserved the ancient vernacular language of Scots. His songs painted an idealising portrait of this 'Scotland' that no longer existed for those who emigrated to the four corners of the British Empire, or, indeed, for those internal economic exiles now living in English towns and cities.

The theme of 'loss,' a necessary component of national nostalgia, underpins many of Burns's songs and poems, paradoxically creating space to keep alive a sense of presence through absence and memory. Enshrined amongst the Victorians' favourite songs were 'Thou Lingering Star' and 'Highland Mary,' morbidly sentimental songs both addressed to Burns's lost love, the dead Margaret Campbell, which formed the heart of the myth that grew up around her tragic relationship with Burns, and which obsessed Victorian Burnsians from near and far, as they travelled to gaze on the landscapes evoked in these same songs while revisiting the land of the Ayrshire bard. Favourite halts on visits to the Land of Burns were the sites where Margaret Campbell and Burns were said to have exchanged bibles and vows of fidelity on either side of a stream near Castle Montgomery, and 'Highland Mary's Thorn,' the tree beneath which Burns bade her farewell for the last time, immortalised in the song 'Highland Mary':[19]

How sweetly bloom'd the gay, green birk,
How rich the hawthorn's blossom;

As underneath their fragrant shade,
I clasp'd her to my bosom! (9–12)[20]

The unfortunate girl was, according to the myth, supposed to accompany the poet to the West Indies, where he planned to take up a position as bookkeeper on a plantation, in the autumn of 1786. However Burns never sailed to Jamaica, but went instead to Edinburgh on the strength of the success of the first edition of his poems, published in Kilmarnock on 31 July 1786, to be fêted as the new natural genius by the literati there. Margaret Campbell died of a malignant fever in Greenock, where she had gone to wait for Burns to join her. The story of the two 'star-crossed lovers' is an integral part of the Burns myth the world over; the statue of Burns placed in New York's Central Park in 1880, for example, depicts the poet on a tree stump, having just composed a poem to his love Mary, which is written on a scroll at his feet.

As the presence of these stops on any tour of the land of Burns suggests, the landscape was saturated with a sense of Burns's biography as much as it was with his literary output, a saturation made more possible by the autobiographical component of the songs. Elements of these proved problematic, however, for many of his idolaters. The Scottish bard had earned a reputation as a drunken womaniser during his short lifetime. The fact that Burns 'talked with Bitches and drank with Blackguards'[21] was a source of unease and embarrassment for his biographers and admirers alike. Wordsworth, for example, had pleaded for God's forgiveness for the bard's profligate life when he visited the latter's grave in 1803: 'Sweet Mercy! To the gates of Heaven/This Minstrel lead, his sins forgiven,'[22] while John Greenleaf Whittier wrote these lines for the Boston celebration of the centenary of Burns's birth in 1859:

Today be every fault forgiven
Of him in whom we joy
We take, with thanks, the gold oh Heaven
And leave the earth's alloy.'[23]

Nevertheless, his character was typically whitewashed by the critics after his death so he could be admired as the sentimental national icon they were so keen to promote, and his bawdy and satirical poems and songs disappeared from the canon. The Victorians read only those deemed decorous, and chose to foreground the image of a successful untutored genius. Many literary pilgrims were led to visit what they often referred to in their writings as consecrated, hallowed ground, and in later accounts there is often an element of pilgrimage, of a voyage of self-discovery and self-improvement in a 'holy' land, a sense of becoming a better person after visiting the scenes made famous by Burns. The stress on piety and self-improvement was disseminated throughout Victorian society; such a didactic tale of triumph in the face of adversity as that of the poet's life could not fail to attract them.

The reputation of Burns was moulded to accommodate the widely-held belief that talent was God-given and not the preserve of noble birth; witness the large number of life-size statues that were erected in his honour, not only throughout his native Scotland, but also in the United States, Canada, Australia, wherever the Scots were emigrating. Thomas Carlyle in his 'Essay on Burns' of 1828,[24] was the first to tell the uplifting story of the poor man's son, 'with no furtherance but such knowledge as dwells in a poor man's hut,' who pulled himself up by the bootstraps to overcome his disadvantaged circumstances. Historian Tom Devine cogently sums up the kind of cultural hero the Victorians made of Burns:

> The historic Burns and his remarkable literary achievement were moulded to suit the political tastes of a Victorian middle-class readership. He was depicted as anti-aristocratic and as a man who had succeeded by his own talent rather than through inherited privilege or noble birth. Burns became the apotheosis of 'the lad o' pairts', a key element in the most influential of Victorian myths, that personal ability alone was enough to achieve success in life.[25]

The Land of Burns held the key to the secret of this myth of the 'Heaventaught ploughman'[26] which continued to have wide currency throughout the nineteenth century, drawing people to visit the surroundings, which were for Archibald Adamson 'eminently calculated to invite the footsteps of a poet'(chapter xix). Literary tourism was not, however, the sole preserve of the English or of exiled Scots. Continental tourists were also interested in British writers and their homes and haunts. French poet Richard De La Madelaine made a pilgrimage to the bucolic country of Ayrshire in search of the revelation of the Scottish bard's genius, and afterwards translated a number of poems and songs by Burns in 1874.[27] In nineteenth-century France, Burns enjoyed the reputation of a poet of an almost ideal simplicity and naturalness; he was the rustic bard *par excellence* who did not look at nature through the spectacles of books.[28] As the bard himself put it in his 'Epistle to Lapraik': 'Gie me ae spark o' Nature's fire,/That's a' the learning I desire' (73–4), and the French, like everyone else, took him at his word. De La Madelaine was one of the first French literary tourists, remarking in the introduction to his translations that his fellow countrymen had hitherto been content to visit Scotland, the land of romance, with the historical Skeleton Tours, the first all-inclusive package tours. They visited famous abbeys, castles and battlefields and the dramatic scenery of the romantic Highlands, but showed no interest in the places associated with the writers of what he referred to as one of the most enlightened countries in Europe. Quoting a Breton proverb *'Kant klevet né dleout ked eur gwelet*, cent lus ne valent pas un vu' ('seeing with one's own eyes is better than reading a hundred books'), De la Madelaine insisted it was time for the French to leave the comfort of their fireside and visit neighbouring countries, in order to enrich French civilisation and ideas and gain a greater understanding of foreign writers and their works. A forerunner in French literary criticism of Burns, he followed in Burns's footsteps, poems in hand, just as Wordsworth had done three-quarters of a century earlier, and embarked on a literary pilgrimage to revive the Scottish bard's muse by reading his poetical works in the places they evoked. His journey led him in search of the poet's soul from the Alloway kirk to the castle of Montgomery, by way of Tarbolton, Mauchline, Ellisland, the banks of the Doon, the Gala, the Nith and the Lugar.

Tellingly, De La Madelaine chose to translate mainly songs, rather than poems from the Burns canon, most of which have a pastoral theme and paint an idealised landscape, idyllic and dreamlike, in conventional neoclassic set-pieces which the Scottish bard superimposes onto real topographical detail. 'Afton Water', 'The Birks of Aberfeldy', 'Now Spring has Clad the Grove in Green' are all songs set in places Burns frequented. Amongst the few poems that are not songs included by De La Madelaine are four set in Burns's native Ayrshire: 'Tam o' Shanter', 'Death and Doctor Hornbook', 'The Brigs o' Ayr' and 'To a Mouse.' 'A Cotter's Saturday Night' is also translated, echoing the Victorians' love of this poem. The Land of Burns which the French translator presented to his readers was therefore designed to perpetuate the myth of the peasant poet, the pastoral piper of the primitive country of Ayrshire, home of picturesque landscapes, timeless rural traditions and superstitions, all of which was received wisdom in nineteenth-century France. The strong tradition of rural life, found in particular in the Scottish song culture, appealed to De La Madelaine, and so did the fact that the Ayrshire ploughmen and shepherds continued their timeless occupations, untouched by the industrialising forces at work in nearby Glasgow and Paisley: 'Le buit des marteaux dans les fonderies de Glasgow, le sifflement des machines dans les filatures de paisley n'y vont point troubler le laboureur à sa charrue, le berger au milieu des bruyères' (xiii). On his first visit to Scotland he was charmed to hear ordinary people singing and reciting poems and songs by their national bard, whose work he was unaware of, and this was what inspired his return on a pilgrimage in search of Burns's poetic genius.

Burns himself, this icon of locality, does not so much describe as inscribe, in order to produce place, to make Ayrshire's 'unkend-of' status known through writing. Penny Fielding suggests that Burns is in fact neither a 'national bard' nor a 'local' bard, since 'as a poet, he is far more interested in exploring the textual determinants of placing, than in positing a lived, pre-textual place' (184). Burns's sense of locality is associated with a nostalgic sense of ideal community, place imagined as the place of shared experience and story-telling. Burns's loco-descriptive poetry and songs created place by inscribing it topographically. By being geographically specific, they contributed to the creation of literary place, the Land of Burns. Yet the Land of Burns was created in the end, not by Burns himself, but by the dissemination and consumption of his poetry, and by the practice of relating poetry to place whether virtually, in books of engravings, or travel-narratives, or by tourists' visits, or by practices of memorialisation.

Notes

1. Auguste Angellier, *Robert Burns La Vie et l'œuvre*. 2 vols (Paris: Hachette, 1893).
2. Principal Shairp, *Robert Burns* (London: Macmillan, 1879), 60.
3. 'Lines Written in the Highlands after a Visit to Burns's Country' (28). *Keats Selected Poems and Letters*, ed. Sandra Anstey (Oxford: Heinemann, 1995), 61.
4. For a full discussion of Keats's visit to Burns's cottage, see Nicola J. Watson, *The Literary Tourist* (Houndmills: Palgrave Macmillan, 2006), 73.
5. Keats wrote about Burns's birthplace in a letter to Reynolds during his Scottish tour. See Sidney Colvin, *John Keats, His Life and Poetry, His Friends, Critics and After-Fame*, ch. 9. http://englishhistory.net/keats/contents.html (accessed 21 November 2007).
6. Archibald R. Adamson, *Rambles Through the Land of Burns* (Kilmarnock: Dunlop and Drennan, 1879), Preface. www.electricscotland.com/burns/indexhtml (accessed 16 February 2007).
7. Hew Ainslie, *A Pilgrimage to the Land of Burns, and Poems* (London: Paisley and Gardner, 1892), 127.
8. John Greenleaf Whittier, 'Fitz-Greene Halleck', 32. *Whittier's Poetical Works* (London: Ward, Lock & Co, 1956), 186.
9. For a full discussion of burial-places as essential components of the literary biography, see Samantha Matthews, *Poetical Remains: Poets' Graves, Bodies and Books in the Nineteenth Century* (Oxford: Oxford University Press, 2004), ch. 2.

10. *Fragments of Ancient Poetry* (1760); *Fingal* (1762) and *Temora* (1763).
11. John Morrison, *Painting the Nation* (Edinburgh: Edinburgh University Press, 2003), 148.
12. Penny Fielding, 'Burns's Topographies' in *Scotland and the Borders of Romanticism*, ed. L. Davies, I. Duncan and J. Sorensen (Cambridge: Cambridge University Press, 2004), 171.
13. Andrew Nash, 'The Cotter's Kailyard' in *Robert Burns and Cultural Authority*, ed. Robert Crawford (Edinburgh: Edinburgh University Press, 1996), 183.
14. Cited by Laurence Buell, *The Future of Environmental Criticism* (Oxford: Blackwell, 2005), 75.
15. Ibid., 64.
16. Carol McGuirk, 'Burns and Nostalgia' in *Burns Now*, ed. Kenneth Simpson (Edinburgh: Canongate, 1994), 32.
17. Dr. James Currie, *The Works of Robert Burns* (Liverpool, 1800), 68.
18. *The Scots Musical Museum*, 6 vols (Edinburgh, 1787–1803).
19. For how these sites were gradually ruined by souvenir hunters and an invasion of commemorative plaques, see Nicola J. Watson, op. cit. 82–3.
20. *The Canongate Burns*, ed. Andrew Noble and Patrick Scott Hogg (Edinburgh: Canongate, 2001), 767.
21. See letter to Reynolds in Sidney Colvin.
22. 'Thoughts Suggested the Day Following, on the Banks of Nith' (55–6). William Wordsworth, *Selected Poems* (Reading: Penguin, 1996), 163.
23. 'LINES, read at the Boston Celebration of the hundredth anniversary of the birth of Robert Burns' (25–8), *Whittier's Poetical Works*, 160–1.
24. In Donald Low, *Robert Burns. The Critical Heritage* (London: Routledge, 1974), 351–93.
25. Tom Devine, *The Scottish Nation 1700–2000* (London: Penguin, 1999), 294.
26. Henry Mackenzie, unsigned essay in *The Lounger*, 9 December 1786, in Low, op. cit., 70.
27. Richard de la Madelaine, *Robert Burns traduit de l'écossais* (Rouen: E. Cagniard, 1874).
28. De la Madelaine writes of Burns's apparent lack of learning and alludes to Dryden's remarks on Shakespeare's natural genius in his *Essay of Dramatic Poetry* (1668): 'He was naturally learned; Shakespeare needed not the spectacle of books to read Nature – he looked inward and found her there.'

4
Literary Biography and the House of the Poet

Julian North

Literary tourism began to develop as a popular pursuit of the middle classes in Britain at the same time as literary biography, marketed in various forms to the same audience, emerged as one of the success stories of publishing. In many ways biography encouraged and sustained the practice of literary tourism. It was one of the most significant means of establishing authors as celebrities and disseminating their homes and habitats to a wide audience. Biographies named and described writers' houses, sometimes including collectable engravings of them, investing these homes with iconic significance and making them desirable and consumable spaces. As I shall show, biographers offered their readers imaginary tours, which functioned as vicarious experience or even as the inspiration to set out on actual literary pilgrimages.

From the 1820s, at least, it is possible to find allusions to literary tourism in *Lives* of contemporary poets. Byron's contempt for sightseers, with their telescopes trained on his house at Lake Geneva, was relayed by Thomas Medwin in his *Journal of the Conversations of Lord Byron* (1824), allowing his readers to feel nicely superior to the 'distorted optics' of the crowd, whilst fully indulging their own voyeurism.[1] Harriett Hughes's 'Memoir' of her sister, Felicia Hemans, included, amongst the extensive personal correspondence printed for the gratification of the readers' curiosity, letters in which Hemans expressed annoyance at the pursuit of autograph hunters, hounding her at her cottage in the Lakes.[2] In his *Homes and Haunts of the Most Eminent British Poets* (1847), William Howitt fused the formats of collective, literary biography and tourist guide and wrote as, himself, an unabashed tourist.[3] He headed the life-story of each poet, from Chaucer to Tennyson, with an engraving of the writer's home, or a location associated with their life and work. These sites formed the symbolic centres of the biographical essays in which Howitt recounted his own pilgrimages to the poets' 'homes and haunts'. His book was a canny experiment in marketing, but it was also fully in keeping with the ways in which biography had developed as a genre from Dr Johnson onwards.[4] Reading a *Life* had long been represented as analogous to the activity of visiting a home and, in some respects, biographical representation of the poet's house extended quite naturally to its eventual construction as a commercial site of tourism. The following discussion will explore the making of the poet's house in nineteenth-century biography, looking, in particular, at what the imaginary tour can tell us of the relationship between the poet and the reading public.

Samuel Johnson defined the special terrain of the biographer as the domestic interior. He wrote famously in 1750 that the 'business of the biographer' was 'to lead the thoughts into domestic privacies, and display the minute details of daily life'.[5]

The unique power of biography was, in his view, to create an intimate relationship between reader and subject by opening up the latter's life at home. The biographer must, in fact or in spirit, be his subject's housemate, for 'nobody can write the life of a man, but those who have eat and drink and lived in social intercourse with him'.[6] He must let the reader see public figures 'in their private Apartments, in their careless Hours, and observe those Actions in which they indulged their own Inclinations, without any Regard to Censure or Applause.'[7] The domestic focus of biography was valuable for Johnson and others after him not just because it caught the great man unawares, but because it did away with a public rhetoric of eulogy and produced, instead, authentic understanding. In entering the home of the great man, the reader of biography would gain an informal and thus a true insight, as the public façade dissolved. By going into the private apartments, biography created a temporarily levelled ground where social differences were erased and the subject and the reader met in the shared space of their common humanity.[8]

Johnson's understanding of biography raised questions which became central, not only to the development of the literary *Life*, but also to the activity of literary tourism. In what senses could either recreate an 'authentic' experience of a writer by opening up their home to view, and in what ways did this affect the dynamics of the author/reader relationship? As the publishing industry expanded in the early decades of the nineteenth century and conceptions of the writer became, in some quarters, defensively focused on the self-determining nature of genius including its capacity to exist independently of the market place, both Johnson's conception of biography and the practice of literary tourism became contentious. Nineteenth-century poets used the writer's house as a metaphor for threatened authorial autonomy rather than openness to audience. For Coleridge and Wordsworth, following Johnson, the domestic space was where the great man's authentic self would indeed be found but, for that very reason, it was to be vigorously defended against the hordes of biographers and readers of literary *Lives* who claimed admission. It was a figure for the writer's vulnerability to a commercialised and democratised print culture that was empowering the new reading public. Coleridge wrote in 1810 of contemporary biography as a criminal invasion of the great man's home, introducing 'the spirit of vulgar scandal, and personal inquietude into the Closet and the Library, environing with evil passions the very Sanctuaries, to which we should flee for refuge from them!'[9] In 1816, in an essay protesting against the exposure of Burns's private life (including his drunkenness) in James Currie's biography of the poet, Wordsworth described the 'coarse intrusions into the recesses, the gross breaches upon the sanctities, of domestic life' inflicted by literary biography.[10] Extending the metaphor, he defended the right of Robert Burns to author himself – to make, in his autobiographical verse, his own 'house'. It was here that the true Burns was to be found, although his biographers were doing their best to convince readers otherwise:

> On the basis of his human character he has reared a poetic one…. Plague, then, upon your remorseless hunters after matter of fact…. when they would convince you that the foundations of this admirable edifice are hollow; and that its frame is unsound! (123)

The figures of domestic invasion in these essays derived from sources other than literary tourism – Coleridge compared biographers and their readers to village gossips, and Wordsworth drew on the nationalistic rhetoric of home and homeland current during the invasion scares of the 1790s. But later in the century, by which time literary tourism had become a widespread and commercialised activity, Robert Browning made essentially the same protest as Wordsworth against biographical intrusion in his poem 'House', which figured the autobiographical poem as the poet's home, opened up to the paying public:

> Take notice: this building remains on view,
> Its suites of reception every one,
> Its private apartment and bedroom too;
> 'For a ticket, apply to the Publisher.'[11]

A poet is unwise to write autobiographically, for he will thereby, inevitably, invite biographical readings of his work. When it comes to his own 'house', Browning politely but firmly closes the door:

> No: thanking the public, I must decline.
> A peep through my window, if folk prefer;
> But, please you, no foot over threshold of mine! (10–12)

The poem draws on what James Buzard has described as a 'rhetoric' of tourism that, from its beginnings around the 1790s, defined the tourist experience, by contrast to that of the 'traveller', as unindividuated, unreflecting and inauthentic.[12] In the concluding stanzas, Browning imagines a house whose interior has been exposed by an earthquake, attracting a crowd who stare and speculate on the secrets of a life, apparently, displayed. The poet mingles with the onlookers, a tourist and yet not a tourist. He deplores their lack of care for the man who lived there ('Oh, he had been crushed, no doubt!' [21]) and the absence of genuine understanding:

> Outside should suffice for evidence:
> And whoso desires to penetrate
> Deeper, must dive by the spirit sense –
> No optics like yours, at any rate! (33–6)

As in Byron's earlier comment, the 'optics' of the tourist are distorted. The biographical perspective encourages pure voyeurism and thus a superficial reading of the work. The authentic view will be gained only by an *imaginative* breach of the exterior walls, that is, by reading the poetry itself. For Browning, as for Wordsworth before him, the public's obliviousness to this – their eagerness to effect a more literal entry into the poet's domestic space – figures a disturbing shift in the politics of the author–reader relationship. The works are sidelined in the drive towards mass consumption of the writer himself.

Coleridge, Wordsworth and Browning imagined the writer's home as an embattled territory, a site of conflict between the author and his works on the one hand, and literary biography and the reading public on the other. Literary biographers of the period also represented the writer's house as a place where an intense and challenging encounter between reader and author occurred, but presented it from the reader's point of view. Access to the writer was, in biography, an allowable desire. Especially after Byron's death in 1824, readers and publishers became obsessed with the private life of genius. Byron's biographers naturally capitalised on his unusually gripping domestic secrets and one of the ways in which they did this was to invite the reader to participate in a virtual visit. Memoirs by Medwin, Leigh Hunt and Lady Blessington were entirely, or almost entirely devoted to recounting the biographers' experiences as the poet's house-guest or daily companion and Medwin used the first sight of the poet at home as the dramatic starting-point for his narrative.[13] The monumental, Boswellian *Letters and Journals of Lord Byron* (1830) by Thomas Moore, dwelt on the biographer's intimate knowledge of the poet and took Byron's domestic life, and particularly the conflict between the demands of love and genius, as its focus.[14] Memoirs of Percy Shelley, Wordsworth, Felicia Hemans and Letitia Landon in the 1830s followed suit, carefully naming and describing the poets' homes, and foregrounding domestic anecdote.[15] *Lives* of the poets at this period sold themselves on their ability to deliver the writer to the reader as a living, breathing person and the home 'visit' was an important moment in substantiating this claim. Literary biographers offered the illusion of an authentic encounter that temporarily levelled the ground upon which the reader and the writer met. The crucial device here was the presence of the mediating guide – often the biographer him or herself. The reader was 'introduced' to the genius by this guide, positioned as the intimate of the poet. It was a technique that clearly borrowed from the theory of Johnson and the practice of Boswell, but one that, as we have seen, held a newly transgressive potential in the context of a Romantic conception of authorial autonomy. There are many possible examples, but I will look here at a few of the most striking, from Medwin's and Hunt's biographies of Byron, Leman Blanchard's of Letitia Landon, and William Howitt's *Homes and Haunts*.

Biographers' accounts of visiting Byron at home in the first, posthumous biographies gratified the unprecedented desire of his public to know the poet as a man. They were scenes charged with an aura of transgression – breaches of Byron's personal and authorial autonomy, enhanced by the crossing of class boundaries and the mystery that still surrounded the precise nature of his sexual relationships and alleged sexual crimes. But the breach of privacy also seemed to have been invited by the poet, by the teasing autobiographical dimension of his poetry, including his apparently shameless revelations of the intimate circumstances of his 'Separation' from Lady Byron.[16] Medwin's *Conversations* capitalised on this ambiguity. The book opens by describing his entrance into the poet's residence, the Lanfranchi Palace in Pisa, as an effortful crossing of boundaries. He stresses Byron's distance from his own (and by extension the reader's) social orbit, describing the poet's entourage of 'seven servants, five carriages, nine horses, a monkey, a bull-dog and a mastiff, two cats, three pea-fowls and some hens', adding '(I do not know whether I have classed them in order of rank).'[17] The joke cuts both ways. Medwin deflates Byron's aristocratic pretensions, but he also adopts the reader's position as a bourgeois tourist, gawping at this splendidly individual 'travelling equipage' (1). The keynote to his description of the visit is Byron's aristocracy, which forms around him a wall as impenetrable to outsiders as the Lanfranchi palace itself. The biographer can only gain entry through the offices of a fellow-poet and member of Byron's intimate circle – Shelley – who is also Medwin's relation and school-friend. As he is led inside the palace by Shelley, so Medwin leads the reader:

> 'It is one of those marble piles that seem built for eternity, whilst the family whose name it bears no longer exists,' said Shelley, as we entered a hall that seemed built for giants. 'I remember the lines in the Inferno,' said I: 'a Lanfranchi was one of the persecutors of Ugolino.' 'The same,' answered Shelley ... (2)

The exchange adds to the sense of Byron's alienation from the common man, both in terms of his genius and his social position – he inhabits a house built for 'giants' immortalised by Dante and associated with a decadent and cruel aristocracy. But the biographer still has to encounter him in person. The hallway is forbidding and the stairs guarded by an English bull-dog. He knows Shelley, growls and lets them pass. At last they arrive at the inner sanctum:

> When we were announced, we found his Lordship writing. His reception was frank and kind; he took me cordially by the hand, and said:
> 'You are a relation and schoolfellow of Shelley's – we do not meet as strangers – you must allow me to continue my letter on account of the post. Here's something for you to read, Shelley, (giving him part of his MS. of "Heaven and Earth;") tell me what you think of it.' (11–12)

It is a rush of intimacy: the poet, in his private chambers, extends his hand and greets Medwin as a friend. The giant shrinks to a human scale, the legend becomes a real man, the social barriers fall and the reader comes into contact with Byron at his least forbidding and most concerned for the response of his audience. Medwin comments, a little later, that 'the familiar ease of his conversation soon *made me perfectly at home* in his society' (14).[18] This is precisely the effect that his account of the entry into Byron's residence aims to create for the reader. It is the fantasy of the literary tourist: to be invited inside by the object of his fascination, to transform, miraculously, from humble pilgrim to the writer's valued companion.

In *Lord Byron and Some of His Contemporaries* (1828), Leigh Hunt, like Medwin, introduced the reader to an intimate relationship with Byron by breaching the walls of his houses, but here, in the least reverent of the early biographies, such intimacy was openly demystifying and politically pointed in its levelling of the relationship between the poet and his public. The tone is set when, in a reversal of Medwin's opening, it is Byron who first visits Hunt – in prison and then in Hunt's modest rooms in Paddington. Hunt's perspective is far from deferential. Byron 'I thought, took a pleasure in my room, as contrasted with the splendour of his great house. He had too much reason to do so. His domestic troubles were just about to become public.'[19]

When Hunt and his family become Byron's guests in Italy, these troubles are fully in evidence. His residence at Monte-Nero was 'the hottest-looking house I ever saw':

> Not content with having a red wash over it, the red was the most unseasonable of all reds, a salmon colour. Think of this, flaring over the country in a hot Italian sun! (9)

The colour is not only vulgar and unsettlingly exotic, it is indicative of sexual impropriety and social revolution going on inside. Hunt is taken into the interior to find the Countess, scarlet like the house: 'Her face was flushed, her eyes lit up, and her hair...looking as if it streamed in disorder' (9). He has arrived in the aftermath of a quarrel amongst the servants, during which the Countess's brother has been stabbed. The angry servant, in the red hat of a sans-culotte, waits outside to attack anyone who dares come out: 'the house was in a state of blockade; the nobility and gentry of the interior all kept in a state of impossibility by a rascally footman' (10). Hunt feels that he has stepped into a scene from *The Mysteries of Udolpho*:

> Everything was new, foreign, and violent. There was the lady, flushed and dishevelled, exclaiming against the '*sceleratio*;' the young Count, wounded and threatening; the assassin, waiting for us with his knife;

and last, not least, in the novelty, my English friend, metamorphosed, round-looking and jacketed, trying to damp all this fire with his cool tones, and an air of voluptuous indolence (10–11)

It is a comic vignette, a Gillray cartoon, or a farcical scene from *Don Juan,* representing the poet as ludicrously unable to control the disorder of his household. He is a man emasculated, an aristocrat deposed, a victim of his own domestic neglect. When Hunt moves into the Casa Lanfranchi, he offers a detailed account of Byron's daily routines that is, by contrast to the account of Monte-Nero, quietly drawn and even affectionate, but the insight into Byron's home life still leaves Hunt with reservations about his host:

> Our manner of life was this. Lord Byron, who used to sit up at night, writing Don Juan (which he did under the influence of gin and water), rose late in the morning. He breakfasted; read; lounged about, singing an air, generally out of Rossini, and in a swaggering style, though in a voice at once small and veiled; then took a bath, and was dressed; and coming downstairs, was heard, still singing, in the court-yard, out of which the garden ascended at the back of the house. The servants at the same time brought out two or three chairs. My study, a little room in a corner, with an orange-tree peering in at the window, looked upon this court-yard. I was generally at my writing when he came down, and either acknowledged his presence by getting up and saying something from the window, or he called out 'Leontius!' and came halting up to the window with some joke, or other challenge to conversation. (Readers of good sense will do me the justice of discerning where any thing is spoken of in a tone of objection, and where it is only brought in as requisite to the truth of the picture). (37–8)

The details accumulate to give the reader a genuine sense of being, like Hunt, Byron's house-guest, knowing and seeing Byron's every movement – Hunt proceeds to describe his dress, 'a nankin jacket, with white waistcoat and trousers and a cap, either velvet or linen, with a shade to it' (38). But he remains a relatively cold-eyed observer of his host's aristocratic airs. He carefully distinguishes himself from the poet, who composes at night on gin and water, where he works more wholesomely in the morning at his desk next to an orange tree. He displays the 'truth' of his own picture, by contrast, to Byron's inflated behaviour. Byron is swaggeringly masculine, but Hunt suggests something fake here – his voice is 'small and veiled.' His joking approach to his guest – 'Leontius!' – suggests a gratifying intimacy, but is part of the whole, exaggerated performance. Even at his most private, Byron is an actor. Hunt has penetrated the poet's inner sanctum, but will still, like Byron's reading public, come up against the impenetrable façade of his posturing.

Byron's biographers were perhaps more intrusive than any others at this period, but they set a trend that affected the posthumous memorialisation of other poets, male and female. Letitia Landon, known as the 'female Byron', was the focus of comparable biographical curiosity, due to the sex scandals surrounding her during her lifetime and the mysterious circumstances of her death in an African castle, to which she had journeyed with her new husband and where her body was discovered, a bottle of prussic acid in her hand. The opening up of a female poet's domestic life was clearly an especially delicate business, but Leman Blanchard's *Life and Literary Remains of L.E.L.* (1841) gave readers what may seem to us now a surprisingly intimate tour of her private circumstances. It was a lively account of Landon from her girlhood to her grim ending, investigating, with forensic detail, the possible causes of her death. Amongst the plentiful domestic insights granted to the reader was this passage, much cited by subsequent biographers, in which Blanchard reported a 'graphic' eyewitness account (by one of Landon's female friends) of the poet's bedroom in her London house:

'Genius' says our accomplished informant, 'hallows every place where it pours forth its inspirations. Yet how strongly contrasted, sometimes, is the outward reality around the poet, with the visions of his inward being. Is it not D'Israeli, in his "Curiosities of Literature," referring to this frequent incongruity, who mentions, among other facts, that Moore composed his "Lalla Rookh" in a large barn? ....Perhaps, to the L. E. L. of whom so many nonsensical things have been said – as "that she should write with a crystal pen dipped in dew upon silver paper, and use for pounce the dust of a butterfly's wing," a *dilettante* of literature would assign, for the scene of her authorship, a fairy-like boudoir, with rose-coloured and silver hangings, fitted with all the luxuries of a fastidious taste. How did the reality agree with this fancy sketch? Miss Landon's drawing-room, indeed, was prettily furnished, but it was her invariable habit to write in her bed-room. I see it now, that homely-looking almost uncomfortable room, fronting the street, and barely furnished – with a simple white bed, at the foot of which was a small, old, oblong-shaped sort of dressing-table, quite covered with a common worn writing-desk heaped with papers, while some strewed the ground, the table being too small for aught besides the desk: a little high-backed cane-chair which gave you any idea rather than that of comfort – a few books scattered about completed the author's paraphernalia.'[20]

The 'graphic' passage claims a newly authentic reading of Landon, in terms that are diametrically opposed to Browning's. As in Browning's poem, there is no easy congruity between the poet's domestic circumstances and their work – the exoticism of *Lalla Rookh* issued from a barn, and from Landon's cell-like bedroom came poetry which, it is implied, was rose-coloured and silver. But, for Blanchard, the truth about Landon is to be found in her bedroom, not in her verse. It is the eyewitness view of her austere chamber that will dispel clichéd understanding in favour of a more complex reality. The bedroom belies the poetry, in being no gaudy, fairy grotto (or kept woman's 'boudoir'), but a mundane, modest space, signifying the hard, economic reality of the life of a professional woman writer. This imaginary visit makes a move that arguably underlies both literary biography and literary tourism – it posits a congruity between life and works only to undermine it and privilege the life. It is Landon and not her poetry that the reader and the tourist really want to know and understand. As writers have repeatedly claimed, in literary biography, as in literary tourism, the work is always in danger of becoming a decorative adjunct to the life. But from the reader's point of view, the writer is brought home to their experience: different, yet familiar, other yet also, potentially, the same.

William Howitt, a more self-conscious tourist than any of the biographers we have looked at so far, showed, by the same token, a more overt sense of the ironic nature of the visit to the poet's house. There is still a remnant of belief in a genuine meeting of souls through the literary pilgrimage. His title page epigraph records that '[a]n indissoluble sign of their existence has stamped itself on the abodes of all distinguished men, a sign which places all kindred spirits in communion with them.'[21]

In this reverential spirit, he accepts a white rose plucked from a tree admired by Felicia Hemans, in the garden of her Lakeland cottage, Dove's Nest.[22] But Howitt is a belated visitor, unlike Medwin or Hunt, and calls only after the poets are dead and gone. Their houses, emptied of the poets themselves, have in some instances been taken over by other occupants who comically disrupt the sense of the visit as a means to authentic understanding, undermining the power of the poet's presence in the encounter. Garrulous landladies show Howitt around Dove's Nest and Coleridge's former cottage at Nether Stowey and it is their chatter that he reports, rather than his feelings of oneness with the shades of the poets. He is amused by peripherals and recognises that these may, in fact, be what the literary tourist recalls as the central experiences of a visit. Hemans's landlady, 'a regular character' (2: 137), reminisces sympathetically about her former tenant, but her talk runs on many other subjects too, especially her hostility to 'steam, railroads, and all sorts of new-fangled things' (2: 137), including Harriet Martineau – 'as I met her the other day walking along the muddy road below here – "Is it a woman, or a man, or what sort of an animal is it?" said I to myself' (2: 140). Reverence is not an attitude that will survive in this democratised culture and this is brought home to Howitt especially forcefully, when he visits Coleridge's cottage and is startled to find that the Somerset landlady is completely ignorant of the concept of a 'poet', let alone of the illustrious tenant who preceded her. The cottage itself has become a 'Tom and Jerry shop' (a low beer house) and this leads Howitt to reflect on the number of other poets whose houses have suffered a similar fate:

> Moore's native abode is a whisky-shop; Burns's native cottage is a little public-house; Shelley's house at Great Marlowe is a beer-shop; it is said that a public-house has been built on the spot where Scott was born ... (2: 113)

Given the personal predilections of Coleridge and Burns this seems, in its way, a fitting fate for their cottages, but the deeper irony in Howitt's reflection is that the private residence of the poet has, in so many cases, quite literally become a public house. The nightmares of Coleridge and Wordsworth have materialised in a form still more nightmarish. The public has invaded and the poet's home has become a place where paying customers find actual, rather than merely imaginative, intoxication.

Clearly the authentic understanding promised by the biographical 'tour', as by the activity of literary tourism, was a precarious fiction. Howitt cheerfully accepted the bathos and fakery of the posthumous visit to the poet's home, as an inevitable consequence of time, but the truthfulness of the eyewitness encounter with a living poet was also, of course, open to question. As Hunt realised, the poet's domestic self might simply be another performance, and even the most intimate biographer was bound to be on some level an unreliable guide – Medwin and Lady Blessington were both thought to have made up much of the 'conversation' of Byron that they claimed to reproduce, word for word. Equally clearly, both literary biography and literary tourism, as they developed in the nineteenth century, were far from simplistically democratising, for they capitalised on the notion of an aristocracy of genius even as they undermined it. Yet, as Hazlitt recognised in an 1820 review of Spence's *Anecdotes of Pope*, the claim of literary biography as well as of literary tourism to offer the public authentic insight into an author's life was a seductive one. The poet's house was made into a place where fantasy was literalised in ways that might be disturbingly or comically deflating, but might, nevertheless, offer the reader of biography or the literary tourist a powerful illusion of companionship with genius:

> Cicero's villa, the tomb of Virgil, the house in which Shakespear was brought up, are objects of romantic interest, and of refined curiosity to the lovers of genius; and a poet's lock of hair, a *fac-simile* of his hand-writing, an ink-stand, or a fragment of an old chair belonging to him, are treasured up as relics of literary devotion. These things are thus valued, only because they bring us into a sort of personal contact with such characters; vouch, as it were, for their reality, and convince us that they were living men, as well as mighty minds. ... We draw down genius from its air-built citadel in books and libraries, and make it our play-mate and our companion.[23]

Notes

1. Thomas Medwin, *Journal of the Conversations of Lord Byron. Noted During a Residence with his Lordship at Pisa, in the years 1821 and 1822* (London: Henry Colburn, 1824), 17.
2. See *The Works of Mrs Hemans; with a Memoir of her Life, by her Sister*, 7 vols (Edinburgh: William Blackwood and Sons; London: Thomas Cadell, 1839), for example, vol. 1, 219.
3. William Howitt, *Homes and Haunts of the Most Eminent British Poets*, 2 vols (London: Richard Bentley, 1847).
4. Howitt's book appeared simultaneously in America (New York: Harper and Brothers, 1847), went into several editions and was still in print in 1903.
5. *The Rambler*, no. 60 (1750), in *The Rambler*, ed. W.J. Bate and Albrecht B. Strauss, *The Yale Edition of the Works of Samuel Johnson*, vol. 3 (New Haven: Yale University Press, 1969), 321.
6. *Boswell's Life of Samuel Johnson*, ed. George Birkbeck Hill and L.F. Powell (Oxford: Oxford University Press, 1934), vol. 2, 166.
7. Review of the *Account of the Conduct of the Duchess of Marlborough, Gentleman's Magazine* (March 1842), cited in Samuel Johnson, *The Lives of The Most Eminent English Poets; With Critical Observations on their Works*, ed. Roger Lonsdale (Oxford: Clarendon Press, 2006), vol. 1, 80.
8. For Johnson's sense of the democracy of biography, see *Idler*, no. 84 (1759), in *The Ilder and The Adventurer*, ed. W.J. Bate, John M. Bullitt and L.F. Powell, vol. 2 of *The Yale Edition of the Works of Samuel Johnson* (New Haven and London: Yale

University Press, 1963), 261–4, esp. 263. See also Robert Folkenflick, *Samuel Johnson, Biographer* (Ithaca: Cornell University Press, 1978).

9. Samuel Taylor Coleridge, 'A Prefatory Observation on Modern Biography', *The Friend*, no. 21 (1810), in *The Friend*, ed. Barbara E. Rooke, no. 4, vol. II of *The Collected Works of Samuel Taylor Coleridge*, Bollingen Series, *lxxv*, ed. Kathleen Coburn (London and Princeton: Routledge and Kegan Paul and Princeton University Press, 1969), 287.

10. William Wordsworth, *A Letter to a Friend of Robert Burns: Occasioned by an Intended Republication of the Account of the Life of Burns, by Dr. Currie* (London: Longman, Hurst, Rees, Orme and Brown, 1816), in W.J.B. Owen and Jane Worthington Smyser, eds, *The Prose Works of William Wordsworth* (Oxford: Clarendon Press, 1974), vol. 3, 111–36: 122.

11. 'House' (1876), 6–9. in *The Works of Robert Browning, Centenary Edition*, intr. F.G. Kenyon (First published London: Smith, Elder and Co., 1912. Reprinted London: Ernest Benn Ltd., n.d.), vol. 9, 30–31.

12. James Buzard, *The Beaten Track. European Tourism, Literature, and the Ways to Culture, 1800–1918* (Oxford: Clarendon Press, 1993).

13. Thomas Medwin, *Journal of the Conversations of Lord Byron. Noted During a Residence with his Lordship at Pisa, in the years 1821 and 1822* (London: Henry Colburn, 1824); James Henry Leigh Hunt, *Lord Byron and Some of his Contemporaries; with Recollections of the Author's Life, and of his Visit to Italy* (London: Henry Colburn, 1828); Marguerite Gardiner, Countess Lady Blessington, *Conversations of Lord Byron*. London: Henry Colburn, 1834 (first published 1832–1833 in the *New Monthly Magazine*).

14. Thomas Moore, *Letters and Journals of Lord Byron, with Notices of his Life*, 2 vols (London: John Murray, 1830).

15. See Mary Shelley's biographical prefaces and notes to *The Poetical Works of Percy Bysshe Shelley*, 4 vols (London: Edward Moxon, 1839); Thomas De Quincey, 'Lake Reminiscences, from 1807 to 1830, by the English Opium-Eater', *Tait's Magazine*, vol. 10 [old series] 6 [new series] (January–August 1839); Henry Fothergill Chorley, *Memorials of Mrs. Hemans. With Illustrations of her Literary Character from her Private Correspondence*, 2 vols (London: Saunders and Otley, 1836); Harriett Hughes's 'Memoir' in *The Works of Mrs Hemans* (1839); and Leman Blanchard, *Life and Literary Remains of L.E.L.*, 2 vols (London: Henry Colburn, 1841).

16. Byron's poems, 'Fare Thee Well' and 'A Sketch from Private Life' were privately circulated in 1816 but widely pirated after being reprinted in the *Champion* newspaper as 'Lord Byron's Poems On His Own Domestic Circumstances'. See Samuel Chew, *Byron in England. His Fame and After-Fame* (1924; New York: Russell and Russell, 1965), 19–26.

17. Thomas Medwin, *Journal of the Conversations of Lord Byron. Noted During a Residence with his Lordship at Pisa, in the years 1821 and 1822* (London: Henry Colburn, 1824), 1.

18. My italics.

19. James Henry Leigh Hunt, *Lord Byron and Some of his Contemporaries; with Recollections of the Author's Life, and of his Visit to Italy* (London: Henry Colburn, 1828), 4.

20. Leman Blanchard, *Life and Literary Remains of L.E.L.*, 2 vols (London: Henry Colburn, 1841), vol. 1, 78–9.

21. The epigraph is from Mary Howitt, *The Citizen of Prague*, 3 vols (London: Henry Colburn, 1846).

22. Howitt, *Homes and Haunts of the Most Eminent British Poets* (New York: Harper and Brothers, 1847), vol. 2, 138.

23. William Hazlitt, Review of 'Spence's Anecdotes of Pope', *Edinburgh Review* (May 1820), in P.P. Howe, ed., *The Complete Works of William Hazlitt, Centenary Edition*, vol. 16 (London: J.M. Dent and Sons Ltd., 1934), 152–81: 153.

5

The Author's House: Abbotsford and Wayside

Erin Hazard

Architectural historians have traditionally criticised nineteenth-century architecture for its 'literary' quality, arguing that its significance results from an abject subordination to historical and literary association rather than, as it supposedly should, from pure form. In *The Architecture of Humanism* (1914), for example, Geoffrey Scott identified a 'literary fallacy' in romantic architecture, which he claimed 'neglects the fact that in literature, meaning, or fixed association, is the universal term; while in architecture the universal term is the sensuous experience of substance and form.'[1] Or, as Robert Furneaux Jordan puts it: 'Mere form or structure – the first of which has been dominant in the eighteenth century and the second of which was to be dominant in the twentieth century – were altogether subordinate to this passionate embracement of the Imagination.'[2] The practice of literary tourism, which emerges at precisely the same time that literature supposedly killed architecture, suggests that objects' and buildings' associative qualities might enhance, rather than subordinate, their material qualities.[3] Association can open up the very thing Geoffrey Scott suggests it destroys, 'the sensuous experience of substance and form.' I will explore this claim through considering two building projects: Sir Walter Scott's building of his house Abbotsford in the Borders, and the renovations to The Wayside in Concord, Massachusetts carried out by its owner, the American author (and visitor to Abbotsford) Nathaniel Hawthorne. These two house building projects demonstrate two very different reactions to the practice of literary tourism, a revelling in its architectural possibilities in Scott's case and a retreat from them in Hawthorne's, but both reveal a commitment to association's possibility to awaken architectural and material form.

As the builder of the most popular (living) author's house attraction in nineteenth-century Britain, Sir Walter Scott would seem the undoubted heir of those eighteenth-century 'painter or poet architects' in whose hands, according to Henry-Russell Hitchcock's narrative of architectural modernism, architecture disintegrated, not to be reintegrated until the modern age.[4] Between 1811 and 1824, Scott collaborated with a variety of architects on the transformation of a Scottish Border farmhouse, Clarty Hole, into a historicist fantasy – Abbotsford. With its silhouette of turrets, stepped gables, battlements, and finials, Abbotsford evokes medieval and early modern Scotland, periods that also figured heavily in Scott's poetry and novels. Furthermore, Scott, a collector of antiquarian objects since his youth, incorporated fragments from historical sites featured in his writings, such as Melrose Abbey, which appears in the poem *The Lay of the Last Minstrel*, or the Edinburgh prison around which much of the action in *The Heart of Mid-Lothian* centres, into the very fabric of his house, thus practicing a kind of literary and historical allusion through building. Scott's use of verifiable locations in his writings and his subsequent use of fragments from those same sites in his building of Abbotsford demonstrate the contribution of the material to literary architecture: on this view, Scott's writings serve as the mediating term between two sites of materiality.

It is not my intention to catalogue Abbotsford's collections, analyse its stylistic influences, or to identify which of Scott's many collaborators authored the building as it exists today; these questions have received ample consideration elsewhere.[5] Rather, in order to demonstrate the material significance of Abbotsford, this discussion will visit the house during each of its many phases of renovation. For the sake of clarity, therefore, a brief survey of Abbotsford's multiple building phases is instructive. Between 1811 and 1814, Scott built a series of service buildings to the west of the house. At this time, he also began to incorporate antiquarian fragments into his architecture and landscape projects, most notably building a well out of 'debris' from Melrose Abbey and attaching a cross from the old Galashiels church to a door.[6] Between 1816 and 1819, Scott, assisted by Daniel Terry, Edward Blore and the architect William Atkinson, built a wing connecting the service buildings to the main block of this house.[7] This wing contrasted strongly with the service buildings and old farmhouse it connected: a stepped gable and crenellated tower dominated its silhouette. In the early 1820s, the old farmhouse was razed and a grand turreted and gabled wing completed Abbotsford. At the western end of the addition, where it joined the earlier connecting wing, an entry porch flanked by storey-high turrets projected onto the courtyard, while a turret marked the southeast corner of the wing, in which Scott's new study was placed. In the mid 1850s Scott's heirs, the Hope-Scotts, built a new wing to the west of the existing structure, which amounted to a house separate from the part of Abbotsford now functioning as a tourist attraction.

Throughout his building project, Scott used fragments from historical buildings as building blocks. In *The Lay of the Last Minstrel* (1805), for example, Scott had described Melrose Abbey as the burial site of the wizard Michael Scott. Beginning in 1812, he used both actual fragments and casts from the building in the interior and exterior of Abbotsford. While it might seem that Abbotsford was thus an afterthought to Scott's literary rendering of the site (with the various fragments from the Abbey embedded in the house fabric gesturing back to his literary text), Scott's depiction of Melrose Abbey had in the first instance resulted from the poet's early contact with the architecture and landscape of the Scottish Borders. Born in Edinburgh, Scott was sent to his paternal grandparents' home in the area, Sandyknowe Farm, to recover from polio as a young child, and later in his youth spent time at his aunt's home in Kelso. The Cistercian Melrose Abbey, erected in the twelfth century and rebuilt in the fourteenth century, is one of the Border's great architectural sites. It had appeared in travel literature and poetry predating Scott's description: for example, John Bower's guide to Melrose Abbey published in 1822 cites J. Copland's eighteenth-century poetic description of the site.[8] As Scott built with fragments from Melrose Abbey, therefore, he not only concretised the imaginative work he had originally performed in writing about the Abbey but he also transferred the material components of the building from their original site to a new architectural context. On this model, Scott's writing becomes a mediating agent between two concrete sites: the Abbey that prefigured Scott's literary depiction of it, and then Abbotsford – the house built from its components.

Might the reading of vivid textual imagery inspire a will to experience those sites described? J.A. Andersen, an early nineteenth-century Danish tourist, travelled to Melrose to witness the Abbey firsthand. At his inn, the night before his excursion, he paged through an album in which visitors recorded their impressions of the site. Andersen writes of their contributions: 'I lay nearly the whole of the night ruminating on descriptions, the very excellence of which only tended to strengthen my belief, that the subject could not be understood from description.'[9] The tourist culture that grew up around sites described in Scott's writing suggests that others shared Andersen's belief and that the conviction in the insufficiency of description might apply even to Scott's own writings, in addition to the tourists' anecdotes collected in such an album. After the publication of *The Lay of the Last Minstrel*, Scott's readers, like Andersen, travelled to see the material precedent to Scott's description. 'Booksellers in the plural number', writes Scott's son-in-law and biographer John Gibson Lockhart, 'were preceded and followed by an endless variety of enthusiastic "gentil bachelors," whose main temptation from the south had been the hope of seeing the Borders in company with their Minstrel.'[10]

As soon as Scott began the work of transforming Clarty Hole into Abbotsford, he began using fragments from recent excavations at the Abbey as building material. In 1810, the year before Scott's purchase of property, the church hitherto established within the precincts left the site for a new church in Melrose and a series of excavation projects followed. Johnny Bower, the keeper of the Abbey, writes, "His Grace the Duke of Buccleugh and Queensberry in 1812 cleared off five solid feet of rubbish."[11] In the summer of 1812, Scott commenced his transformation of Clarty Hole into Abbotsford, starting with the well built with 'some debris from the Abbey.'[12] Scott employed this strategy in his construction of the house fabric proper itself. Washington Irving, who visited Abbotsford in 1817, recalled looking out of his Abbotsford bedroom window and seeing Scott in the yard surrounded by workmen and stones. 'About the place,' writes Irving, 'were strewed various morsels from the ruins of Melrose Abbey, which were to be incorporated in his mansion.'[13] Irving's anecdote points out how pieces of the Abbey constituted building blocks of Abbotsford's second building phase connecting the new service buildings to the west with the old farmhouse to the east.

Scott's acquisition of the door from the old Edinburgh prison, or the Heart of Midlothian, illustrates how the fragments Scott acquired for his house contributed to his writing process. Scott's descendant, Mary Monica Maxwell-Scott, who published a catalogue of Scott's collections in 1893, states that the Magistrates of Edinburgh presented the door and its keys to Scott in 1817 following the razing of the old prison.[14] The Scottish inventor and engineer James Nasmyth remembers watching the inauguration of the demolition in the form of the removal of the door with Scott in attendance.[15] Scott's acquisition of the fragment corresponded with the second phase of building at Abbotsford when the wing connecting the old farmhouse with the service buildings was erected. Abbotsford visitor John Morrison, recalls, 'Sir Walter pointed out to me, with considerable triumph, the door of the Heart of Mid-Lothian – that is, the old prison-door of Edinburgh – which he had procured and erected as the gateway from his mansion house to the offices.'[16] Scott's acquisition of the tollbooth door corresponded temporally with Scott's renovations of his house and with the writing of *The Heart of Mid-Lothian*.[17] The novel, like Scott's *Lay of the Last Minstrel*, intervened between two physical sites: the old Edinburgh prison building and Scott's connecting wing at Abbotsford.

In 1819, at the end of this second phase of building, the American author George Ticknor visited Abbotsford and commented on Scott's use of fragments: 'His house itself is a kind of collection of fragments of history; architectural ornaments, – copies from Melrose in one part, the old identical gate of the Tolbooth, or rather the stone part of it, through which the Porteus mob forced its way, in another, – an old fountain before the house, and odd inscriptions and statues everywhere, make such a kind of irregular, poetical habitation as ought to belong to him.'[18] Ticknor makes the connection between the object (the piece of the Tolbooth) and the historical incident and literary rendering it gestured to (the Porteus riots depicted in *The Heart of Mid-Lothian*). As Ticknor observes, Scott's collection constituted the very fabric of his house, rendering its architecture a variety of cabinet or museum. Kryzstof Pomain has argued that a collection is, by definition, a set of objects taken out of circulation and displayed in a protected space, which mediates between an audience and something invisible.[19] Ticknor's account suggests that Abbotsford existed simultaneously as architecture and as a collection mediating the 'invisible' of Scottish history and the 'invisible' of Scott's writing.

Ticknor's characterisation of Abbotsford as the 'kind of irregular, poetical habitation as ought to belong to' Scott, with its implicit invocation of the character of the author, foreshadows a significant shift in emphasis that occurred with Scott's final building phase in the early 1820s. At this time, the old farmhouse was replaced with Abbotsford's grand eastern wing. The new addition provided an entrance hall where Scott's antiquarian collections, exceeding the space allotted to them in the armoury of the second phase of building, could be displayed to visitors upon their entry to the house. The design of the study, located in the southeast corner of the new wing, indicates an increased recognition of popular interest in Scott as 'the Minstrel of the North' and 'the Author of Waverley,' rather than simply in his antiquarian collections and historicist house. Built-in bookcases line the study's walls, whose regularity is interrupted by a small alcove, or oratory. The room's flexible planning meant it could serve either as an isolated work place or as an exhibition site. With its door closed, Scott could write in a private corner of his house and move between his desk and the upstairs family quarters via a staircase, accessible from the study's gallery level, communicating with the upstairs family quarters. The plan of the room, however, also concedes Scott's potential as an author-attraction. When the study and hall doors were open, the tourist, arriving upon entry at the hall, could look straight east to Scott's workplace.

As Irving's and Ticknor's visits to Abbotsford indicate, many visitors to the house during Scott's lifetime were American, and Abbotsford accordingly exerted a strong influence on the conception and construction of the American author's house as tourist attraction. While it is not within the scope of this discussion to detail the sway Abbotsford held over the American culture of literary tourism, it should be noted that James Fenimore Cooper and Washington Irving, both of whom visited Abbotsford, both built early American authors' house attractions on the Abbotsford model: Cooper's Otsego Hall (renovated 1834) in Cooperstown, New York, and Washington Irving's Sunnyside (1835–1847) outside Tarrytown, New York, were fantastic historicist structures built by their author-residents and consciously set into the landscapes depicted in their writings. My subject here is another American author who visited Abbotsford some years after Scott's death, Nathaniel Hawthorne, and his reaction as embodied in the building of his own house in Concord, Massachusetts.

Hawthorne visited Abbotsford twice in the years of 1856–1857 in the midst of the Hope-Scotts' final addition of family quarters to the west of Scott's building, first in May of 1856 with a second visit in July of 1857.[20] Upon Hawthorne's first approach to the house, he experienced disappointment, seemingly provoked by the surprisingly diminutive size of the house, as well as its architectural playfulness:

> It is but a villa, after all; no castle, nor even a large manor house, and very unsatisfactory when you consider it in that light. Indeed, it impressed me not as a real house, intended for the home of human beings – a house to die in, or to be born in – but as a plaything, something in the same category as Horace Walpole's Strawberry Hill (341).

In the absence of the living presence of Scott which would have conferred meaning on the collections, Hawthorne perceived his collections as cacophony ('every inch of the walls is covered with claymores, targets, and other weapons and armor, or old-time curiosities, tastefully arranged, many of which, no doubt, have a history attached to them – or had, in Sir Walter's own mind' [341]). Without the attraction of Scott at his desk in the sight-line of the approaching tourist – the figure whose creative process bound together house, collections, and writings – the family exhibited the former casings of his person, most notably his clothing and a plaster cast of his death mask. The mask profoundly disturbed Hawthorne: 'I wonder that the family allows this cast to be shown; the last record of Scott's personal reality, conveying such a wretched and unworthy idea of it' (343).

Hawthorne returned to Abbotsford in the summer of 1857 after the completion of the Hope-Scott addition. His description of this second visit expresses a more categorical concern with what sort of place Abbotsford had become after Scott's death:

> The feeling in visiting Abbotsford is not that of awe; it is little more than going to a museum. I do abhor this mode of making pilgrimage to the shrines of departed great men; there is certainly something wrong in it, for it seldom or never produces (in me, at least,) the right feeling. It is a queer truth, too, that a house is forever spoiled and ruined, as a house, by having been the abode of a great man. His spirit haunts it, as it were, with a malevolent effect, and takes hearth and hall away from the nominal possessors, giving all the world (because he had such intimate relations with all) the right to enter there (540).

Hawthorne's categorical disappointment with the practice of visiting and preserving 'the shrines of departed great men' owes something to the very materiality of Abbotsford, that simultaneous house and collection ('little more than going to a museum'). In limbo between the public and private realms, Abbotsford, in Hawthorne's view, had ceased to function as a domestic space. If Scott's spirit haunted Abbotsford, it did so at the bidding of his survivors who substituted former containers of his body, like his clothes and his death mask, for his presence, summoning his spirit to fill them.

When Hawthorne returned to America in 1860 after seven years spent abroad he undertook house renovations of his own. His building project was exemplary of a well-identified tendency in nineteenth-century American domestic architecture to extend the house into the landscape and include the outdoors in the environment of the house.[21] In 1853 Hawthorne and his family had moved into The Wayside, a colonial-period two-storey wood farmhouse with a central entrance, gable and chimney in Concord, Massachusetts. Upon the family's return from Europe, Hawthorne – with the help of local carpenters and neighbour Bronson Alcott – converted the original central door into a bay window with glass panes spanning the height of the first storey of the house on all sides. The door was moved to the left side of the house and a second storey was added to the wing on the left. And then there was Hawthorne's tower study, rising from the centre of the house into Concord's treetops. Whereas Scott had used the house surface – interior and exterior – as a display space, Hawthorne moved by contrast toward dissolving the house surface. With windows running the height of his tower study, the room was – and is – suspended in sky and sunlight.

Like Scott, Hawthorne's house-building aesthetic and writing were closely inter-linked. Between his 1860 house renovations and his death in 1864, for example, Hawthorne worked on 'Septimius Felton,' an unfinished work set in Concord during the Revolutionary War.[22] 'Septimius Felton' explores the sinister lure of immortality, as its protagonist walks upon a Concord hilltop path planning to create a potion guaranteeing eternal life. The action of the story is set in the landscape with which The Wayside, following Hawthorne's renovations, communicated. In addition to their common location, both Hawthorne's house renovations and 'Septimius Felton' considered the problem of immortality. But if the character Septimius Felton desired eternal life, Hawthorne's house renovations suggest a will to evade the posthumous transformation of his house into a shrine. At Abbotsford, faced with the playfulness of the architecture, excessiveness of its collections, and abundance of artifacts linked to Scott, Hawthorne had concluded with distaste that the house no longer functioned as a house, but rather as a variety of museum whose displays enabled its haunting by Scott. By reducing the materiality of his house and opening it up onto the landscape, Hawthorne might prevent The Wayside from becoming a spectacle akin to Abbotsford. As for what might remain as Hawthorne's own memorial, the author himself reportedly located it in the landscape which his tower study overlooked. His neighbour, Ralph Waldo Emerson, recalled after Hawthorne's death that 'One day, when I found him on top of his hill, in the woods, he paced back the path to his house, and said, "This is the only remembrance of me that will remain."'[23]

From the perspective of architectural history, Hawthorne's architectural work not only critiques Abbotsford and the version of authorship it performs, but participates in a larger historical trajectory. The dissolution of the mass of the house, the opening up of the interior to the exterior, and the exterior to the interior foreshadow the modernist reduction of architecture to its structural elements. According to this view, architectural work like Hawthorne's marks a primitive moment in the history of the demise of contaminated 'literary' architecture and the restoration of an architecture committed to its most essential characteristic, structure. Certainly, a house like Abbotsford does not meet the precepts of a modernist understanding of architecture committed to a purist differentiation between art forms. Yet, to reduce Abbotsford, or literary architecture in general, to its imaginative and associative characteristics misses the consequence of its material fabric. An implicit acknowledgment of the real allure of a site like Abbotsford is evident in Hawthorne's commitment to limit the materiality of The Wayside and thus reduce its potential as a public spectacle. If Hawthorne's dissolution of his house surface amounts to an effort to reduce the spectacle of his house then implicit in this project is a reaction against – and hence a recognition of – the constituent, but rarely acknowledged, materiality of literary architecture.

Notes

1. Geoffrey Scott, *The Architecture of Humanism: A Study in the History of Taste*, rev. edn (New York: Charles Scribner's Sons, 1924), 62.
2. Robert Furneaux Jordan, *Victorian Architecture* (Harmondsworth, Middlesex: Penguin, 1966), 48.
3. The literature on literary tourism, like that on nineteenth-century architecture, demonstrates a tension between the materiality of authors' houses and their immaterial literary associations. Stephen Bann examines literary tourism through Washington Irving's essay 'Abbotsford and Newstead Abbey' in a larger study of representations of history in the romantic period, identifying a renewed cultural investment in the material environment during this historical period. In her compelling and comprehensive study of the phenomenon of literary tourism, Nicola Watson argues that the literary text is the driving factor in literary tourism: visits to literary sites, with their inability to concretise the authorial imagination or the reveries of reading, are, for Watson, affairs of absence. Stephen Bann, 'The Historical Composition of Place: Byron and Scott' in *The Clothing of Clio* (Cambridge: Cambridge University Press, 1984), 93–111, and Nicola J. Watson, *The Literary Tourist* (Basingstoke: Palgrave Macmillan, 2006).
4. Henry-Russell Hitchcock, *Modern Architecture* (New York: Payson and Clarke, 1929), 11.
5. See Clive Wainwright, *The Romantic Interior* (New Haven: Yale University Press, 1989), 147–207; James Macauley, *The Gothic Revival, 1745–1845* (Glasgow: Blackie and Son Ltd., 1975), 223–8; and Iain Gordon Brown, ed., *Abbotsford and Sir Walter Scott: The Image and the Influence* (Edinburgh: Society of Antiquaries of Scotland, 2003).
6. Scott to Daniel Terry, September 1812, *The Letters of Sir Walter Scott*, ed. Sir Herbert Grierson, vol. 3 (London: Constable & Co., 1933), 153–4 and Scott to Daniel Terry, 10 November 1814, *The Letters of Sir Walter Scott*, vol. 3, 514.
7. John Gibson Lockhart, *Memoirs of the Life of Sir Walter Scott*, rev. edn, vol. 3 (Boston: Houghton Mifflin, 1901), 121–6.

8. John Bower, *Description of the Abbeys of Melrose and Old Melrose, with their Traditions*, 2nd edn (Edinburgh: printed for the author, 1822), 36–7 and 44–6.
9. J.A. Andersen, *A Dane's Excursions in Britain*, vol. 2 (London: Printed for Mathews & Leigh by W. Clowes, 1809), 25.
10. Lockhart, vol. 1, 442. See vol. 2, 171 on the similar tourist frenzy following the 1810 publication of Scott's *The Lady of the Lake*.
11. John Bower, *Description of the Abbeys of Melrose and Old Melrose, with their Traditions*, 2nd edn (Edinburgh: printed for the author, 1822), 84.
12. Scott to Daniel Terry, September 1812, *The Letters of Sir Walter Scott*, vol. 3, 153–4.
13. Washington Irving, 'Abbotsford' in *The Crayon Miscellany* (Boston: Twayne, 1979), 143. Irving's account of his 1817 visit was published in 1835.
14. Mary Monica Maxwell-Scott, *Abbotsford. The Personal Relics and Antiquarian Treasures of Sir Walter Scott* (London: A. and C. Black, 1893), 63.
15. Samuel Smiles, ed. *James Nasmyth, Engineer: An Autobiography* (London: John Murray, 1883), 85.
16. John Morrison, 'Random Reminiscences of Sir Walter Scott,' *Tait's Edinburgh Magazine*, vol. 10 (1843): 569–78, 576.
17. David Hewitt and Alison Lumsden suggest that Scott most likely began work on *The Heart of Mid-Lothian* in the spring of 1817 but that he 'might have written the first chapter at any time before January 1818.' Hewitt and Lumsden, eds, 'Essay on the Text,' *The Heart of Mid-Lothian* (Edinburgh University Press, 2004), 473. Nasmyth dates the destruction of the building to late in 1817 (85). Thus, Scott's acquisition of the fragment from the building and work on the novel corresponded chronologically, though it is likely he started writing before securing the object.
18. George Ticknor, *Life, Letters, and Journals of George Ticknor*, vol. 1 (Boston: James R. Osgood and Co., 1876), 283.
19. Krzystof Pomian, *Collectors and Curiosities: Paris and Venice, 1500–1800* (Cambridge and London: Polity Press, 1990), 9, 23.
20. Nathaniel Hawthorne, *The English Notebooks* (New York: Russell and Russell, 1962), 341, 538.
21. See Vincent Scully, *The Shingle and Stick Style*, rev. edn (New Haven and London: Yale University Press, 1971).
22. Hawthorne writes in December 1860 of his completed tower study. Hawthorne to Bennoch, 17 December 1860 in *The Letters, 1857–1864, The Centenary Edition of the Works of Nathaniel Hawthorne*, ed. Thomas Woodson et al., vol. 18 (Columbus: Ohio State University Press, 1987), 352.
23. Edward Waldo Emerson and Waldo Emerson Forbes, eds, *Journals of Ralph Waldo Emerson, 1864–1876*, vol. 10 (Boston and New York: Houghton Mifflin Co., 1909–1914), 40.

6
Bringing Down the House: Restoring the Birthplace

Julia Thomas

As any literary tourist knows, Shakespeare's birthplace stands in Henley Street, Stratford-upon-Avon, its ancient timbered beams evoking a sense of its history and uniqueness, its iconic status amongst other literary shrines. The property, the guide books confidently assert, was purchased by Shakespeare's father, John Shakespeare, in 1556 and remained in the possession of the Shakespeare family until 1806. But this account tells only part of the story. While the property appears as a testament to its Tudor past, it silently erases another, far more recent, history. Shakespeare's birthplace, I want to suggest, is, quite literally, a Victorian construct; the building that we see today and the tourist industry that has developed around it was created in the mid nineteenth century.[1]

The Victorian history of the birthplace began in 1847 when the building was bought at public auction by a joint London and Stratford committee. At the time of its purchase for 'the nation', the birthplace was not one but three premises forming part of a terrace: there was a cottage on the left which was built onto the north-west end of the house, a butcher's shop, complete with open hatched window, in the middle, and, on the right, a pub called the Swan and Maidenhead. In the decade following its acquisition, some outbuildings were demolished to prevent damage from fire and the Swan and Maidenhead was let to a tenant, with strict instructions that no alcohol was to be sold, but the committee did not have enough funds to make any significant alterations to the premises. Then in 1856 a benefactor appeared in the form of one John Shakespeare – not a glover from Stratford-upon-Avon, but a scholar of Hindustani from Ashby de la Zouch. Shakespeare gave the committee £2500 and left a further £2500 in his will when he died the following year (although this bequest was later contested).

With this money the committee was, at last, able to invest in the birthplace, but it was not obvious what form this investment should take. As early as 1835, when the self-styled Shakspearean Club met in Stratford to formulate an appeal to restore the bust and monument of the bard in the Holy Trinity Church, it was indicated that if enough money were raised the Club would 'gladly extend their care to the preservation of the house in which Shakespeare's father resided, in Henley Street, the presumed birthplace of Shakspeare.'[2] In the months leading up to and following the purchase of the house at auction, discussions about the future of the birthplace became more urgent, the writer Douglas Jerrold expressing his hope that 'the local authorities will endeavour to maintain the predominance of a style of architecture of an Elizabethan character.'[3] But exactly what this 'preservation' or 'maintenance' might entail was highly problematic. After the committee received John Shakespeare's donation, John Payne Collier, the Shakespearean scholar and editor, wrote to the Chairman, imploring him to proceed with caution: 'we must be especially careful in what is usually called "restoration",' he writes.[4] 'What I am most anxious about is, that no scrap of the original fabric should be removed, and that whoever may undertake the restoration should have sufficient reverence for the smallest relic that can be preserved. All ought to be kept, as far as possible, in the state in which it now is.'[5]

Collier's remarks are suggestive of a growing Victorian concern about restoration projects, and the different values and meanings of restoration (turning the building into what it once was) and preservation (maintaining it in its current state). These differences were framed as oppositions by John Ruskin, who was dismayed at restoration work carried out on monuments and buildings in Italy and frequently criticised such projects, coining the aphorism that restoration is 'the worst manner of Destruction'.[6] Indeed, according to Ruskin, restoration was actually impossible: an old building could never be 'restored' because the very act of restoration would obliterate its oldness, its spirit and life:

> Do not let us talk then of restoration. The thing is a Lie from beginning to end. You may make a model of a building as you may of a corpse, and your model may have the shell of the old walls within it as your cast might have the skeleton, with what advantage I neither see nor care: but the old building is destroyed, and that more totally and mercilessly than if it had sunk into a heap of dust.... But, it is said, there may come a necessity for restoration! Granted. Look the

necessity full in the face, and understand it on its own terms. It is a necessity for destruction.[7]

For Ruskin, the solution was not to restore but to preserve buildings, replacing decaying brickwork, or propping up parts of the structure that were essential to its stability. And even here the new work should be strictly differentiated from the old, with any stonework added to the building having the date of its insertion engraved on it so that future historians would be able to identify it.[8] Ruskin's suggestion was that a group be set up with the aim of keeping an eye on old monuments and preventing unnecessary restoration,[9] a scheme that was adopted in 1877 when William Morris established the Society for the Protection of Ancient Buildings, nicknamed the Anti-Scrape society. In a letter published in the *Athenaeum,* Morris reiterated the connection between restoration and destruction that Ruskin had made almost 30 years earlier: restoration was an act of 'barbarism' and this new Society would 'protest against all "restoration" that means more than keeping out wind and weather.'[10]

When the birthplace trustees received the money from John Shakespeare[11] there were two alternative possibilities open to them: either to preserve the house in its current condition; or to 'restore' it, with all the meanings that critics like Ruskin attached to this activity. The trustees called in as an advisor the architect Edward Barry, the son of Charles Barry, who had designed the new Houses of Parliament. Barry outlined these two options in his preliminary inspection of the birthplace:

In dealing with the exigencies of the case, there are two courses open, one to uphold strictly all that now exists, removing nothing, and restoring nothing, but remaining content with upholding the building against the ravages of time, and transmitting it to posterity as far as may be, in its present shape; the other, is to remove with a careful hand all those excrescences which are decidedly the result of modern innovation, to uphold with jealous care all that now exists of undoubted antiquity, not to destroy any portion about whose character the slightest doubt may exist but to restore any parts needing it in such a manner that the restorations can never be mistaken for the old work, though harmonizing with it, and lastly to adopt such measures as modern science enables us to bring to our aid, for the perfect preservation of the building, and perhaps to make Shakespeare's House a nucleus of such an institution as might prove eventually not unfit to bear so illustrious a name.[12]

What Barry is proposing, then, is either to leave the building alone, making only those repairs and additions necessary to preserve it in its current state, or to perform a sort of 'anti-scrape' scrape, removing the modern additions of the building in order to reveal the ancient features beneath. Far from the binary opposites presented in Ruskin's writing, in Barry's report preservation and restoration are seen as complementary: restoration is itself a type of preservation. Perhaps even Ruskin would have been content with Barry's recommendation that any repairs should be flagged up as new, although exactly how recent work could be presented as contemporary while 'harmonizing' with the old is left unsaid.

The trustees' decision to follow Barry's second option and restore the building is not surprising considering the architect's remarks about the future tourism potential of the birthplace, his indication that it could serve as the 'nucleus' of an institution. Barry himself was quite clear about his own preference, warning that 'If the first plan above named were adopted it would be necessary to uphold those portions of the building which in their modern ugliness so distress and confuse the present spectator.'[13]

The restoration of the birthplace, therefore, would involve removing its 'ugly' modern aspects, leaving behind the ancient fabric. But while the old skeleton of the building gave some clues as to how it might have appeared at the time of Shakespeare's birth, so little was surviving that its original appearance was difficult to ascertain. The birthplace was to be restored, but restored to what? With the architectural clues insufficient to indicate what the birthplace looked like, the restorers turned instead to a picture. As one committee member wrote, the aim of the project was to 'restore the House to the state it is supposed to have been at the birth of the Poet according to the oldest Print extant and as it appeared at the time of Garrick's Jubilee in 1769.'[14]

The 'print' referred to here, which was used as the template for the restoration, accompanied a letter written by 'T. B.' to the *Gentleman's Magazine* in July 1769 where it was intended to coincide with David Garrick's jubilee festivities in Stratford. T.B.'s letter discusses the pleasures of visiting the burial sites and birthplaces of great men and refers to the picture of Shakespeare's first home: 'My worthy friend Mr Greene, of this place, hath favoured me with an exact drawing of it (here inclosed), which may not possibly be an unacceptable present to such of your readers as intend to honour Stratford with their company at the approaching jubilee'.[15] The 'Mr Greene' responsible for this drawing was the antiquarian Richard Greene, who had himself contributed some 30 letters to the *Gentleman's Magazine* between 1751 and 1792. Greene was famous for his Museum of Curiosities, an eclectic collection of shells, stones, Roman coins and other interesting objects, which had many admirers including Samuel Johnson. Significantly, Greene's museum also consisted of items related to Shakespeare given to him by a neighbour, Peter Garrick, the brother of David. An even closer connection to Stratford came in the form of Greene's brother, who was headmaster of Stratford-upon-Avon grammar school and with whom he was in frequent correspondence. It is probable that Richard Greene drew this impression of the birthplace on one of his visits to Stratford.

Greene's drawing shows a detached, timber-framed, gabled building with dormer windows and porch, set in the middle of a field. Indeed, the success of the restorers in matching the building to this particular picture is demonstrated in the fact that the house we see in Henley Street today so perfectly mirrors this engraving. However, despite the apparent stark veracity of the image, this picture is anything but documentary evidence of how the building looked at the time of Shakespeare's birth, or, indeed, at the time of Garrick's jubilee two hundred years later. When this image was drawn, the birthplace was not a single house, but was made up of three premises, as it was at the time of the auction. Nor was it detached from its neighbouring dwellings or positioned in the middle of the countryside. Greene's picture relies on an artistic convention, common to topographical images from the seventeenth century onwards, which stressed the importance of buildings by setting them apart and isolating them from their surroundings. The Greene brothers, who were interested in drawing and printing techniques and collected images of buildings as well as drawing them, would have been familiar with these conventions, which are also reflected in the decision to focus on the front profile of the building, to exclude any extraneous detail (people, for example), and to represent the house, despite its age, in such a remarkably good state of repair. Shakespeare's birthplace was meant to appear in the picture as it might have done to its contemporaries, not necessarily as it was at the time it was drawn.[16]

But how the birthplace might have appeared to the Tudor residents of Stratford is not necessarily how it did appear. Even at the time that this engraving was published, there were no consistent accounts or visual records of what the birthplace looked like. Other images diverge widely, showing the building as either ramshackle or in pristine condition, as detached or terraced, and with or without the gabled roof and porch. What is significant, however, is that the trustees chose Greene's particular picture as the one that was to serve as the model for the restoration.

Ostensibly, this was because Greene's was the oldest known engraving, but it also happened to represent the birthplace in the most imposing way. In Greene's image, Shakespeare's birthplace was the dwelling of a fairly prosperous Elizabethan landowner rather than a modest and unassuming country cottage.

It was the faithful transformation of the actual house into how it appeared in this picture that was the priority of the restoration project. When advertisements were put out for local architects, potential applicants were encouraged to view a copy of Greene's image at the local stationers. Indeed, there was considerable anxiety when the picture and the architectural features of the building failed to coincide. After Barry submitted his report to the trustees, they queried the fact that his drawing of the house was at variance with the engraving. The minutes of the trustees' meeting record 'that Mr Barry be asked whether as his drawing differs in some respect from the old drawing there is any and what objection to introduce the dormer windows and porch as represented in that drawing.'[17] The conversation with Barry is not recorded, but the trustees must have won the day because the restored house does feature the dormer windows and porch. Such anxieties about the conformity of the building to the 1769 engraving seem to have continued well into the twentieth century. Following architects' reports in 1922, the porch gable was remade at a slightly higher pitch and the roof was replaced with old, handmade tiles consistent with Greene's picture. As Levi Fox comments, at the time of the original Victorian restoration 'it was not realised that the drawing showed a tiled roof and not a weather-boarded one, such as was then put on, and there were one or two other points of detail that had not been interpreted correctly.... These alterations, the Trustees were convinced, ensured that the appearance of the front entrance to the Birthplace was in strict keeping with the earliest known representation of the building.'[18]

With Greene's picture as the template, one of the first aspects of the restoration to be undertaken was the destruction of the buildings on either side of the property and the old stabling and a cottage behind. This particular course of action had been suggested after the auction when the committee appealed for money to 'remove certain premises adjoining, which injure the appearance, and endanger the safety of the house.'[19] Significantly, it was this 'injury', not to the structure, but to the appearance of the house that was marginalised in later accounts when it was the risk from fire that the connected buildings posed that was emphasised; no fire or candle was now allowed into the building, which was heated by hot water pipes. Of the committee members, only

John Payne Collier admitted that the isolation of the house should be undertaken for aesthetic reasons: 'not merely for the sake of the property, but as an attractive site to the visitors of Stratford.'[20] In one fell swoop, then, the birthplace was transformed from a terraced house to a detached one. This would have implications, as Collier noted, for how future tourists viewed the building, but it also had implications for how they viewed Shakespeare. This detached residence was more like the home of an aspiring bard. As one writer commented, the dwelling was a 'fit residence for one of the thriving aldermen of the borough'.[21]

Taking Greene's picture as their guide, the restorers aimed to follow Barry's advice and to remove not only the houses on either side of the birthplace, but also any modern additions, while marking the restoration work as new. This architectural philosophy was supported by the press. The local newspaper reported that 'any new features which, for safety's sake, may be introduced, shall be distinctly stamped as new, and not be allowed to mislead the pilgrims who may visit the shrine of an intellect so vast and noble…. we may as well worship the Blarney stone at once as pay our devotions to imitative bricks and mortar which the fanciful eye of an architect may happen to select as resembling the original object of our admiration.'[22]

Paradoxically, in a restoration project that relied not on Shakespeare's past but on an engraving of 1769, it was this notion of 'authenticity' that was paramount. By removing the modern additions, revealing the old structure, and, moreover, maintaining an absolute distinction between the old and new, the 'real' house could be discovered, or so it was suggested. Problems arise, however, as this newspaper article suggests, when the modern additions masquerade as the old, when tourists unwittingly 'worship' elements that are not original. Unfortunately, it was not always easy to identify recent additions to Shakespeare's birthplace. While it was its apparent 'originality' that was the deciding factor as to whether an aspect of the building should be removed or retained, repeated discussions amongst the architects, builders and trustees as to what was and was not 'original' suggest that this distinction was not always obvious. Nor was it necessarily desirable to identify what had actually been restored. Indeed, such a strategy was at odds with the other aim of the project: to renovate the ancient fabric. When alterations had to be made, there was a concerted effort to secure old materials. A delay in the work was caused when the builders attempted to source timber from a demolished house of the Earl of Warwick. Where the floorboards needed replacing, seasoned oak boards were acquired which looked older and more weathered.

The absolute distinction between the modern and the ancient on which the project depended was never clear-cut. Despite the aims of the restorers, the 'modern' had a nasty habit of encroaching on the old. This was recognised by one of the earliest tourists to the restored birthplace. John Mounteney Jephson visited Stratford in 1863 and wrote despairingly of the house:

> I was not prepared to see it look so smug and so new. Many of the old timbers remain, and the house is, indeed, substantially the same house as it was; but new timbers have been inserted where the old were decayed, everything has been scraped and polished up, and the place looks as if it had been 'restored,' a word to strike terror into the heart of an antiquary, not to speak of a man of taste. The propensity to stain, and polish, and varnish, and substitute new work for old unnecessarily, is much to be deprecated. Perhaps the committee, who hold the property in trust for the nation, could not avoid giving to Shakspere's birthplace its present holiday appearance; but how often is the artistic eye offended by seeing a fine old building vulgarised by restorers! ... Perhaps a few years' exposure to the weather may tone down the 'neat' look of the house in Henley Street.[23]

For Jephson, the attempt of the restorers to retain the old and eradicate the new actually had the opposite effect: so much 'new' work has been added to the old structures that the house had assumed a 'holiday appearance.' And Jephson's comments about the vogue for restoration suggest another way in which the 'modern' encroaches on the antiquity of the birthplace: it is manifest not only in the specifics of the restoration work that Jephson criticises, but also in the very decision to restore rather than preserve the house. As Jephson's remarks imply, these projects employed particular methods for uncovering the past that were bound up in contemporary, mid nineteenth-century notions about restoration and what it involved. Although restoration, by definition, implies a return to a past state, the idea of such a return, and how it is achieved, is always informed by the present.

Even the idea of history that the birthplace embodied was constituted by Victorian values. The overriding aim of the project to reveal the Tudor structure of the house takes place in the context of a nineteenth-century fascination with 'merrie olde England,' which can be seen in numerous paintings and literary texts of the period. The trend for Tudor architectural styles had been signalled as early as 1834 in the competitions held to rebuild the Houses of Parliament after a fire. Following the report of a Royal Commission, it was agreed to design the new building either as an Elizabethan or Gothic structure, both of which were regarded as specifically national styles. The Gothic, in the form of Charles Barry's plans, was eventually chosen, but the resultant building was famously described by his fellow architect, A.W.N. Pugin, as 'Tudor details on a classic body.' And it was not just grand designs that looked back to the sixteenth century. In the year of the Westminster competition, James Hakewill's *An Attempt to Determine the Exact Character of Elizabethan Architecture* attempted to reclaim Elizabethan street architecture and expose the 'hideous' and overloaded imitations which were 'disgracing our streets and public places.'[24] One of the first talks given at the newly-founded Decorative Art Society in London in 1844 was on Elizabethan furniture, the speaker, George Fildes, discussing the 'prevalence of the Elizabethan style, both in the exterior and interior decorations of the present day.'[25] Certainly, by the end of the nineteenth century and the emergence of the Arts and Crafts Movement, the so-called Tudorbethan or Jacobethan style, with its characteristic half timbering, mullioned windows and jettied first floors, was a familiar sight in many British towns, including, of course, Stratford-upon-Avon.

The birthplace, then, might have appeared as a Tudor dwelling, but the ideologies and values informing the restoration project were specifically Victorian. Despite Barry's assertions that they would remain distinct, the past and present were always conjoined, even down to the fabric of the birthplace's walls where the framed oak quarterings were filled in between with Portland cement. But these modern encroachments went largely unseen. Jephson's recognition of the 'newness' of the building seems to have been an exception. As he predicted, the British weather did its work and the birthplace soon came to be regarded as a genuinely old and authentic building, the traces of its Victorian renovation more or less invisible. In 1903, the romantic novelist Marie Corelli, who had moved to Stratford and could often be seen floating down the Avon in a gondola she had brought over from Venice, called for the restoration of the whole town. Corelli's enemies were the 'jerry builder,' who had made Stratford look like a cheap bit of Clapham,[26] and the stucco that had been plastered over the fifteenth-century carved house-fronts in the reign of Queen Anne. Corelli was acutely aware of the economic potential of Stratford: 'Modern progress is decidedly not the cue for Stratford,' she proclaimed. 'Its good measures of gold, its full purses, its swelling bank-books, will be best and most swiftly attained by setting its back to the wall of the Sixteenth century and refusing to budge.'[27] Corelli's words predict with some accuracy the growth of the tourist trade in Stratford. But what is so significant about her appeal is that the birthplace was held up as the 'real' thing, the one historic building in Stratford that had not been plastered over or otherwise defaced. By the end of Victoria's reign, then, the fact of the restoration of Shakespeare's birthplace had been erased. Indeed, the building that we see in Henley Street today has become the enduring symbol of Stratford's sixteenth-century heritage, despite its hidden nineteenth-century foundations.

Notes

1. The Victorian history of the birthplace has rarely been examined, critics tending to focus on the emergence of the Stratford tourist trade in Garrick's Jubilee of 1769. Levi Fox provides a documentary account of the building in *The Shakespeare Birthplace Trust. A Personal Memoir* (Stratford: Shakespeare Birthplace Trust, 1997). Where the birthplace is discussed, it is usually within the general contexts of the Shakespeare cult, for example, Barbara Hodgdon, *The Shakespeare Trade: Performances and Appropriations* (Pennsylvania: University of Pennsylvania Press, 1998); Graham Holderness, *Cultural Shakespeare: Essays on the Shakespeare Myth* (Hertfordshire: University of Hertfordshire Press, 2001); and one of the earliest accounts, Ivor Brown and George Fearon, *Amazing Monument: A Short History of the Shakespeare Industry* (London and Toronto: William Heinemann, 1939).
2. Shakspearean Club, *A Circular Relative to the Restoration and Preservation of the Bust and Monument of Shakspeare* (Stratford upon Avon, 1835).
3. Douglas Jerrold, 'Shakespeare's House. (1847)', *Specimens of Douglas Jerrold's Wit: Together with Selections, Chiefly from His Contributions to Journals, Intended to Illustrate His Opinions* (Boston: Ticknor and Fields, 1858).
4. John Payne Collier to Dr Thomas Thomson, 9 September 1856, unpublished letter.
5. John Payne Collier to Dr Thomas Thomson, 17 October 1856, unpublished letter.
6. John Ruskin, *The Seven Lamps of Architecture, The Works of John Ruskin*, ed. E.T. Cook and Alexander Wedderburn, 39 vols., vol. VIII (London and New York: George Allen; Longmans, Green and Co., 1903–1912), 242.
7. Ibid., 244.
8. John Ruskin, 'A Letter to Count Zorzi', *Works*, vol. XXIV: 405–11, 410–11.
9. John Ruskin, *The Opening of the Crystal Palace Considered in Some of its Relations to the Prospects of Art*, *Works*, vol. XII: 415–32, 431.
10. 'Society for the Protection of Ancient Monuments', *Athenaeum*, 10 March 1877.
11. A committee of Trustees of the John Shakespeare Fund was set up to administer the trust.
12. Report to Dr Thomson from Edward M. Barry, 29 June 1857, unpublished.
13. Ibid.
14. W.O. Hunt to Lord Carlisle, undated, unpublished letter.
15. *Gentleman's Magazine*, July 1769, 345.

16. For details of these conventions, see Lucy Peltz, 'Aestheticizing the Ancestral City: Antiquarianism, Topography and the Representation of London in the Long Eighteenth Century', *The Metropolis and Its Image: Constructing Identities for London, c. 1750–1950*, ed. Dana Arnold (Oxford: Blackwell, 1999), 6–28, 16.
17. Minutes of the proceedings of the trustees acting under a Deed of Gift by John Shakespeare, 6 July 1857.
18. Fox, 51.
19. 'Covent-Garden Theatre. Shakspeare's House', *The Times*, 8 December 1847, 5.
20. J.P. Collier to Thomas Thomson, 17 October 1856, unpublished letter.
21. Samuel Neil, *The Home of Shakespeare* (Warwick: H.T. Cooke and Son, 1871), 16.
22. *The Royal Leamington Spa Courier and Warwickshire Standard*, 24 April 1858.
23. John Mounteney Jephson, *Shakspere: His Birthplace, Home, and Grave. a Pilgrimage to Stratford-on-Avon in the Autumn of 1863. With Photographic Illustrations by E. Edwards. A Contribution to the Commemoration of the Poet's Birth* (London: Lovell Reeve and Co., 1864), 35.
24. James Hakewill, *An Attempt to Determine the Exact Character of Elizabethan Architecture* (London: J. Weale, 1835), 20.
25. George Fildes, *On Elizabethan Furniture* (London: F.W. Calder, 1844), 5.
26. Marie Corelli, ed., *The Avon Star: A Literary Manual for the Stratford-on-Avon Season of 1903* (Stratford-on-Avon, 1903), 4.
27. Ibid., 5.

7
Ghosting Grasmere: the Musealisation of Dove Cottage

Polly Atkin

In the summer of 1889, Stopford Augustus Brooke – Queen Victoria's chaplain, dedicated Wordsworthian, critic and poet – went on holiday to Grasmere with his brother. Whilst there they made a visit to the cottage that William Wordsworth and his sister Dorothy had moved to 90 years earlier, in December 1799. This was the 'Home at Grasmere' of Wordsworth's eponymous poem, the cottage Wordsworth called 'our happy castle,'[1] and 'a home within a home,'[2] where Dorothy wrote her Grasmere journal, and where William wrote or conceived much of his most highly considered work. It was the house in which Wordsworth's three eldest children were born, after his marriage to Mary Hutchinson in 1802; the house they still called 'our cottage'[3] long after they had moved out and Thomas De Quincey had made it his. For Brooke, visiting in that late-nineteenth-century summer, it was already full of ghosts and echoes of the past. The Wordsworths' lives there had been recorded as they were being lived, in Dorothy's journal and in William's poems. They had also been recalled and evoked for public consumption by Thomas De Quincey in his *Reminiscences of the English Lakes and the Lake Poets*, first published in Tait's *Edinburgh Magazine* between 1834 and 1840. It was the cottage of these writings that Brooke and his brother came to see, and it was the cottage of the writings that they found. Bought only a few months beforehand by a gentleman from Bradford 'who had written a pleasant and graceful book on Dorothy Wordsworth',[4] the cottage appeared perfectly to fit its literary descriptions. To the Brooke brothers the cottage appeared unkempt, but authentically Wordsworthian. Brooke later writes: 'It remains almost as it was left by Wordsworth when, in 1808, he went away from it to Allan Bank' (12). During this visit, a plan formed in Brooke's mind. The next summer the cottage opened its doors to the public, as Dove Cottage,

The Wordsworth Museum; and by 1893, visitors from as far away as Massachusetts, Montreal and Singapore were flocking to it, to pay their sixpence, see inside the former home of the famous poet, and sign their names in the visitors' book.[5]

The story of how this came about is one which belongs to, and originates from, a particularly nineteenth-century vision of literary heritage and tourism. It is a story which revolves around the desire of Victorian admirers of Wordsworth to keep something of him in the world after his death; something tangible, and, crucially, something transferable. Both the story of the museum and 'the Wordsworth Story' that founded it, are precipitates of the specific cultural moment in which they arose. 'The Wordsworth Story' is a phrase first used by Brooke in a pamphlet he wrote in 1890, detailing and disseminating the idea he had had that previous summer, that a dedicated group could arrange the purchase of the cottage, and turn into a Wordsworth memorial museum. The pamphlet, snappily entitled *Dove Cottage: Wordsworth's Home from 1800–1808* is unassuming as an object. A little smaller than A5, 75 pages long, and with a plain biscuit-coloured cover, it appears more like a political tract than a tale of poetic inspiration and hauntings. In reality, it is both these things. Brooke wrote the pamphlet as a kind of manifesto, with the hope of gaining support and financial backing for his plan. It works hard to convince the reader why such a plan is desirable, and indeed, necessary, which is where 'The Wordsworth Story,' the particular version of the Wordsworths' Dove Cottage life that Brooke presents, comes in. This 'story' works to tap into seams of its contemporary culture, as much as it emanates from them. In doing so, it promulgates a myth of the Wordsworths' life in Dove Cottage and the cultural implications of such a life, which essentially create the site as a museum well before the physical work of turning it into one actually begins.

I am using the term *musealisation* to describe this multi-dimensional museum-making. First coined by Wolfgang Zacharias in the 1980s, it refers to a wider, more active museum-making than that which occurs in single, dedicated buildings.[6] *Musealisation* encompasses more than merely the physical business of creating archives or collections and housing them, suggesting an extensive archiving of everyday things and places, even of whole towns. It is particularly appropriate in the case of Dove Cottage, where the cottage can be seen as the epicentre of a broader musealisation of the whole of Grasmere, and even of the whole Lake District. The musealisation of Dove Cottage, what Stephen Gill has called 'The Dove Cottage Project,'[7] was complicated enough in itself, encompassing the appropriation of an actual building and grounds, physical objects and the space they occupy, but also imaginative space, and the space of memory. I will be investigating here how this Dove Cottage Project was managed and brought into action, starting with the literary and imaginative musealisation that Brooke effects with his pamphlet, and following on to how this was extended into physical space and place.

Brooke's 1890 pamphlet opens with a semi-mythologised tale of the genesis of the Dove Cottage Project in that 1889 vacation. The figures of the Brooke brothers, contemporary tourists and lovers of English poetry, are inserted into the Grasmere landscape, both physically (by their tourist activities) and literarily (by the recounting of their visit in the pamphlet). This immediately and evocatively makes the case for musealisation: Dove Cottage is a place of historic importance that can be visited, lived, enjoyed and turned into a personal experience. Moreover, it displays in action the inspirational quality of the place, for it is being there that affords the idea. Brooke presents the birth of the Project in what will become a standard conceptualisation of the importance of Grasmere. He writes:

> We had walked up to Easedale Tarn in the morning and the whole of that lovely and joyous piece of poetry in which Wordsworth describes the delightful goings on of the Easedale stream on that 'April Morning'[8] was in our ears as we stood by the wooden gate which opens on to the low-roofed porch. It seemed that he and his sister Dorothy were standing with us and that we heard him say to her, 'Come in: I will dictate to you the verses I made to-day in Easedale.' And in our mind's eye we saw the place as it was in his time. (5–6)

This short passage manages to combine comment on the perceived inspirational effect of walking, on Wordsworth's poems and their sense of place, on a sense of co-presence between present visitors and 'the past,' on the importance of specificity of location, and on the power of auratic landscape and objects/artefacts in the landscape.

For Brooke, Dove Cottage above all is 'the haunted place' (41), haunted by its past occupiers and associations. But he sees a problem: Dove Cottage 'is now uncared for; no sentiment presides over it; it is hard to see the ghosts that as evening falls must inhabit it' (9). Brooke envisions the possibility of manifesting those ghosts, of making the special quasi-supernatural experience he had accessible to others. According to Anja Nelle, this evocation of the past in the present is an essential aspect of musealisation; she identifies it as 'the journey into the past' function,[9] but it might be more usefully thought of here as a co-presencing. For Brooke, the importance is not just in '[seeing] the place as it was in [Wordsworth's] time', but that he, his brother and his *own* time were also there: he does not describe a journey back into the past so much as the past continuing to be existent in the present. This co-presencing 'ghosts' Grasmere. 'Ghosting' in this sense refers not just to the spectrality frequently evoked by Brooke, but also to a more general sense of presencing, such as that suggested by De Quincey when he wrote of the 'sense of mysterious pre-existence, by which ... I viewed myself as a phantom-self – a second identity projected from my own consciousness, and already living [in Grasmere].'[10] Here we see De Quincey using the language of haunting to evoke a layering of people and place, regardless of chronological time, a sense which, as we shall see, became pervasive in Brooke's conceptualisation of Grasmere.

In *The Poetics of Space* Bachelard writes of 'the house' that:

> If we have retained an element of dream in our memories, if we have gone beyond merely assembling exact recollections, bit by bit the house that was lost in the mists of time will reappear from out the shadow. We do nothing to reorganise it; with intimacy it recovers its entity, in the mellowness and imprecision of the inner life. It is as though something fluid had collected our memories and we ourselves were dissolved in this fluid of the past.[11]

It is precisely this kind of relationship between tourist and house that Brooke worked to create and promote. It is one in which all the elements of Grasmere past – the place, its inhabitants, artefacts and objects, but also events and emotions – may be recalled and re-experienced by the later visitor. The pamphlet works to people the cottage, its gardens, and the whole of Grasmere, with spectres of the Wordsworths, their friends, and their literary creations, giving the reader a virtual tour of Grasmere and its special places, 'the pool where Wordsworth met the Leechgatherer' and 'the pine grove where John Wordsworth paced to and fro, remembering his ship at sea, and made the path among the trees, of which his brother wrote the poem' (7). The description of John's Grove offers an excellent example of how the places, the poems about them, and the process of writing are conflated to create a triple-layered associative magic: 'There, evening after evening, Dorothy rested and William built his verse. There is not a line of all the poems which is not linked by sentiment to this quiet piece of woodland' (8). Most importantly, it is presented as if, by being there in those places, one might enter into the poems. We are told 'It was down this road, down the hill, that the "Waggoner" came,' but also that 'The famous horses stopped almost of their own accord before the gate at which now we stood' (8). Fictions and biographical facts become co-existent and equally accessible. Being in situ offers a kind of time travel, doubly fantastic as it includes travelling back into both the imagined 'real' past and into the fictionalised past of the poems.

Brooke thus presents literature as an extension of memory, a kind of transmissible public memory, which allows the past to remain visible in the present. Dorothy Wordsworth therefore becomes crucial because of her close observation of Dove Cottage life. For Brooke, she 'is the figure which, as much as Wordsworth, haunts this cottage' (32). This haunting is so powerful that it is tantamount to a reanimation: 'In this cottage, every room of which her presence fills, in this orchard garden, every flower of which breathes of her, she is alive and delightful, and beloved for evermore' (28–9). Yet this is a complicated possession. The Dorothy-figure filling the cottage is not just Dorothy Wordsworth, the woman and writer in her own right, but the version of Dorothy Brooke perceived to have been represented in Wordsworth's poems of that era. The cottage 'breathes of her' because she was both written into it, and wrote it herself, building herself into it as a permanent fixture: 'The tales of Dorothy... people the house with love and joy' and allow the initiated visitor to 'see with her eyes the view from the windows' (47, 48). Most importantly, they 'will endear the house to those who visit it hereafter; it will be peopled with memories' (52) through the process of reading.

In this sense the house and its garden, presented as the epicentre of this cross-temporal Grasmere, become like writings themselves, filled with information that may be legible to the lucky visitor equally well acquainted with the biography and poetry. For those attuned to the scent, 'the whole house is perfumed with their memories' (11). Memories of the past inhabitants, like those of their writings, become peculiar spectral presences, haunting the visitor. This is a place properly auratic in the sense Benjamin writes of,[12] actively observing the observer and 'invest[ed]...with the ability to look at us in return.'[13] Memory, literature and place are blended together in a cocktail of archival information, so that place becomes almost sentient. The landscape and its features have retentive powers, absorbing and holding information: it is 'a lovely land, scarcely a rock, or slope of grass, or sheep-fed nook of which had not heard Wordsworth murmuring his poems' (7). But it is also able to give information back. Writing of the beck in the garden, Brooke quotes 'The Rime of the Ancient Mariner': 'Underneath the grass flows the rill that fed the well, "a hidden brook...its quiet soul on all bestowing"' (12).

As the quotation of Coleridge's poem implies, this archival capacity of the cottage is not limited to the Wordsworths themselves: the place is 'an island of literature' still populated by the many literary figures who visited – Southey and Lloyd among them (72). These famous transients become more powerfully palpable in Dove Cottage than elsewhere, even their own homes: 'we do not find ourselves elsewhere so closely bound up with these visitors as we are in the cottage rooms of the Wordsworths, or in the garden, which was so small that they seem cloistered in it for our quiet observation.' (21)

For Brooke, this powerful spectrality and aurality bleed seamlessly into sacrality, so that Dove Cottage becomes a place of worship, even more sacrosanct when quiet and still:

> When all the visitors swim away from our eyes, we still see in the quiet sacredness of home, Dorothy flashing in and out, the three children playing around Wordsworth as he wrote, and among them, moving quietly ... Mary 'the phantom of delight.' (28)

It is this domestic sacredness which Brooke presents as the reason it must be preserved. Even before it becomes an actual museum and archive, the cottage is conceived as an archive or museum of the immaterial. Brooke's mission is to manifest those ghosts he feels sure *must* be there, indeed that he claims to feel there himself, not just for himself, but for and on behalf of 'all those to whom the work and memory of the poet are dear' (15). Dove Cottage is constructed by Brooke in 1890 as a geographically locatable repository of multifarious 'sacred' knowledge, and therefore important to all, and part of the national heritage. This is where the 'story' feeds into the manifesto:

> 'There is no place,' we said, 'which has so many thoughts and memories as this belonging to our poetry; none at least in which they are so closely bound up with the poet and the poems; almost everything in this garden has been written of beautifully; almost every flower has been planted by his or his sister's hands; in almost every tree some bird has built of which he has sung. In every part of this little place he has walked with his sister and wife or talked with Coleridge. And it is almost untouched. Why should we not try to secure it, as Shakespeare's birthplace is secured, for the eternal possession of those who love English poetry all over the world?' (14)

In presenting Dove Cottage as a spiritual and material centre, Brooke is drawing on and adding to the popularly held view of Wordsworth as a tantamount to a secular saint. Gill tells us that even within his own life-time, 'Wordsworth became a cultural icon, to be visited, written about, and, by disciples, revered.' (Gill, 3) Wordsworth's earliest disciple was the young De Quincey, the first person to be drawn to live in Grasmere because of Wordsworth's influence. After the Wordsworths outgrew Dove Cottage, he rented it for 27 years. Importantly, he also wrote about it at length, both in the *Confessions* and in the *Reminiscences*. He wrote of it as 'my beloved cottage', 'Cottage, immortal in my remembrance', and, vitally, as a place whose 'associations with Wordsworth, crowned it...with historical dignity' (De Quincey, 293). Brooke draws heavily on De Quincey, quoting long passages directly from the *Reminiscences*, treating them as a primary (and reliable) source comparable to Dorothy's journal or Wordsworth's poems. To De Quincey's hyperbolic exclama-tions can be traced Brooke's belief in the numinosity of the cottage and its significance as an archive. Although the cottage obviously gained meaning for De Quincey as the locations of important moments in his own life, it never lost its association for him with Wordsworth. If any-thing, this association grew stronger over time, swelling his feelings for the cottage to extremes. Dove Cottage becomes 'this cottage, so memor-able from its past tenant to all men...' (299). He writes of it as the home of all homes, 'endeared...to my heart so unspeakably beyond all other houses, that even now I rarely dream though four nights running that I do not find myself (and others besides) in some of those rooms, and most probably, the last cloudy delirium of death will re-install me in some chamber of that same humble cottage' (293). These sentiments of De Quincey's echo, perpetuate and re-generate the mythos of 'Home at Grasmere,' and predict (or set into motion) the generation of admirers and visitors who would follow.

In the preface to the selected works commissioned by The Wordsworth Society, Wordsworth's biographer William Knight wrote of the enduring need for Wordsworth's guidance: 'We do not wish him back amongst us, but we desire that his influence should increase, for nothing is more needed in our time' (Gill, 242). This quasi-sanctification seems to have led to the extra-textual mission of the evolving Wordsworth Trust in the last decades of the nine-teenth century; that of 'ensuring that what evidence remained of Wordsworth's actual life [in the Lake District] should be preserved' (Gill, 242). For his Victorian followers, Wordsworth's life was as inspi-rational as his writings; his places as important as his poems; his eve-ryday possessions as important as his treasures. Through association with Wordsworth, Grasmere became a place of numinous or auratic significance, and therefore Dove Cottage should be constituted as a monument or 'memorial' (Brooke, 15).[14]

Throughout his manifesto Brooke draws on the example of The Shakespeare Birthplace Trust. It is both an obvious comparison to make, and a very clever one. Obvious, because it is the principal precursor site in England, and so presents a 'convenient and safe guide' (17) to the potential investors at whom this pamphlet is aimed. It is also the seat of national literary pride, so if The Wordsworth Story can be aligned with Shakespeare and Stratford, it compliantly becomes another story of an English literary hero domiciled in an English landscape. Carefully ignoring the inconvenient existence of Cockermouth, Wordsworth's actual birthplace, Brooke posits Dove Cottage as the birthplace of the *poet* Wordsworth, constructing it as the birthplace of the poems: 'All the lovely band of brother poems 'On the Naming of Places' once inhabited, at their birth, this cottage.' (Brooke, 54) The poems become, in this story, living things, which 'ran to and fro in Wordsworth's mind while he sat dreaming over the fire'. (Brooke, 56) In an extraordinary passage Brooke hypothesises:

> that together [the poems] form a body of memories and thoughts to which it is well by the purchase of this place to give a local habitation and a name; some home where we may fancy that the poems may gather – glad to see once another – and hold converse when all the world of England is asleep; for it seems no dream to think that great poems have a being of their own, and move as they please about the place where they were born and shaped into their beauty. (59–60)

They are literally children of the poet's mind, independent souls, which deserve to have the cottage as their inheritance and heritage secured and protected. Hence the act of musealisation becomes an affordance of a bizarre family reunion:

> If the 'Cuckoo' and the 'Green Linnet' meet in the orchard; if 'Michael' and the 'Recluse' sit over the fire by night in the upper room, they will be glad to think that their birth-place is to be theirs for ever. (60)

These 'ifs' remind us of the purpose of this peculiar fantasia: it is, after all, a business proposal. At all times Brooke is working on the imaginations of his readers, selling them his vision.

The vindication of all of his efforts came when, in 1898, Knight decided to give his Wordsworth collection to the nascent museum ('relics and portraits, sketches and engravings, as well as of original MSS., and letters of Wordsworth and of more than 2,000 letters from men of note concerning Wordsworth and his work'). Brooke calls it 'this gift of yours to the Cottage', positioning the cottage itself as the beneficiary, 'and through Dove Cottage...the nation.' The poems are, in their physical manuscript form, to be reunited with the place from which they came. Because of this enrichment, 'the garden, the rooms where the Wordsworths dwelt, will have a new value and new associations.' The addition of all these genuine relics must have worked to magnify the already powerful aura of the cottage. The need to properly house the relics promptly outstripped the need to maintain structural integrity. Provision was made quickly for the 'adaptation of two of the rooms in the Cottage into one to form a library and Museum [and] to secure the proper lighting, heating and ventilation of this room' to store and display the new acquisitions.[15] Accounts reveal this included a 'fire proof door' (*DCMB*, 46). Brooke may have done a good job of imaginatively ghosting Grasmere, but the newly formed Trust together had to work on filling the space they had acquired with more tangible presences. At a meeting of 14 October 1891, it was agreed:

> That the Trustees of the Capital Fund be authorised to expend a sum not exceeding One Hundred Pounds...in the purchase of furniture, pictures, books, and other memorials of the Poet such as may form the basics of a museum, and to arrange for structural repairs. (*DCMB*, 16)

It was made a priority to replace the 'modern sash-windows with casement and leaded light' in order to be more 'in fair harmony with the place' (*DCMB*, 23), and to furnish the cottage 'in a manner that will truthfully indicate its appearance when occupied by the Poet' (*DCMB*, 24). This was all to fulfill the guidelines laid out by Brooke in his pamphlet, for preserving and reconstructing the place which had suffered 'no fatal change' (9) and could easily be 'arrange[d]...as it was in Wordsworth's time' (16). Intrinsic to this endeavour was the collection of genuine Wordsworthiana, including 'the gifts of important relics' such as 'an old four-post bed and bedding said on good authority to have been used by Wordsworth himself' (*DCMB*, 23). A contemporary tourist guide of 1891 even carries a postscript to its details of Dove Cottage ('now shewn to visitors') telling the reader that 'MSS., or other mementoes of the poet are gladly received on loan.'[16] This, like Brooke's mission statement and the early minutes of the Trust, reveal the extent to which literary tourism and tourism in general were already established. Brooke's constant reference to The Shakespeare Birthplace Trust, combined with the minutes, displays certain expectations as to what visiting and maintaining such a site should involve:

> The Committee shall have power to appoint and remove a Caretaker...they shall make provision for the reception of visitors, and regulate the hours during which the Cottage and ground shall be open and the fees for admission, which shall not be *less than 6d per* person.

Moreover, 'A visitors' book shall be kept at the cottage, in which the names and addresses of all visitors shall be entered' (*DCMB*, 12). Investors need to know where their money has gone, whether the scheme is proving successful, whether it can keep itself afloat. A report ten months after opening (signed G.F. Armstrong) details admissions and projected visitor figures as carefully as a modern marketing report. The 'total prospective income for the year' is calculated at £28:

> This result it must be pointed out has been attained without the assistance of outside advertising or the help of guide book and press notices etc. ... when the fact of the Cottage being open to the public becomes more generally known ... we may safely count upon something approaching double the present number of admissions in future years ... (*DCMB*, 21)

There is even mention of getting work done 'before the summer rush of visitors sets in.' As a business and as a working museum it was as successful as any of the originators might have hoped. By 1898 Brooke was able to boast that:

> Dove Cottage is no longer unknown to distant lands, or to the remoter parts of Great Britain and Ireland. It occupies, as a goal of pilgrimage, a place in this country second only to Stratford-on-Avon.[17]

The Dove Cottage Project, like Wordsworth's poems, had achieved independent life.

If you were to visit Dove Cottage today you will find exactly what Brooke dreamt of:

> a low-roofed, simple museum, shaded by trees; the little cottage beside it, with its orchard-garden, [which] form, standing together, a pretty and historic group of buildings, and recall, amidst the newer Grasmere, the homely mountain village of the last century. (17)

And if you were then to go into the cottage, and wait in the first room for your guided tour to begin, you might notice the picture over the fireplace: not a portrait of Wordsworth, but a photograph of Stopford Augustus Brooke, reclining on a chair in Dove Cottage garden, a book in one hand, and his hat flung nonchalantly behind him.

Notes

1. William Wordsworth, 'Stanzas Written in my Pocket-Copy of Thomson's "Castle of Indolence"', *The Major Works* (Oxford World's Classics, 2000), 1.
2. Wordsworth, 'Home at Grasmere', *The Major Works*, 261–3.
3. Dorothy Wordsworth to Catherine Clarkson, March 1817 (Wordsworth Trust Archive).
4. Stopford A. Brooke, *Dove Cottage: Wordsworth's Home from 1800–1808* (London: Macmillan and Co., 1890), 15.
5. Recorded in the Dove Cottage visitors books. MSS., courtesy of The Wordsworth Trust, Grasmere.
6. See Wolfgang Zacharias, ed., *Zeitphänomen Musealisierung: Das Verschwinden Der Gegenwart Und Die Konstruktion Der Erinnerung* (Essen: Klartext Verlag, 1990).
7. Stephen Gill, *Wordsworth and the Victorians* (Oxford: Oxford University Press, 2001), 244.
8. A reference to 'It was an April Morning', the first of Wordsworth's 'Poems on the Naming of Places.'
9. Anja B. Nelle, 'Mapping Museality in World Heritage Towns', Hermes vol. 1, (www.swkk.de/hermes/lang.en/seites5–1.html), 5–7.
10. Thomas De Quincey, *Recollections of the Lakes and the Lake Poets* (London: Penguin, 1972), 292.
11. Gaston Bachelard, *The Poetics of Space* trans. Maria Jolas (Boston: Beacon Press, 1994), 57.
12. See Walter Benjamin, 'The Work of Art in the Age of Mechanical Reproduction' (1936), http://www.marxists.org/reference/subject/philosophy/works/ge/benjamin.htm (accessed 30 May 2008).
13. Walter Benjamin, *Illuminations*, ed. Hannah Arendt, trans. Harry Zohn (New York: Schocken, 1969), 188.
14. Printed insert in *Dove Cottage Minute Book* (Grasmere: Wordsworth Trust Archive).
15. *Dove Cottage Minute Book*, transcript from handwritten book (Grasmere: Wordsworth Trust Archive), 37–40. (*DCMB* hereafter).
16. M.J.B. Baddeley, *Thorough Guide to the English Lake District* (London: Dulau & Co., 1891), insert between 106–7.
17. From a copy of letter to Professor Knight from Stopford Brooke (co-signed by all trustees), 13 July 1898 (*DCMB*, 39).

8
Women Re-Read Shakespeare Country
Gail Marshall

The nineteenth century saw the official establishment of Shakespeare as a national treasure, as his birthplace was bought for the nation in 1847; the Birthplace Trust was formed in 1866, and in 1891 was incorporated by act of parliament. By 1900, 30,000 visitors a year were visiting Stratford.[1] But this official commercial adoption belies the variety of Shakespeare's meanings for these visitors, and for Victorian women in particular. Both establishment bard and a voice adopted by radicals, Shakespeare's sheer variety made him peculiarly suitable for adoption by politically various Victorian women in need of a mouthpiece who could be both responsive to their situation and sufficiently weighty to carry authority in a period in which their own voices benefited from the supplement of his. But there is also discernible in the responses of many Victorian women to Shakespeare, a personal element which exceeds political or literary utility, and which speaks instead of their emotional responsiveness to his work, and of the gratitude with which they welcome his ability to recognise and to voice aspects of femininity which would otherwise go unacknowledged.

These responses go beyond the semi-official realm of literary and biographical criticism, theatrical display, and political and commercial utility, and exceed the usual limits of literary tourism in their adherence to a poet whose voice and characters might sound forth their own emotions. In this essay I examine the work of three such late-Victorian women, whose links with Stratford in the 1890s and early twentieth century attest to the almost visceral nature of their affiliation to Shakespeare, and their concomitant repudiation of the burgeoning commercialism of the town's Shakespeare sites. This type of commercialism is exposed by Henry James's 1903 story 'The Birthplace', in which the birthplace phenomenon is exposed as a blind, a simulacrum, bound up with the credulity upon which commercialism is based. For James, the existence of Shakespeare the man scarcely mattered; what was important to him, as he writes in his 1907 preface to *The Tempest*, was his work as an artist, 'the monster and magician of a thousand masks'.[2]

The grounds of James's rejection of the birthplace cult are, however, very far removed from the experience of the biographer, poet and translator Mathilde Blind, the political activist, teacher and writer Eleanor Marx, and the novelist Marie Corelli, for whom Stratford was the site of resonances which were both emotional and political. So intense was their identification with Shakespeare that these women forsook the usual limits of literary tourism by actually going to live in Stratford, and thus investing in the town as a form of living memorial to the writer who was so crucial to both their lives and writings. As will become clear, the oxymoronic quality of the term 'living memorial' denotes some of the ideological complexity of Shakespeare's significance for these women, who actually contested the submergence of both Shakespeare and Stratford within modern commercialism, and whose attachments themselves derive from a recognition of the very real previous existence of both Shakespeare and his Stratford.

The evocation of place is central to Blind's 'Shakespeare Sonnets' (1895). Blind uses the places associated with Shakespeare to conjure up his spirit in order that she can commune with the long-dead writer, even projecting herself into a vicarious romantic memory, as she fantasises about how Shakespeare might have come to woo Anne Hathaway:

> IS this the Cottage, ivy-girt and crowned,
> > And this the path down which our Shakespeare ran,
> > When, in the April of his love, sweet Anne
> Made all his mighty pulses throb and bound;
> Where, mid coy buds and winking flowers around,
> > She blushed a rarer rose than roses can,
> > To greet her Will – even Him, fair Avon's Swan –
> Whose name has turned this plot to holy ground!
> To these dear walls, once dear to Shakespeare's eyes,
> > Time's Vandal hand itself has done no wrong;
> > This nestling lattice opened to his song,
> When, with the lark, he bade his love arise
> In words whose strong enchantment never dies –
> > Old as these flowers, and, like them, ever young.[3]

Blind rather cloyingly imagines the love-struck young Will and his Anne in a process of commemoration which is literally grounded in the bricks and mortar of the cottage, artefacts which act to guarantee the parallel perpetuity of his work and renown. Nature and Time perpetually re-enact the scene of Shakespeare's domestic drama and remain, as do his words and love, 'ever young'.

Blind's is a Shakespeare embedded fundamentally in the land in which he was born, and shaped and inflected inescapably by that topography. In 'The Avon', Blind writes of a leaning willow, 'That hath not ceased to weep,/Whence, hanging garlands, fair Ophelia sank;/ Since Jacques moped here the trees have had a tongue;/And all these streams and whispering willows keep/The moans of Desdemona's dying song' (ll. 10–14, 114). The songs emitted by the willows have remained with them, a testimony in this case to the perpetuity of sorrow in love, and to Shakespeare's sympathetic witness of that sorrow. In 'Evensong (Holy Trinity Church)', Shakespeare's spirit is 'pervasive' round the 'old familiar things' (l. 14, 115) in the churchyard and in 'Shakespeare' he is the ultimate cartographer, unrolling 'before our sight', 'the world of men', which:

> Showed like a map, where stream and waterfall
> And village-cradling vale and cloud-capped height
> Stand faithfully recorded, great and small;
> For Shakespeare was, and at his touch, with light
> Impartial as the Sun's, revealed the All. (ll. 10–14, 116)

In a fin de siècle spin, Blind makes Shakespeare the mirror of nature; life imitates art as she accords to the poet a critical power so potent that it becomes a determining force.

The continuity between Shakespeare and place pervades these poems in a far from inert way. Nature and Shakespeare perpetually reinvest each other with resonance for the contemporary moment, albeit a resonance which has its affective roots in the past of Shakespeare's own day. This may at first sight appear to be a prime example of what Philip Dodd has described as the stabilisation of the growing conviction between 1880 and 1920 that:

> English culture was to be found in the past [...] The past cultural activities and attributes of the people were edited and then acknowledged, as contributions to the evolution of the English national culture which had produced the present. Nowhere was this more

evident than through the establishment of a national literary tradition within the emergent discipline of English literature.[4]

Shakespeare may then conservatively be invoked as a form or manifestation of national consciousness which is simultaneously coercively present and outmoded. Yet this is far from articulating the visceral Shakespeare of Blind's poems, which is actively present in her work, as in so many Victorian women's accounts of him. Her Shakespeare is not a lapidary national treasure, but a lover, a lambent Laureate, a mapper of emotions, whose authority derives from, and is embedded in, the connotations of the geography which represents a mode of anti-authoritarian, resistant identification.

In order fully to appreciate Blind's response to Shakespeare, we need to be aware of the ways in which her contemporary fellow-thinkers were also invoking the notion of a pastoral ideal in the midst of late-Victorian modernity, and to take account of her socialist affiliations. Blind was the stepdaughter of the German radical Karl Blind, who was an acquaintance of Karl Marx's, a leader in the Baden Insurrection of 1848, and, like Marx, a political émigré who took refuge in London after fleeing several other European countries. Once in London, Karl Blind became a journalist, and his home was a natural meeting-place for visiting radicals, including Mazzini, with whom Mathilde struck up a close acquaintance. As Simon Avery writes, 'Mathilde Blind was brought up in a household constantly involved in revolutionary and socialist discussion, where she was in continuous contact with many of Europe's leading political thinkers and activists'.[5]

Blind's life from childhood through to adulthood is one lived through a profound affiliation with concepts of stringent intellectual enquiry and social justice, and through a commitment to literature which could sound out those principles. Clearly she sees those principles as made manifest in Shakespeare, but her affinity with him has further personal dimensions. In September 1894, she writes to Richard Garnett, the Keeper of Printed Books at the British Museum:

> The charm of Stratford grows upon me the longer I remain. I drove to Wilmcote this afternoon, and saw Mary Arden's house, a sweet old cottage said to be four or five hundred years old. The timbered walls and mighty oaken beams of roof and ceiling show that it must have been a place of some importance in Shakespeare's day. It strikes one everywhere hereabouts how plentiful wood must have been at that time, when all these villages and hamlets were still embosomed in

the green recesses of the Forest of Arden. One seems to come upon Shakespeare's tracks here, and to get into closer touch with him and such plays as 'As You Like It' and 'A Midsummer Night's Dream'.

Memories and echoes of merry old England seem to have survived in Warwickshire longer than anywhere else [...] The inhabitants seem to be more cheerful than is generally the case in little provincial towns. They love the theatre.[6]

Blind's letters and the writings from the 1890s in her commonplace book attest to an enjoyment of nature, the rural world, and small country towns, perhaps as a respite from London. Stratford – and Shakespeare, who underwrites the town's effect – exemplifies the relief from modernity.

Blind was briefly living in Stratford when she worked on the Shakespeare sonnets, the last poems she wrote. Their elegiac quality derives perhaps from her own age, and declining health, and from her sense of sharing a last experience of Stratford with the Shakespeare who returned to the town at the end of his own life, but it also derives from a mournful sense of how the country had deteriorated since Shakespeare's day. John Lucas has identified a tendency in socialist writers of the period to hanker after a rural vision with, as he puts it, 'its implicit politics of containment and hierarchical structures.'[7] Blind's hankering, however, like that of Eleanor Marx as we will see below, is for a countryside which was precisely not redolent of those structures and hierarchies, which were anyway probably less oppressive than the structures in place in capitalist, industrialised Victorian Britain, but which actively opposed by its very existence a capitalist ethos. In *Merrie England* (1894), Robert Blatchford describes the industrial counties of England as 'ugly, and dirty, and smoky, and disagreeable.' By comparison, he suggests that the Southern counties have:

pure air, bright skies, clear rivers, clean streets, and beautiful fields, woods, and gardens; you will get cattle and streams, and birds and flowers, and you will know that all these things are well worth having, and that none of them can exist side by side with the factory system.[8]

The countryside takes on broader political, as well as literary and personal connotations, as both Blind and Blatchford envisage a harmonising of nature and man's efforts, a harmony which for Blind had been achieved in Shakespeare, and of which she could find faint echoes in the countryside of the 1890s.

In many respects, Blind's affinity with Shakespeare is echoed in that of her contemporary and acquaintance Eleanor Marx, whose life is imbued with references to Shakespeare which have their roots in her émigré childhood. It is clear that for Eleanor Marx the playwright's significance was born out of a close-knit family life in which Shakespeare played an important role, both as provider of family entertainments and as a source of the English language. As an adult, Eleanor consolidated her interest in Shakespeare by being the only one of her family to join the New Shakspere Society which was established in 1874 by the philologist and scholar of early texts, F.J. Furnivall, and also taught Shakespeare to working-men's evening classes.

For both Eleanor Marx and her father, Shakespeare signified and was indivisible from a notion of Englishness that was not necessarily coterminous with the England in which they lived. In Eleanor Marx's critiques of contemporary society, particularly of the place of women and workers in that society, Shakespeare represents a prelapsarian, pre-industrial voice signalling possibilities of regeneration for all through the recuperation of a past characterised by emotional integrity and generosity. For Marx, however, the recuperation of that past is also tinged with a poignant personal longing. She found a brief taste of such a recovery in the cottage which she and Aveling found, just outside Stratford, in 1887:

> One day, walking from Stratford to Bidford, (one of Shakespeare's well-known walks) we saw a farm – near the farm two cottages, one unlet. We inquired, found the rent was two shillings a week and [...] decided to rent this lovely little place. It is two miles from Stratford and Dodwell and consists of this farm and its two cottages. [...] There's plenty of room [...] I can't tell you how charming this country life is after the hurry and worry and tear of London [...] Think of it Laura, Shakespeare's Home! We work two or three times a week at his 'birth-place' (by permission of the Librarian of the place) and we have been over this home, and seen the old guild Chapel that stands opposite 'New Place', and the old grammar school – unchanged – whither he went 'unwillingly to school'; and his grave in Trinity Church, and Ann Hathaway's cottage, still just as it was when master Will went a-courting, and Mary Arden's cottage at Wilmecote – the prettiest place of all. Now that I have been in this sleepy little Stratford and met the Stratfordians I know where all the Dogberries and Bottoms and Snugs come from. You'll meet them here today. Just near our 'Kastle' is a bank – many think it Titania's for it is covered with wild

thyme and oxlips and violets [...] I never knew before how Stratfordian Shakespeare was. All the flowers are Stratford ones and Charlecote I would wager is Rosalind's Arden [...] we are settled here till our lessons and other work call us back to London [...] Then we get back to Chancery Lane to our teaching and usual dreary round of work.[9]

The potential sentimentality of this letter is redeemed by the anguish which underlies and even impels it. This injects an extraordinary pathos into the personal relief afforded by the cottage, a relief clearly made possible for Marx by its Shakespearean connections. Her rural vision confirmed her access to Shakespeare, and enabled a visceral satisfaction in shared labour which temporarily overcame her emotional isolation.

Jonathan Bate has convincingly demonstrated the ways in which the burgeoning concepts of the 'genius' of Shakespeare and of his status as national poet were ineluctably linked with his roots in Stratford and the Warwickshire countryside. His strategic embedding in his native environment, argues Bate, enables the construction of Shakespeare as one distinguished by his epitomising Englishness, so that the English countryside becomes the root of creativity and of the imagination, especially in the late eighteenth and early nineteenth centuries, when the 'Romantic idea of authorship locate[d] the essence of genius in *the scene of writing*'.[10] In some ways then, Blind and Marx, in their specific affiliations to the countryside, might seem to be reviving an earlier understanding of the significance of Stratford and its environs in the face of the town's increasingly commercial status at the hub of a developing tourist industry. Yet, the oppositional nature of the affiliation which is created fundamentally disrupts the harmony Bate cites between poet, rural identity and nation. Rather the women find in Shakespeare a voice out of tune with their times, although not their own aspirations. What had previously signalled the poet's national standing and identity now becomes a measure of his, and the women's, lack of affiliation with their late nineteenth-century moment. Variously disenfranchised by romantic disappointment, ill health, the disdain of the literary establishment, late-Victorian women could make Shakespeare into an ally in a manoeuvre which simultaneously bereft the establishment of one of its cornerstones.

Marx and Blind did so, as we have seen, by effecting their own alliance in nature with a poet who seemed to them able to voice an anti-capitalist identification with their contemporary dissatisfactions. Marie Corelli, to whom we now turn, did so rather by taking on the forces of capitalism, as manifested in the local interests of tourism and civic identity, and exposing their inadequacy as guardians of the memory of Shakespeare as it was manifested in the buildings which his presence had sanctified. Arguably Shakespeare's best-known female champion at this period, Corelli, the best-selling author, self-determined scourge of the new and dedicated controversialist, was a leading figure in Stratford in the 1890s. Corelli was renowned for the personal gondola – and gondolier – she maintained on the Avon, for her daily promenades amongst her adoring fans, and for the celebrities she entertained at her home, Hall's Croft, now appropriately part of the Shakespeare Institute at Stratford. Corelli and her friend Bertha Vyver fell in love with Stratford when they recuperated there following the final illness of Bertha's mother in 1890. A few years later Corelli wrote to a Mrs Corker, the then owner of Hall's Croft, from whom she hoped to rent the house, that 'I [...] am only seeking peace and comfortable surroundings in dear Shakespeare-land in order to finish my new book'.[11] Once installed in Stratford, Corelli became an indefatigable campaigner for the protection of the relics and memorials in, through and by which the town remembered its playwright.

Her energies were most fully exercised during what she labelled the 'Stratford-on-Avon controversy', whereby, taking confident advantage of her own fame and the extent of her popularity, Corelli took on the Trustees of Shakespeare's birthplace in their attempts to create a new Carnegie library for the town in Henley Street on the site of some cottages which were contemporaneous with Shakespeare, and which thus, as she believed, should not be altered. Corelli published her version of events in:

THE PLAIN TRUTH OF THE STRATFORD-ON-AVON CONTROVERSY: CONCERNING THE FULLY-INTENDED DEMOLITION OF OLD HOUSES IN HENLEY STREET, AND THE CHANGES PROPOSED TO BE EFFECTED ON THE

National Ground of
Shakespeare's Birthplace

MARIE CORELLI

'Fear not my truth; the moral of my wit
Is "plain and true".'

SHAKESPEARE
Troilus and Cressida[12]

Corelli's is a detailed narrative of the attempts of the members of the Shakespeare Birthplace Trust to enable the demolition of two houses on Henley Street (also the street on which the birthplace was to be found), and the alteration of a third in order to enable the construction of a Carnegie library for Stratford. During the ensuing controversy, Corelli set herself firmly against both the Trustees, many of whom were also councillors in Stratford, as well as against the substantial wealth of Andrew Carnegie, whose generosity had seen 2811 free libraries established worldwide. Corelli's opponents are chided for their lack of respect for their Shakespearean heritage, and in Carnegie's case, for the vulgarity of his attempting to use his substantial wealth to ride roughshod over local opinion. The newness of American money blunts the appreciation of time-hallowed associations which nothing can replace, and modernity threatens the authority of history in a contemporary battle for culture which sees the socially aspirational author opposing the free libraries which might have benefited some of her own readers, and arguably even augmented her readership. Corelli was, however, careful to position herself as a voice of the people in opposition to both Carnegie and his local representatives. Using the local and national press to maximum effect, and even briefly setting up her own newspaper to promulgate her views to a local readership, Corelli professed to express 'a very general and deeply felt opinion by saying that when there are so few old-world towns remaining unspoilt in England, the Birthplace of Stratford should at least be guarded more sacredly for the nation at large than that a portion of its most historic street should be left open to the easy purchase of the mere millionaire'.[13] Authorised by her affiliations with Stratford itself and its people, Corelli goes on to contend that 'I do not think I am mistaken in believing that the smallest and most traditional scrap of Shakespearean times is dearer to the world than a wilderness of Free Libraries' (*Plain Truth*, 45).

And it is indeed the case that the controversy was over a 'scrap' of Shakespearean times, two cottages adjacent to and contemporaneous with the Birthplace, and which Corelli suggests 'must' have been familiar to the young Will. The cottages are hallowed by an association which Corelli suggests Carnegie and the local Trustees are too callow to appreciate. Eventually, Corelli won the day: the cottages were saved, local people were denied their library and Henley Street remained intact. The whole exercise had proved Corelli's energy, her skills in managing public opinion, and a degree of combativeness which was also in evidence in her public controversies with a literary establishment which kept her firmly positioned as a popular rather than serious author.

Much of her 1895 novel, *The Sorrows of Satan,* is taken up with this debate as Corelli exposes contemporary reviewing to be a venal trade and critical opinion ready to be cheaply bought. Luckily for her and her alter ego Mavis Clare, public opinion is too wise to be similarly easily swayed and retains its integrity in preferring the works of the woman writer to those puffed by periodical reviewers. As we have seen, this form of demotic authorisation is also in evidence in the Henley Street controversy where Corelli purports to speak for and of the people of Stratford, and to make them the most virtuous and proper protectors of the name of Shakespeare in the face of the philistinism of local leaders and the national press. Curiously then, Corelli espouses a form of radical democratisation, albeit for a fundamentally conservative end as she and the 'people' of the town set out to protect Shakespeare. Shakespeare commensurately then becomes a popular rather than an establishment figure, joining Corelli in her oppositional state. There may then be more common ground between Eleanor Marx, Mathilde Blind and Marie Corelli than has previously seemed apparent, united as are all three in their attempts to realise Shakespeare and his continuing presence in the late-Victorian and early twentieth-century periods.

It is only possible to speculate about what James might have made of Corelli's zealously aggrandising efforts to protect the Shrine, or of Marx and Blind's more private experiences of making contact with something fundamentally Shakespearean in believing that they were experiencing the natural world that he grew up in. They might for James simply have been variations on the kind of literary tourist, creeping parasitically and destructively around the Shrine at which they professed to worship and which he creates in 'The Birthplace.' One might argue that Corelli was such a parasite in using the renown and stature of Shakespeare to increase her own status and standing, but for Marx and Blind, and those other women throughout the century who had revered the possibility of Shakespeare's relics, those mementoes were significant not in their own right but because they enabled an act of connection which was transhistorical, rather than ahistorical, a connection which went beyond the material in an attempt to connect emotionally with a form of authenticity that Shakespeare could provide. For them the relics and places are a form of visceral reminder of the words which had brought Shakespeare alive to them in the first place, and as such I would suggest that James would do a disservice to Blind and Marx in bracketing them with other literary tourists of his day. Far from disregarding Shakespeare's words, it was those words themselves which acted as the stimulus to trying to find a relic of the man and of the moment in which those words were created, and thus effecting a more concrete connection with a more sympathetic time than their own. James overlooks the fact that literary relics, literary tourism, are about more than a spatial connection, but that they can involve a temporal connection too, and as such that they can retain intact at their heart the figure of the inspirational writer.

Notes

1. Nicola J. Watson, 'Shakespeare on the Tourist Trail' in Robert Shaughnessy, ed., *The Cambridge Companion to Shakespeare and Popular Culture* (Cambridge: Cambridge University Press, 2007), 199–226 (213).
2. Preface to *The Tempest*; quoted in Leon Edel, *Henry James: A Life* (London: Collins, 1987), 562.
3. Mathilde Blind, *Birds of Passage: Songs of the Orient and Occident* (London: Chatto and Windus, 1895), 109–10.
4. Philip Dodd, 'Englishness and the National Culture' in *Englishness: Politics and Culture, 1880–1920*, ed. Robert Colls and Philip Dodd (London: Croom Helm, 1986), 22.
5. Simon Avery, 'Eleanor Marx and Mathilde Blind' in *Eleanor Marx (1855–1898): Life, Work, Contacts*, ed. John Stokes (Aldershot: Ashgate, 2000) 175.
6. Letter from Blind to Richard Garnett, 21 September 1894; quoted in Garnett's memoir of Blind in *The Poetical Works of Mathilde Blind*, ed. Arthur Symons (London: T. Fisher Unwin, 1900), 40.
7. John Lucas, *England and Englishness: Ideas of Nationhood in English Poetry, 1688–1900* (London: Hogarth, 1990), 204.
8. Robert Blatchford, *Merrie England* (London: Scott, 1894), 21.
9. Quoted in Yvonne Kapp, *Eleanor Marx, Volume II, The Crowded Years (1884–1898)* (London: Lawrence & Wishart, 1976), 209–10.
10. Jonathan Bate, *The Genius of Shakespeare* (London: Picador, 1997), 82.
11. Quoted in Teresa Ransom, *The Mysterious Miss Marie Corelli: Queen of Victorian Best-Sellers* (Stroud: Sutton, 1999), 98.
12. Published in 1903 by Methuen.
13. Letter by Marie Corelli, which appeared in the *Morning Post* on 11 February 1903; quoted in *The Plain Truth* (London: Methuen and Co., 1908), 9.

9
John Murray's *Handbooks to Italy*: Making Tourism Literary
Barbara Schaff

In the course of the nineteenth century, the Murray handbooks became formative for a distinctive way of cultured and educated travelling to the Continent, and were embraced by the British middle class not only as guidebooks but also as models for tourist practice: next to giving up-to-date and precise information about sites and the tourist infrastructure, a central concern of the handbooks was making tourists read the right thing on the spot, which not only meant reading what could be associated thematically, but also what was considered as being culturally valuable and aesthetically edifying. This paper will analyse the function of literary references in Murray's Italian handbooks,[1] particularly their use of Byron's works and persona, and finally the ways in which tourists, largely with the help of Murray, absorbed and performed Byronic experiences and poses on their Italian travels. Murray's extensive use of Byron not only provided tourists with cultured, elitist, anti-touristic gestures in the emerging age of mass tourism, as James Buzard has claimed, but also appropriated, familiarised and marketed Italy as a product of English Romanticism.

With the publication of his *Hand-Book for Travellers on the Continent* in 1836, John Murray invented a new genre: the modern guidebook. In the introduction, he distinguished two types of – in his opinion – deficient guidebooks: a first group by authors who were not acquainted with the places they wrote about, and which was therefore faulty and often antiquated, a second written by local authors who in fact knew too much about their localities, being therefore incapable of separating useful from useless information. Murray then defined his own objectives:

> The writer of the Hand-book has confined himself to matter-of-fact descriptions of what ought to be seen at each place, and is calculated

to interest an intelligent traveller, without bewildering his readers with an account of all that may be seen. [...] He has adopted as simple and condensed a style as possible, avoiding stilted descriptions and exaggerated superlatives. As he is by no means ambitious of showing off any powers of fine writing, he has preferred availing himself of the descriptions of others, where they appeared good and correct, to obtruding extracts from his own journals. Whenever an author of celebrity, such as Byron, Scott, Southey, or Bulwer, has described a place, he has made a point of extracting the passage, knowing how much the perusal of it on the spot, where the works themselves are not to be procured, will enhance the interest of seeing the objects described.[2]

Murray here makes a stylistic distinction between two separate forms of discourse, which together form the indispensable basis of a successful guidebook: sights are presented both in plain style as matter-of-fact descriptions and in the form of quotations from famous literary works. It is, however, misleading, to regard these discourses as completely unrelated. Rather, in order to highlight the complex alterity of the guidebook's objects (and to render them more attractive for the tourist), the description of the mundane was to be complemented with the literary, and especially with Romantic visions of the sublime and picturesque.

The Murray guidebooks, of course, were not to remain the only available sources of tourist information available to British travellers. Hand in hand with the increasing tourism industry in the nineteenth century went the further diversification of guidebooks, aiming at different destinations, different groups of tourists and their different interests, but none of the newly created series laid the same emphasis on cultured travelling and on literary tourism as did Murray's publications. Even Murray's main competitor Karl Baedeker, whose first guidebook was very much modelled on Murray's *Hand-Book for Travellers on the Continent*, did not present his factual information as so deeply embedded in a network of literary references as did the Murray guides. Equally targeted at the travelling middle classes, the Baedeker guides laid more emphasis on what was to be seen and on the detailed presentation of the tourist infrastructure than on linking their information to literary works and poet travellers.

Another proliferating British series was the Black's guides, published by the Edinburgh publishers Adam and Charles Black from the 1840s onwards, but becoming really popular only in the later nineteenth century. The series started with a guidebook to Scotland, *Black's*

Picturesque Tourist of Scotland, in 1840, and mostly confined itself to the British Isles, publishing guides to cities, countries and regions. Black's guides were primarily factual and informational guides; literary references and stylish embellishments were scarce. Black did occasionally publish guidebooks to European countries – such as an Italian guidebook in 1869 – but otherwise concentrated firmly on the British Isles. With prices ranging from 2*s.* for a city guide to 10*s.* for a regional and illustrated guide, the Black's guides were certainly more affordable than the Murray guidebooks, which started at 8*s.* and went up to 16*s.* for the larger volumes such as Ford's *Handbook for Spain.* Leisure travel in the nineteenth century is, of course, also particularly linked to the name of Thomas Cook, the founder of popular tourism and conducted tours. His strategy of popularising travel, that is making it more affordable and easier, started as a philanthropic project to keep away the working people from drink by offering them better diversions. Originating in an excursion from Leicester to a temperance meeting in Loughborough in 1841, Cook's tours became more and more diversified and sophisticated in the course of the century, first offering excursions to Scotland, and then from 1863 onwards, to the Continent: first to France, then to Switzerland and Italy, and culminating in tours to Egypt in 1869 and 1872 in an tour round the globe, which Cook himself undertook with eight people. But although the vast expansion of Cook's system of tours and excursions can truly be said to have democratised tourism in the nineteenth century, as far as nineteenth-century guidebook publications are concerned his importance is negligible. For his early tours, he published factual travel brochures and it was not until 1900 that the Cook guidebooks really gained a significant share of the market. In general, therefore, it can be said that although by the end of the nineteenth and certainly during the twentieth century the guidebook market became much more diversified, for most of the nineteenth century it was a close head-to-head competition between Murray and Baedeker as the two outstanding publishers of guidebooks for the educated and more privileged. It was certainly John Murray who set the standard for educated and culturally well-informed travelling, which in his time clearly meant embracing literature as a main source and model for the right perception of places.

Why did Murray so strongly emphasise the importance of the literary for his readers – mainly the emerging class of educated middle-class British tourists? The answer partly relates to the innovative quality of the medium of the guidebook: its target group would be more familiar with literary presentations of foreign places than with the yet unknown matter-of-fact descriptions that would become typical of the guidebook as a genre. Before Murray introduced factual, simple and impersonal depictions, travel accounts had been personal and subjective – in felicitous cases poetical and original, in less felicitous cases, as he put it, 'stilted' and full of 'exaggerated superlatives.' By integrating the literary in his handbooks, Murray in fact created a hybrid genre, harmonising the familiar tone of subjective travelogues with the form of the modern guidebook. Literature, and to be more precise, poetry would complement the sober seriousness of the given facts with the evocation of sublime emotions and refined perspectives, it would ennoble factual information and shape the tourist's perception according to the accepted cultural norms of the middle class. Thus the guidebook would also, as Jan Palmowski has argued, serve as a mediator of high culture, a translator of Romantic notions of the sublime into middle-class awareness, commodifying Romantic poets as prestigious properties of the emerging tourist industry. The simultaneous experience of sublime European sites, *in situ* and in literature, was of course much facilitated by the progressive development of a tourist infrastructure on the Continent in the post-Napoleonic era, which helped to proliferate notions of Romantic European landscapes; as Palmowski notes:

> Murray's active advocacy of the Romantic poets at precisely the point at which Romantic emotions could be verified and authenticated 'first hand', where they had first been felt, gave Byron and Shelley new levels of popularity. Images became internalised by the middle classes, such as Byron's impression of Mont Blanc as the 'monarch of mountains,' which is replicated not just in the guidebook, but in virtually every recorded traveler's sentiment.[3]

In terms of content, the integration of Romantic literature was far from secondary or merely supplementary, but had far-reaching consequences for the development of tourist itineraries: as Palmowski has shown in his comparison of Baedeker's and Murray's guides to Switzerland, Murray actually created routes along literary locations, that is he preferred places described by poets to places without any literary associations.[4] In the case of Italy as well as Switzerland, Murray mainly resorts to the English Romantics and to Byron in particular.[5] Consequently, touristic sights, as selected in the Murray handbooks, were not only chosen in relation to their historical, geographical or cultural significance, but also in relation to existing literary representations.

The frequent and extensive literary quotations in the Murray hand-books by far exceed the creation of a merely aesthetically pleasing add-on effect. They have a deep impact on the experience and understanding of foreign places, inasmuch as, through literature, sites and works of art are represented as spectacles, which immediately evoke an emotional response along the prescribed norms set by the given literary context. When, for instance, in a rather factual enumeration of paintings in the Pinacoteca di Brera in Milan, Murray singles out one painting by Guercino with the remark that 'Ever since Lord Byron was so much struck by this picture, numberless travellers have been struck too,'[6] this clearly indi-cates the prescriptive quality of the anecdote: even more important than Byron's spontaneous appreciation of this work of seventeenth-century religious art is his construction as an arbiter of taste who sets the norms for the educated British traveller. The following passage from Murray's *Handbook for Travellers in Central Italy* demonstrates the general principle of literary references: the reflection as well as the normative determina-tion of the tourist experience. After giving some practical information about guides and their prices, and having suggested ideal positions from which to contemplate the falls of Terni, Murray writes:

> The falls of Terni have been so frequently described, that we shall merely add such historical and other facts as may be useful, and quote the beautiful passage from Lord Byron, in whose judgement 'either from above or below, they are worth all the cascades and tor-rents of Switzerland put together; the Staubach, Reichenbach, Pisse Vache, Falls of Arpenaz &c., are rills in comparative appearance.' –

> 'The roar of waters! – from the headlong height
> Velino cleaves the wave-worn precipice;
> The fall of waters! rapid as the light
> The flashing mass foams shaking the abyss;
> The hell of waters! where they howl and hiss,
> And boil in endless torture; while the sweat
> Of their great agony, wrung out from this
> Their Phlegethon, curls round the rocks of jet
>   That guard the gulf around, in pitiless horror set ... .'
>   Childe Harold

> Lord Byron, in a note to these stanzas, remarks the singular circum-stance 'that 2 of the finest cascades in Europe should be artificial – this of the Velino and the one at Tivoli.'[7]

The handbook's guiding principle of selection, that it should not describe everything which might be seen, but only that which ought to be seen, is affirmed by the prescriptive judgement of the poet, who rates the Falls as one of the top sights on the tourist itinerary. Through his historical and geographical knowledge, Byron is presented as an authority to guarantee the perfect sublime experience, and in addition, his poetical view of the falls, presented as the sublime account of his poetical persona Childe Harold, testifies to the possible depth and universality of the tourist experience. Thus, the actual conditions of a visit to the Falls in the nineteenth century – as a most frequented attraction, where tourists continuously stepped on each other's toes – were discreetly camouflaged as a sublime experience with the perusal of the literary on the spot. Clinging to their Murray's, reading and reciting Byron on the spot, Victorian tourists could distance themselves from the hordes of fellow tourists and Italian Ciceroni, still enjoying the pose of the solitary Romantic even in the age of emerging mass tourism.

James Buzard has argued that this extensive use of the picturesque in nineteenth-century travel literature created an authenticity effect: European alterity, Buzard maintains, is represented (and felt rather than seen) as a primarily aesthetic essence:

> Coleridge had given travellers a maxim on picturesqueness: one may find it 'where parts only are seen and distinguished, but the whole is felt' (qtd. in Price 280). Indeed, for tourists, the picturesque vision is a Coleridgean symbol, shot through with the essence of the whole for which it stands.[8]

It is of course the primary purpose of any guidebook to present its objects in a frame of attractive alterity, and over the centuries different strategies have evolved to achieve this. Buzard locates the main underlying motif of the authenticity effect in picturesque conventions, claiming that this literary style – which, in the context of travel books, could also be described with the Russian formalist's technique of остранение – serves to produce the view of a touristic Europe, consisting of distinctive, essential features that mark off foreign places from familiar domestic society: in short, that the picturesque constructs alterity. Looking at Murray's frequent use of extracts from Byron, and among them the most colourful and picturesque passages from *Childe Harold* or *Manfred*, I would maintain rather that this strategy does not accentuate Italian alterity, but on the contrary familiarises it by positioning it within an accustomed, received, canonical and distinctively British literary framework. The otherness of Italy is much lessened, when perceived through the gaze of a Byronic persona, so well embedded in the British cultural consciousness. What is more, through these quotations Italy is not only familiarised, but even appropriated for the British, as Italy is marked off as cultural capital for British writers or perhaps even as part of British literary heritage.

The appropriation of Italy in the framework of English Romantic aesthetics is, however complemented by a wider set of literary references which puts Byron's dominance and Byron's views of Italy in the Murray *Handbooks* into perspective; although among all literary references, Byron is definitely the most frequently and extensively quoted author, I would not diminish the fact that the Italian handbooks do in fact cite a fair share of classical Latin and Italian authors: Cicero, Livy, Pliny, Ovid, Ariosto, Petrarch, Tasso and others. These authors appear as historical points of reference, but also as poetic authorities in the same ways as the English Romantic poets do, and quite often Murray juxtaposes references to classical Roman authors with a passage from, for instance, *Childe Harold*. The handbooks' insistence on elaborate literary links and cross-references to classical authors is neither accumulative nor arbitrary: it is a strategy which in fact turns Italy into a web of European literary allusions and complements the descriptions of classical works of art as signifiers of the origins and riches of European cultural history. Embedded in the wider framework of classical Latin and Italian literature, Byron is connected with its tradition rather than singled out as the English national bard per se. This also reflects on the construction of the tourist in the Murray handbooks: the educated tourist, or ideally 'the classical tourist'[9] as envisaged by Murray, was certainly not one with limited, parochial insular views, but a tourist with a profound knowledge and esteem of a shared European cultural heritage.

Two distinctive qualities make Byron particularly useful in the context of a tourist guidebook: one is the often theatrical quality of his poetry, characterised by an acute sense of place and history as well as a sense for lively dramatic scenes, the other is the scandalous reputation of the libertine and freedom fighter, which at the time when Murray published the Italian guidebooks, was still very much part of the British cultural consciousness. Murray's handbooks make frequent and ample use of references to both Byron the man and to his works, familiarising the tourist not only with Byronic views of Italian landscapes and history, but also with biographical information about the poet's Italian sojourns.[10]

For Victorian British tourists, Italy had long had theatrical Byronic resonances. During his Italian years, Byron had served as a spectacle for British tourists. Byron's friend Richard Hoppner, the British Consul in Venice, gave a rather comical account to Murray about how English celebrity hunters were on the look out for Byron during his daily ride on the Lido:

> The spot, where we usually mounted our horses had been a Jewish cemetery; but the French, during their occupation of Venice, had thrown down the enclosure, and levelled all the tombstones with the ground, in order that they might not interfere with the fortifications upon the Lido, under the guns of which it was situated. To this place, as it was known to be that where he alighted from his gondola and met his horses, the curious amongst our country-people, who were anxious to obtain a glimpse of him, used to resort; and it was amusing in the extreme to witness the excessive coolness with which ladies, as well as gentlemen, would advance within a very few paces of him, eyeing him, some with their glasses, as they would have done a statue in a museum, or the wild beasts at Exeter 'Change. However flattering this might be to a man's vanity, Lord Byron, though he bore it very patiently, expressed himself, as I believe he really was, excessively annoyed at it. The curiosity that was expressed by all classes of travellers to see him, and the eagerness with which they endeavoured to pick up any anecdotes of his mode of life, were carried to a length which will hardly be credited. It formed the chief subject of their inquiries of the gondoliers who conveyed them from terra firma to the floating city; and these people who are generally loquacious, were not at all backward in administering to the taste and humours of their passengers, relating to them the most extravagant and often unfounded stories. They took care to point out the house where he lived, and to give such hints of his movements as might afford them an opportunity of seeing him.[11]

This is one of the earliest statements about the ways the emerging Italian tourist industry responded to the Byron hype. Byron's importance as symbolic cultural capital was quickly recognised, and everything was done to create the specific sort of Byron which would satisfy the needs of British tourists. After Byron's death, the dead poet was quickly commodified into as valuable a touristic asset as the live one had been. The English pilgrimage to a Byronised Italy was supported and intensified by Italians in the familiar Catholic forms of hagiography and relics. In his *Pictures from Italy* (1846), Charles Dickens relates how a waiter in a hotel in Bologna, as soon as he had recognised that the traveller was from England, hastened to regale him with anecdotes about Milord Beeron:

> He knew all about him, he said. In proof of it, he connected him with every possible topic, from the Monte Pulciano wine at dinner which was grown on an estate he had owned, to the big bed itself, which was the very model of his. When I left the inn, hecoupled with his final bow in the yard, a parting assurance that the road by which I was going, had been Milord Beeron's favourite ride [...].[12]

This reads like an explicit strategy of Byronisation: for the English tourists, not only the celebrated sites of Italy, but even its more mundane aspects, like hotel beds, food and modes of transport are all turned into Byronic devotional objects along an emergent Byronic literary trail. The posthumous Byronisation of Italy, however, perceptibly shifted balance away from the attraction of the spectacle of scandalous celebrity to the perception of places of natural beauty associated with Byron, and thus to a far more sanitised and abstracted version of a Byronised Italy. This shift is principally due to Murray's exploitation of Byron's verse in his Italian handbooks. Byron, the publisher's most prestigious literary property, figures as the exemplary itinerant, and his protagonists as model spectators. Byron's acute sense of place and his performative style helped Murray to aestheticise Italian sites and sights with poetical quotes.

The theatrical quality of Byron's poetry provided Murray with plenty of descriptive passages, inviting emulation. For example, the famous first lines of Canto IV of *Childe Harold* turned the Bridge of Sighs into a major attraction for tourists ever since: 'I stood in Venice on the bridge of sighs, a palace and a prison on each hand,'[13] is above all a stage direction, and accordingly, these lines were appropriated by generations of tourists, who, for a moment, could rehearse the pose of the poet and the protagonist in a performative speech act on the spot.[14]

In accordance with the handbooks' objective of supplying 'matter-of-fact descriptions of what ought to be seen at each place,' Murray, referring to the Coliseum, claims in the first edition of *Murray's Handbook to Central Italy* (1843): 'We shall not attempt to anticipate the feelings of the traveller, or obtrude upon him a single word which might interfere with his own impressions, but simply supply him with such facts as may be useful in his examination of the ruin.'[15] This attempt at objectivity is, however, belied by Murray's deployment of Byron to supplement the experience. A few pages later, after having provided the reader with the detailed historical facts and measurements of the Coliseum, Murray's description metonymically culminates in the view from the summit, and this view is encoded as a Byronic scene: 'The scene from this summit is one of the most impressive in the world, and there are few travellers who do not visit this spot by moonlight in order to realise the magnificent description in "Manfred," the only description which has ever done justice to the wonders of the Coliseum.'[16] This is complemented with an extract from *Manfred*, establishing a dramatic contrast between the well preserved Coliseum as a symbol of death and cruelty, and the scarce ruins of the palace of the Roman emperors, the 'Augustan halls' as a symbol for culture. Murray again chooses a quote which enables the tourist to identify with the narrative persona and provides instructions even on when to visit and where to stand:

> I do remember me, that in my youth,
> When I was wandering, – upon such a night
> I stood within the Coliseum's wall,
> Midst the chief relics of almighty Rome;
> The trees which grew along the broken arches
> Waved dark in the blue midnight, and the stars
> Shone through the rents of ruin ... [17]

Murray's instructions for how to experience the Coliseum taken whole therefore do not read as mere matter-of-fact description; rather, this strategy of quoting Byron super-added sentiment to dry, factual information, thus modelling the British tourists' view of Italy.

This concept, however, had its limits, and the actual circumstances of travelling soon ceased to guarantee anything like a solitary romantic experience. As Beard and Hopkins point out, the experience of the Coliseum by night had, by mid nineteenth-century standards mostly turned into a vulgar mass event by the late 1850s. The tourists' posing as the solitary Byronic wanderer – sometimes even with a Murray guide in their hands – became a standard subject for parody in Victorian literature. Nathaniel Hawthorne, in *The Marble Faun* (1860), paints a vivid picture of English-speaking tourists doing the Coliseum by moonlight and 'exalting themselves with raptures that were Byron's and not their own.'[18]

Murray's influence in designing the literary appropriation of Italy for the British, in shaping distinctive modes of perception, was decisive. Murray provided tourists with what they desired, he enabled them to perceive themselves or even perform not as mere tourists, but rather as travelling readers. As Hawthorne's sour remarks suggest, due to the democratisation of travelling and modern means of transport, Victorian middle-class tourists were now able to travel extensively, but they still willingly relied on literary sources as guidance to the right perception of place, thereby hoping to mimic the aristocratic Grand Tour of the eighteenth century. This embrace of the older model of travel-experience as culturally more valuable exhibits nineteenth-century tourists' class-consciousness, their anxieties and social frictions. Through the knowledge of Byron's poems, they hoped to distinguish themselves from non-literary tourists, and to be classified as members of the cultured elite.[19] This kind of Victorian pretentiousness, inextricably linked to the dissemination of Byron's works through Murray, is portrayed in E.M. Forster's *Where Angels Fear to Tread* (1905): here, Mrs Herriton wants to find out about Monteriano, a little town in Italy where her daughter-in-law is staying. She consults three different works: first an atlas, then *Childe Harold*, then Twain's *Tramp Abroad*, and last, because 'Byron had not been there,' she literally leaves the territory of literature, and resorts to her son's room where she finds Baedeker's *Guide to Central Italy*. This book is not to her taste: 'Some of the information seemed to her unnecessary, all of it was dull.'[20] If one reads Mrs Herriton's choice of reference books as consciously typical of the average middle-class British tourist in the late nineteenth century, one could construct two hypotheses from Forster's gently ironic description; firstly, that *Childe Harold IV* was the urtext of the Italian experience for the British tourist, acknowledged as a normative model for the perception of Italy, and secondly, that a guidebook designed for the use of the educated middle classes, should not limit itself to factual description, otherwise its readers would be bored – a maxim John Murray had already formulated in 1836. If Baedeker failed to live up to the standard of the literary taste of Mrs Herriton, Murray's handbooks certainly would have suited her ideally.[21]

Ultimately, the sophisticated Victorian tourist would resort to Byron's self-portrayal as the exile par excellence to stand out from uncultivated mass tourism. Childe Harold's proud world-weariness – 'in the crowd/ They could not deem me one of such; I stood/Among them, but not of them; in a shroud/Of thoughts which were not their thoughts' – served as the model pose for such a tourist.[22] Thus, Byron, by epitomising an idea of the cultured elite traveller lent himself and his work as a role model for the target group of the Murray handbooks, namely the British middle class. 'Byron furnished', as James Buzard has put it, 'post-Romantics with accredited anti-touristic gestures that were performable within tourism.'[23]

The significance of Byron's works in the emerging tourist practices of the nineteenth century can certainly be hardly understated, but one should not forget to mention that this is mainly the result of Murray's intelligent and strategic placement of Byronic quotes in respective tourist literature, and what is more, his provision of the material conditions, by which the reception of Byron was facilitated for the tourist. Murray had taken utmost care to capitalise on Byron – after all, his most valuable literary asset – as much as possible in his various books for tourists. Taken together, Murray's commodification of Byron, through the extensive Byronic references in the handbooks, the 1843 portable edition of Byron's works for tourists and *The Beauties of Byron's Poetry and Prose* (1853) in the Railway reading series, presented Italy largely as a Byronic construction, as a spectacle which served to shape and regulate the tourist experience in complex ways. Thus, the handbooks also served as manuals for literary pilgrimage, by turning the itinerary of the Giro d'Italia itself into a hagiographic exercise of literary routes which perhaps were enjoyed not only by those tourists who wanted to perform anti-touristic gestures, but also by those who embraced a concept of collective literary worship. By claiming it as a part of the national literary heritage, Murray's literary portrayal of Italy in the frame of Byronic Romanticism familiarised and appropriated Italian alterity into the familiar tradition of canonised British literature, thus supporting the identity of an imagined British literary community abroad.

Notes

1. Despite the complex bibliography of the Italian handbooks, which involved not only various authors for the single books but frequent collaborations and different editors and contributors for the subsequent editions over the years, I shall for the sake of simplicity not refer to single authors but to John Murray as the organising head and chief editor of the series.
2. John Murray, *A Hand-Book for Travellers on the Continent, Being a Guide through Holland, Belgium, Prussia and Northern Germany* (London: John Murray, 1836), 2.
3. Jan Palmowski, 'Travels with Baedeker – The Guidebook and the Middle Classes in Victorian and Edwardian Britain' in *Histories of Leisure*, ed. Rudy Koshar (Oxford and New York: Berg, 2002), 111 ff.
4. See Palmowski, 108.
5. The importance Murray laid on the tourist practice of 'reading on the spot' is further demonstrated by the publication of a pocket-sized travel edition of Byron's works, supplementing Murray's requirements of a successful tourist guidebook. This edition was advertised in the 1843 edition of *The Handbook to Central Italy* as 'The traveller's complete and portable edition of Lord Byron's Poetical Works in one volume,' clearly targeted for use *in situ*.

6. *Murray's Handbook for Travellers in Northern Italy: Comprising Piedmont, Liguria, Lombardy, Venetia* (London: John Murray and Son, 1843), 195.

7. *Murray's Handbook for Travellers in Central Italy Including the Papal States, Rome, and the Cities of Etruria* (London: John Murray and Son, 1857), 269.

8. James Buzard, 'A Continent of Pictures: Reflections on the Europe of Nineteenth-Century Tourists,' *PMLA*, vol. 108, no. 1 (January 1993), 30–44; 33.

9. *Murray's Handbook for Travellers in Central Italy* 1843, 273.

10. See also Barbara Schaff, 'Italianised Byron – Byronised Italy' in Ralf Hertel and Manfred Pfister eds, *Performing National Identity: Anglo-Italian Cultural Transactions* (Amsterdam and New York: Rodopi, 2008), 103–21.

11. Quoted in Fiona MacCarthy, *Byron. Life and Legend* (New York: Farrar, Straus and Giroux, 2002), 342.

12. Charles Dickens, *American Notes and Pictures from Italy* (Oxford: Oxford University Press, 1957), 325.

13. Lord Byron, *The Major Works*, ed. Jerome J. McGann, Oxford World's Classics (Oxford: Oxford University Press, 1986), vol. 1, 124.

14. James Buzard, *The Beaten Track: European Tourism, Literature and the Ways to Culture 1880–1918* (Oxford: Oxford University Press, 1993), 117.

15. *Murray's Handbook for Travellers in Central Italy* 1843, 294.

16. Ibid., 296.

17. Ibid.

18. Quoted in Mary Beard and Keith Hopkins, *The Colosseum* (Cambridge Mass.: Harvard University Press, 2005), 7.

19. Buzard, *The Beaten Track*, 121.

20. E.M. Forster, *Where Angels Fear to Tread* (1905) (Harmondsworth: Penguin 1975), 29.

21. Forster never mentions the Murray handbooks, confining his digs at British tourist practices to the Baedeker guides.

22. Byron, *Childe Harold's Pilgrimage*, Canto III, Stanza 112/113, in *The Major Works*.

23. Buzard, *The Beaten Track*, 117.

10
Selling Literary Tourism in *The Bookman*

Margaret D. Stetz

Literary tourism may have promoted nation-building, canon-building, and other lofty ideals, but nothing associated with culture in the late Victorian period was innocent of the profit motive. Certainly, anything in which print culture in general, or the world of periodicals in particular, took an interest was sure to be tied directly to business concerns. In the final decade of the century, one of the chief disseminators of information about literary tourism and of visual images related to its pursuit was the *Bookman*, a British magazine that, in ways both subtle and effective, encouraged, fuelled, and capitalised on the new interest in writers' houses and fictional landscapes.

In October 1891, William Robertson Nicoll (1851–1923) proved that a sixpenny British monthly could be an enormous popular success if it took as both its subject and its target audience the world of the so-called bookman. Creating a periodical that talked explicitly about the literary marketplace, Nicoll found that he had an immediate hit on his hands. As Claude A. Prance records, 'Of the first number, an edition of 10,000 copies was quickly sold, to be followed by a further 5,000 and even a third printing.'[1] The intended readers certainly included the general book-buying public, but the main consumers that Nicoll tried to reach were his compatriots in what George Gissing called (in the title of the novel that also appeared in 1891) *New Grub Street* – that is, publishers, owners of new and second-hand bookshops, editors of periodicals, and, most of all, authors or would-be authors across the British Isles. To these groups, Nicoll's magazine offered professional gossip, advice, and a sense of community, along with a wide range of opportunities for promotion of their wares and publicity for their doings. Early on, moreover, the *Bookman* showed itself equally concerned with identifying and recording the activities of *bookwomen*. Through reviews of their work, reports

119

of their ongoing projects, 'puffs' of their travels abroad, and especially through reproductions of their faces in glamorous portraits, it reached out to attract, as well as to exploit, women who wrote for a living.[2]

The *Bookman* presented an inventive take on the genre of the trade journal, recognising and celebrating what Gissing bemoaned in his fiction of the same year: the transformation of literature, in the late nineteenth century, into a trade and, moreover, into an industry.[3] Many of Robertson Nicoll's innovations centred upon making visible the links between literary work and commerce already in place, as well as on forging new ones. In this regard, no development was more significant than his creation, beginning with the initial issue in October 1891, of the first bestseller list, titled 'Sales of Books During the Month,' which included reports from booksellers across Britain (from the West End of London to Edinburgh) of 'the best selling books'[4] and thus employed the same phrase we still use today. The chief currency of a literary trade journal, as Nicoll knew, was currency itself – that is, the impression of up-to-date-ness, especially in terms of knowledge; as Robertson Nicoll himself put it, in his capacity as editor, 'Great pains are taken to make our intelligence as far as possible fresh.'[5]

Providing timely information about sales could and would influence what authors wrote, what publishers released and what bookshops stocked. The inaugural 'Sales of Books During the Month' column highlighted this last function by ending with a list, not repeated in subsequent issues of the magazine, of the most popular 'Stock Authors,' according to 'a very large bookselling house in Central London.' The names of these writers were numbered in descending order, from most to least profitable, and consisted of '1. Scott. 2. Dickens. 3. Thackeray. 4. George Eliot. 5. Carlyle. 6. J.M. Barrie.'[6] That the last of these was a living author and, moreover, a young and very active one, proved, as we shall see, a significant fact that would affect other features of the *Bookman* in its early years, especially those related to literary tourism.

Amongst the novelty goods that Nicoll sold to this audience was the idea of literary tourism – a concept that, as Alexis Easley notes, had been fuelling an 'emerging industry' since the middle of the nineteenth century.[7] Thanks to this new form of recreation, according to Nicola Watson, 'travellers developed a taste for visiting a range of sites of purely literary interest ... [and] a new desire to visit the graves, the birthplaces and the carefully preserved homes of dead poets and men of letters. This fashion extended to the practice of visiting sites that writers had previously visited and written in or about.'[8] One could, of course, view the purchase of the *Bookman* as itself an exercise in literary tourism, especially for those who lived outside either the literal or the metaphorical 'New Grub Street' of 1890s London. After all, the magazine took the uninitiated and offered them an immersion experience in *la vie litteraire*, complete with exposure to important persons, instruction in the rules of journalism, lists of new merchandise, accounts of London bookselling in the past and present, and so on, while also providing occasional news about the foreign equivalents, from New York to Paris.

But the early numbers of the *Bookman* also defined themselves through literary tourism in the narrower sense that scholars such as Easley and Watson mean, when employing the term. Nicoll's magazine presented this concept in two ways: by linking imaginary landscapes, chiefly from recent fiction, to actual places that could be visited; and by detailing the sites (including the interiors of houses) where successful writers of the past had lived, as well as where their present-day counterparts resided. This double-faceted approach began with the *Bookman's* first issue, which contained the opening chapter of a multi-part series titled 'The Carlyles and a Segment of Their Circle: Recollections and Reflections' and 'Thomas Hardy's Wessex,' the latter with a map. Both were published anonymously, though John Stock Clarke has identified the writer of the former as Francis Espinasse,[9] while Nicola Watson has identified the writer of the latter as Clive Holland.[10] The article on the Carlyles featured descriptions of their 'little house' in Chelsea (as well as a mention of its address, for those who cared to walk by it themselves), while the one on 'Wessex' encouraged readers to visit 'our south and south-western counties' and assured them that there were 'few better guides than Mr. Hardy' to this region: 'To follow the fortunes of the people of his fancy through their native Wessex would be as good an itinerary as any need desire.'[11]

Certainly, it was no coincidence that the inaugural number of the *Bookman* functioned as a sort of guidebook and also extolled literature that mapped a region, for Nicoll's venture engaged in many kinds of mapping of the literary field. Each issue of the magazine opened with a lengthy collection of seemingly disconnected fragments, labelled 'News Notes,' combining puffs (evidently from their publishers) of books being planned or already in print; announcements (evidently from their editors) of new periodicals or of the contents of special issues; and reports (evidently from authors) of their health, their work-in-progress, and their journeys abroad. As a typical entry in January 1892 read:

> Miss Mathilde Blind, the first edition of whose recent volume of verse, 'Dramas in Miniature,' has been sold out, has just left London

for Egypt, where, by medical advice, she will spend the first three months of the year. Miss Blind has been indisposed for some time past, and a dry and sunny atmosphere is considered essential for her well-being. She hopes to finish there a novel of contemporary life upon which she has been long engaged.[12]

Alongside these details about an individual figure might be more general and practical information, aimed at aspiring writers, regarding the formal or informal rules of journalistic practice:

> Where a person not on the staff of a newspaper, say the writers, sends a manuscript to the editor without any invitation either to himself personally or to the public generally to do so, he sends it at his own risk, there is no obligation on the part of the newspaper proprietor or editor to preserve it, and if it be lost the sender cannot recover its value.[13]

But some of the items clearly were little more than gossip, meant to make the reader feel like a privileged insider, with access to the latest events and *contretemps* in the literary world:

> Provincial clubs are always glad of 'distinguished strangers' at their feasts, but it is inconsiderate on the part of the honoured guests to fight out their private quarrels on such occasions. Not very long ago a local Pen and Pencil Club entertained Mr. Harry Furniss [the caricaturist] in the course of his lecturing tour, and were entertained by him in turn with his grievances against Mr. G. A. Sala and the editor of the *National Observer* [i.e., W. E. Henley]. It was reported that his audience did not much like it.[14]

Though Laurel Brake rightly situates the *Bookman* amongst a number of 'specialised trade journals in the news and books trades in the late nineteenth century,'[15] it was more than that. In many ways, it anticipated what would be called, in the 1970s, the genre of the 'lifestyle' magazine, for what it sold was entrée into a whole way of life centred upon the production and consumption of texts. An important facet of that 'lifestyle' was the image of authorship itself. Through its longer articles, many of which were profiles of writers (complete with portrait photographs), the *Bookman* manufactured an illusion – designed to appeal, in particular, to those not yet part of the profession – of intimacy with authors and with the spheres in which they moved, in order to make outsiders *wish* to be authors themselves.

One of the most effective ways to give readers the sense of being insiders was to allow them to traverse the neighbourhoods and cross the thresholds of the places where celebrated writers lived and worked. As John Stock Clarke notes á propos of 'Thomas Hardy's Wessex,' in the very first issue, 'The Wessex article inaugurated literary topography as a special theme of *The Bookman* over the years, with articles and illustrations on the homes and settings of the Brontës, Dickens, and many other authors'.[16] Clarke does not exaggerate. The June 1892 number, for instance, contained an article by Harold Spender, 'The Browning Palace at Venice,' written in the breathless, awe-filled voice of a guide leading his party into and through a sacred space:

> Since his [Robert Browning's] death ... young Mr. Browning has very wisely and piously filled its great rooms with memorials of the mighty dead ... You are escorted up a narrow winding staircase ... into a spacious anteroom. Thence you pass directly into a great, lofty drawing-room ... On the side table of the sitting-room, as if to consecrate it, is a small copy of the large portrait of Mrs. Browning in her maturity and beneath it a presentation copy of her works in very precious and beautiful binding.[17]

'Shelley as Poet,' a literary assessment by William Watson (who was, of course, a poet himself) for the August 1892 issue included a photograph captioned 'Tomb of Shelley in the Protestant Burial-Ground, Rome' – the sort of souvenir photo that a fan of the great Romantic might bring back from a pilgrimage. And most temptingly, the 'News Notes' feature for July 1892 reproduced an engraving titled 'Sir Walter Raleigh's House in Youghal,' accompanied by the information that the very house where 'Sir Walter is said to have smoked the first pipe of tobacco in Ireland' had been 'put up for sale lately, but only £1, 250 was offered, and it was bought in.'[18] Not only could one tour a historic property, but, egged on by the *Bookman,* one might even consider purchasing it. In later issues from 1893 and 1894, W. Robertson Nicoll himself signed a series of articles called 'The Literary Associations of Hampstead' that went house by house, identifying not only famous sites ('Keats' Lodgings in Well Walk' appeared in the November 1893 number), but more obscure and unexpected ones ('Where Mrs. Coventry Patmore Died' appeared in the October 1894 number). This series was notable, moreover, for its interest in identifying current writers' homes – indeed, even the very newest. In October 1893, it described Frognal End, for instance: 'This house, built in 1892, is the residence of Mr. Walter Besant, the celebrated novelist.'[19]

Such attention to a house belonging to a living writer was no anomaly for the *Bookman*. Earlier in 1893, the April number had contained two images: 'Max Gate, Dorchester, The Residence of Mr. Thomas Hardy' and 'The Residence of Mr. Rudyard Kipling, Brattleboro, Vermont.' These were not tied to an article or, indeed, to any text whatsoever. Readers would, presumably, understand without explanation that to be a *bookman* (or a *bookwoman*) – to experience fully the literary scene – required not only news of current texts and of their authors, but visual knowledge, including the spectacle of how writers lived. If subscribers were unable to travel across Britain themselves to gain this knowledge, then the magazine would function as a vicarious tour. Thus, the June 1893 issue featured two more photographs, now labelled part of a series called 'Novelists' Homes, II': 'Mr. Hall Caine's Late Residence at Keswick' and 'Mr. J. M. Barrie's Residence at Kirriemuir.'

Throughout the first three years of the *Bookman*'s existence, the name of J.M. Barrie appeared again and again. As we have seen already, there was indeed a good explanation for this. Though a young man in his early thirties, Barrie, whose success as a playwright still lay ahead of him, was already a bestseller as a writer of fiction and essays and the only living 'Stock Author' to make the *Bookman*'s list of the top six. To feature him so prominently was, presumably, to give the public what it wanted. The February 1892 number, therefore, offered a panegyric by A.T. (that is, Arthur) Quiller-Couch to Barrie's works about Kirriemuir – the place he renamed 'Thrums.' Accompanying the article were two photographs linked to those same works – 'The Window in Thrums' and 'The Auld Licht Kirk' – photographs that encouraged readers' interest in the original sites that supposedly served as inspiration. Such sites could, in fact, be visited. Quiller-Couch, nevertheless, warned potential sightseers that 'Thrums itself, I suspect, will disappoint the tourist. ... But Mr. Barrie probably knows better than the tourist, for it is his birthplace, and he is a Scot.'[20] Thrums/Kirriemuir, it seems, was best encountered through Barrie's prose and through the *Bookman*'s photographs; knowledge of a location was important, but not as important as the mediated knowledge provided by *experts* and acquired through the purchase of books and magazines.

The magazine's emphasis upon presenting photographs of the homes and haunts of living writers – Barrie's house, R.L. Stevenson's 'Vailima' in Samoa (in the January 1894 issue), Swinburne's 'The Pines' in Putney (in the June 1894 issue), and many others – was not attributable merely to a desire to satisfy readers' curiosity about popular authors. There was more at stake, and literary tourism was only one piece of a larger package. Ultimately, what the *Bookman* held out to readers – both to those who already were part of the professional literary scene and to those who wished to be – was hope: the dream of celebrity. Features about Hardy's 'Wessex' or Barrie's 'Thrums,' like the photographs of writers' residences, represented something for novices and seasoned professionals alike to envy and to work toward.

By the 1890s, literary fame in Britain no longer meant merely the possibility of wealth; it also meant the possibility that one's house might be turned into a shrine and the settings of one's own texts into sites of pilgrimage. Series such as 'The Literary Associations of Hampstead' were integrally linked to monthly features such as the magazine's 'The Young Author's Page,' which offered evaluations of manuscripts sent by fledgling writers. The latter column dangled before eager novices the promise of discovery. If one were discovered, then photographers presumably would soon be setting up their cameras outside one's own house, in order to immortalise it.

But the *Bookman* did more than lure potential authors who wished someday to be 'toured' themselves; it also connected literary tourism to advertising. The inclusion, for instance, of the article on 'Hardy's Wessex' began a concerted campaign to puff Hardy in many ways – from a lengthy appreciation, 'The Work of Thomas Hardy' by 'Professor Minto' (that is, William Minto) in December 1891, to frequent mentions in the 'News Notes' column – culminating at last in Hardy's publisher, Osgood and McIlvaine, buying a half-page advert in March 1894 and in subsequent issues. Puffery paid off. This purchase of advertising space guaranteed a steady income for the *Bookman* of £4.40 every month. In the case of J.M. Barrie, however, the magazine's inclusion of a photograph of his house in June 1893 – as well as an illustrated article in February 1892 by Arthur Quiller-Couch, about the connections between Barrie's writings and his Scottish homeland – all came *after* Barrie's publishers, Hodder and Stoughton, had started running a quarter-page advert devoted solely to 'Mr. J. M. Barrie's Works: "Racy, humorous, delightful" ' from the first issue of the *Bookman* onwards. In the world of late Victorian print culture, literary tourism provided a splendid opportunity for *quid pro quo* promotional efforts. Encouraging readers to tour sites associated with living writers – and to do so either virtually, through the pages of the magazine, or in actuality – was tied directly to monetary arrangements with publishers.

Seen through the lens of the present, when we take for granted the commodification of all varieties of fame, including the literary sort, W. Robertson Nicoll's monthly looks all too modern and familiar. It was a trade journal, a 'lifestyle' magazine, and a celebrity rag that glamorised the book world, at the very moment when the production and sale of books was becoming a domain of often brutal industry. For the grim realities of the factory and the warehouse, on which the literary market increasingly depended, the *Bookman* substituted the appealing image of the writer's house and took its awestruck, envious readers on a tour. Just as it does today, literary tourism made good business sense at the end of the nineteenth century, and the proprietors of magazines such as the *Bookman* were shrewd enough to know this and profit from it.

Notes

1. Claude A. Prance, 'The Bookman,' *British Literary Magazines: The Victorian and Edwardian Age, 1837–1913*, ed. Alvin Sullivan (Westport, CT: Greenwood, 1984), 44.
2. For more about the strategic use of women as textual subjects and as visual objects in the *Bookman*, as well as in other contemporary periodicals, see Stetz, 'The New Woman and the British Periodical Press of the 1890s,' *Journal of Victorian Culture*, 6: 2 (Autumn 2001), 272–85.
3. The employment of the word 'industry' in connection with literature and with publishing alike was, at the end of the nineteenth century, both commonplace and contested. For more on this subject, see Stetz, 'Publishing Industries and Practices,' *The Cambridge Companion to the Fin de Siècle*, ed. Gail Marshall (Cambridge: Cambridge University Press, 2007), 113–30.
4. 'Sales of Books During the Month,' *Bookman*, 1: 1 (October 1891), 31.
5. 'News Notes,' *Bookman*, 1: 3 (December 1892), 88.
6. 'Sales of Books During the Month,' 31.
7. Alexis Easley, 'The Woman of Letters at Home: Harriet Martineau and the Lake District,' *Victorian Literature and Culture*, 34: 1 (2006), 291.
8. Nicola J. Watson, *The Literary Tourist: Readers and Places in Romantic and Victorian Britain* (Houndmills, UK: Palgrave Macmillan, 2006), 5.
9. John Stock Clarke, 'The Bookman,' *The 1890s: An Encyclopedia of British Literature, Art, and Culture*, ed. G.A. Cevasco (New York: Garland, 1993), 72.
10. Watson, 181.
11. [Claude Holland], 'Thomas Hardy's Wessex,' *Bookman*, 1: 1 (October 1891), 26.
12. 'News Notes,' *Bookman*, 1: 4 (January 1892), 126.
13. Ibid., 129.
14. 'News Notes,' *Bookman*, 1: 6 (March 1892), 199.
15. Laurel Brake, *Print in Transition, 1850–1910: Studies in Media and Book History* (Houndmills, UK: Palgrave, 2001), 76.

16. Clarke, 72.
17. Harold Spender, 'The Browning Palace at Venice,' *Bookman*, 2: 9 (June 1892), 81–2.
18. 'News Notes,' *Bookman*, 2: 10 (July 1892), 103.
19. W. Robertson Nicoll, 'The Literary Associations of Hampstead,' *Bookman*, 5: 25 (October 1893), 16.
20. A.T. Quiller-Couch. 'J. M. Barrie.' *Bookman*, 1: 5 (February 1892), 169.

11
Elizabeth Gaskell and Literary Tourism

Pamela Corpron Parker

Eighteenth- and nineteenth-century Britain saw a rapid growth of international print culture. Women writers were increasingly defined as literary celebrities, and their homes became popular destinations for a rising number of British and American visitors. Earnest readers knocked on the Brontë Parsonage door in Haworth, peeked into Harriet Martineau's Ambleside window at teatime, and retraced Elizabeth Gaskell's steps in Knutsford, her girlhood home and last resting place. In the expanding consumer culture of Victorian Britain, successful female authors became marketable literary personalities. The popular presses eagerly supplied a growing number of memoirs, guidebooks, periodicals, and maps focusing on Britain's literary heritage. Then, as now, the national heritage industry, particularly literary tourism, augmented the popular and critical reputations of British writers such as Charlotte Brontë and Elizabeth Gaskell. As the author of *The Life of Charlotte Brontë* (1857), Gaskell in particular legitimated literary tourism as a cultural practice and created some of the central myths surrounding the British Woman of Letters. Throughout her 25-year publishing career (from 1840 to her death in 1865), Elizabeth Gaskell was a promoter, participant, and subject of literary tourism.

Nicola J. Watson's recent study, *The Literary Tourist: Readers and Places in Romantic and Victorian Britain,* demonstrates clearly nineteenth-century readers' engagement with Britain's urban and rural landscapes through the lens of literature. By supplementing reading with travel, the literary tourist reconstituted Britain through a proliferating number of literary signifiers.[1] Far from the metropole of London, villages such as Brontë's Haworth and Gaskell's Knutsford were transformed into monuments to Britain's literary history and cultural superiority. In James Buzard's influential study, *The Beaten Track,* he argues that increased affluence, mobility and literacy amongst the middle and working classes encouraged their participation in literary tourism.[2] Their activities bolstered Britain's national pride and the commercial interests of the burgeoning transportation and publishing industries. Eager to appropriate the cultural markers of the literate classes, tourists collected postcards, writers' autographs, portraits, personal relics, and related souvenirs. These artefacts mark the shift from what Loren Glass has called a 'genteel culture of publishing' largely characterised by a cottage industry of several family owned presses, to a highly commercialised industry engaged in the mass marketing of the literary personality.[3] Though traditional literary sources (such as fiction, poetry, and biography) certainly undergirded writers' public acclaim, more popular forms and practices, such as the 'homes and haunts' genre and the subsequent prevalence of literary tourism amplified the reading public's engagement with writers as celebrities.

Homes, haunts and *The Life of Charlotte Brontë*

Literary tourism encouraged the production and consumption of popular print culture, while reciprocally these materials furthered the activities of literary tourism. Both promoted the international renown of British writers and advanced the Victorian cult of personality. As a popular subgenre of literary biography, the 'homes and haunts' guides integrated biographical and geographical information about literary personalities. William Howitt is often credited with establishing this subgenre through his popular *Homes and Haunts of the Most Eminent British Poets* (1847). Indeed, Howitt's book provides one of the earliest attempts to map a comprehensive literary history of Britain for popular reading audiences. His contributions to British literary history and travel writing have been greatly underestimated. As Alison Booth has recently argued, *Homes and Haunts* helped to launch a 'lucrative line of biographical piecework that continues to support literary tourism to this day.'[4] However, Gaskell's *The Life of Charlotte Brontë* arguably represents the pinnacle of the 'homes and haunts' genre as well as being one of the first book-length portraits of the British woman of letters. Gaskell herself would become the subject of such writings; by the turn of the century, numerous 'homes and haunts' guides to Gaskell were appearing in print, including George Payne's *Mrs. Gaskell and Knutsford* (1900) and Mrs. Ellis Chadwick's *Haunts, Homes, and Stories of Mrs. Gaskell* (1913).

From her earliest publications onwards, Elizabeth Gaskell acquired a regional identity through her emphasis on north-western British settings, particularly Lancashire, Yorkshire, and Cheshire counties. Indeed, her earliest writings adopted the travel-writing genre. She described Clopton Hall for Howitt's *Visits to Remarkable Places* (1840) and contributed 'Notes on Cheshire Customs' to his *Rural Life of England* (1840). Later, her nostalgic account of 'The Cumberland Sheep-Shearers' appeared in Dickens's *Household Words* (1853). While some Gaskell scholars dismiss these early writings as inferior 'apprenticeship' or 'journalistic' pieces, their discursive imprint is foundational to Gaskell's entire body of work. Throughout her career, Gaskell incorporates the discourses of rural nostalgia, travel writing and national historiography within her fiction. Her vivid travelogues of the geographies and inhabitants of England's northern villages and cities remain central to her fictional masterpieces, particularly *North and South* (1855), *Wives and Daughters* (1866) and *Sylvia's Lovers* (1863), and they are equally central to *The Life of Charlotte Brontë* (1857).

With its atmospheric opening of her journey into Haworth and its gothic rendition of the parsonage and surrounding graveyard, *The Life of Charlotte Brontë* effectively transformed Haworth into a place of pilgrimage for the Brontë faithful; in 1877 Sir Thomas Wemyss Reid testified to this success:

> One great change resulted from the publication of Mrs. Gaskell's work: Haworth and its parsonage became the shrine to which hundreds of literary pilgrims from all parts of the world began to find their way to see the house in which the three sisters had spent their lives and done their work, to stand at the altar at which Charlotte Brontë was married, and beneath which her ashes now rest, and to hear her aged father preach one of his pithy, sensible, but dogmatic sermons, was what all literary lion-hunters aspired to do.[5]

By Wemyss's account, *The Life* was the book that launched a thousand tourists. The literary lion-hunter aspired 'to do' Haworth; that is, to physically inhabit the existential place of the author ('to see,' 'stand,' and 'hear' the remaining relics of the Brontës).

The Life of Charlotte Brontë positions readers as fellow pilgrims alongside Gaskell. The opening train ride on the Leeds and Bradford railway is advertised as providing the 'peculiar smack and flavour of the place'[6] and is followed by careful directions for travelling on to Keighley and Haworth: 'Right before the traveller on this road rises Haworth village; he can see it for two miles before he arrives, for it is situated on the side of a pretty steep hill, with a background of dun and purple moor, rising and sweeping away yet higher than the church, which is built at the very summit of the long narrow street.'[7] Gaskell's present-tense descriptions direct the reader's gaze and physical location, suggesting the visitor's bodily presence alongside her own entry into Haworth: 'as the visitor stand[ing] with his back to the church, ready to enter in at the front door belonging to Mr. Brontë's study, the two on the left to the family sitting room.'[8]

Throughout the text, the trope of literary pilgrimage guides Gaskell's mobile, dynamic narrative and dramatises the psychic and geographical landscapes of the Brontë sisters. Using the by now familiar discourses of the 'homes and haunts' genre, Gaskell writes into existence a less familiar subject, the British woman of letters. By locating Charlotte Brontë in Haworth, Gaskell creates a more coherent portrait of the woman writer as a cultural icon. *The Life* performs what Chandra Talpade Mohanty has called a 'politics of location,' in which a woman's *place* – that is her home, landscape, region, and national identity, provide her with 'historical, geographical, cultural, psychic, and imaginative boundaries' for the construction of her political self-definition.[9] This notion of a woman's *place* – as a particular geographical region, home, or social position – thus converges with *placing* or locating a woman within a specific historical, professional, and familial context. As Gaskell puts it, 'For a right understanding of the life of my dear friend, Charlotte Brontë, it appears to me more necessary in her case than in most others, that the reader should be made acquainted with the peculiar forms of population and society amidst which her earliest years were passed.'[10] In doing so, Gaskell acts as a surviving witness and narrator of Brontë's life, death and literary legacy. She does this not only as Brontë's 'dear friend,' but also as a fellow woman of letters. Even as she obscures Brontë's mobility and agency within the shifting historical contexts of nineteenth-century publishing by dramatising her regional and domestic setting, Gaskell validates her own active presence and literary production as a woman of letters.

Gaskell's contributions to nineteenth-century literary biography and tourism thus disclose her insistent engagement with the Woman Question, the Victorians' unresolved debate regarding women's vocation or *place* in British culture. The nineteenth-century ideology of separate spheres located women as private, familial, spiritual and peripheral to the rough-and-ready world of economic, political, and cultural production inhabited by men. Middle and upper-class women's gentility and femininity rested upon assumptions of their financial and emotional dependence, as well as their separation from ongoing, remunerated labour. However, visiting a woman writer's home and environs collapsed those boundaries between her domestic and professional identities, and thus disrupted complexly gendered notions of woman's vocation. Elizabeth Gaskell's guided tour of Haworth Parsonage locates Brontë in a specific geographical setting even as it positions her within a highly codified gender system. In attempting to 'honour her as a woman, separate from her character of authoress,'[11] Gaskell's *Life of Charlotte Brontë* reveals the limitations of these binary oppositions even in her attempt to integrate them through her narrative of Brontë's 'wild, sad life.'[12] By foregrounding specific geographic locations in north-west England, Gaskell places herself in proximity to Charlotte Brontë as a northerner, woman and professional writer. She is both the subject and the object of the narrative, aligning herself with the reader even as she maps out the homes and haunts of the sisters. Yet Gaskell's account is more remarkable for its indeterminacy than coherence. Her narrative interpolates numerous letters as well as her own self-referential narrative, offering multiple perspectives that sometimes fail to distinguish between herself as woman of letters and her biographical referent.

Mrs. Gaskell and the perils (and privileges) of lionizing

Ten years or so before the publication of *The Life of Charlotte Brontë, and* shortly after the publication of *Mary Barton* (1848), Elizabeth Gaskell travelled to London for a whirl of meetings, introductions, and dinner parties with her publisher, Edward Chapman. Upon her return she received a bracing letter warning her against the altering effects of fame, or what the Victorians called 'lionizing'. She responded to her correspondent with somewhat dubious sincerity: 'I hardly understand *what* is meant by the term; nor do I *think* anything could alter my own self; but I will be on my guard ... it would ill become me to say I might not be materially altered for the worse by this mysterious process of "lionizing." How am I to help it? There are people I really want to see as well as things.'[13] Gaskell was not only lionized herself, but a great lionizer. Her entry into the higher realms of literary culture afforded her greater opportunities to meet other notable Victorians. Ever on the defensive regarding her genteel femininity, these opportunities were, she considered, the 'privileges accorded to acquaintanceship or friendship.'[14]

As her fame grew, Gaskell extended her professional influence through the social mechanisms available to women of her time and class: writing letters, attending cultural events, participating in philanthropic projects, and exchanging social visits. Her talents for discreet professional networking and self-promotion were impressive, and she managed a wide range of requests for autographs, patronage and professional advice throughout her career. As the wife of a prominent Unitarian minister and a published author, she mingled with many of the leading intellectuals of her day. She and her husband William hosted many literary figures at 42 Plymouth Grove, their large Manchester home, including Charles Dickens, Charlotte Brontë, Harrriet Beecher Stowe, and Richard Monckton Milnes. Likewise, her travels to London, Paris, and Rome expanded her professional contacts and publishing markets even further. She negotiated the translation of her works into Continental languages and participated in the salons of French intellectuals, such as Madame de Staël and Madame Mohl.

Closer to home, Gaskell frequently rented a cottage in the nearby Lake District to escape the heat and commotion of Manchester and focus on her writing. Gaskell and many other self-consciously literary people and their followers were drawn not merely by the picturesque beauty of the Lake District but by its associations with the Romantic poets, and, more pragmatically, by the presence of other well-known literary figures. In *Homes and Haunts of the Most Eminent British Poets* (1847) William Howitt warns against the 'Tourist Vandals' in the vicinity of Ambleside:

> If anyone wants to set up for a lion or lioness, let him or her go and take a cottage in the Lake Country, there they will be lionized to their heart's content. There in the height of the summer, the whole region is alive with tourists and idlers who are all on the lookout for any novelty; a literary creature is a fascinating monster, more piquant to the tribe than badger or fox to the old race of Nimrods. If I heard of a literary person settling at the Lakes, I should say at once that person is anxious to be lionized.[15]

Although Gaskell deeply resented the intrusive habits of literary lion-hunters and curiosity-seekers herself, she eagerly followed the news, reviews and gossip surrounding her literary contemporaries. Her lively letters recorded her candid assessments of their writings and public readings, as well as her meetings (and near-meetings) with well-known figures, such as Florence Nightingale, Lord Tennyson, and Thomas Carlyle. While these working holidays in the Lake District were some of Gaskell's most productive, her letters also recite a regular round of visits and teas with her famous neighbors Matthew Arnold, John Ruskin, and Harriet Martineau. In 1850, Gaskell recorded her first meeting with Charlotte Brontë at the Lake District home of Sir James Kay-Shuttleworth. A swift succession of letters breathlessly described her first impressions and rehearsed her later role as Brontë's biographer: 'Such a life as Miss B's I never heard of before Lady K[ay]-S[huttleworth] described her home to me as in a village of a few grey stone houses perched up on the north side of a bleak moor – looking over sweeps of bleak moors.'[16]

In addition to regaling her many correspondents with first-hand accounts of meeting famous writers, Gaskell frequently sought information about other literary figures, and took a particular interest in other women writers besides Brontë. After the 1859 publication of *Adam Bede*, for instance, she obsessively sought to uncover the identity and gender of George Eliot. With help from Harriet Martineau, she eventually confirmed 'Miss Mary Ann Evans' as 'Madam Adam' and then badgered her publisher, George Smith, into providing more information: 'Send us PLEASE a long account of what she is like &c&c&c&c&c, – eyes nose mouth, *dress* &c for *facts*, and then – if you would – your impression of her, – which we won't tell anybody. *How came she to like Mr. Lewes so much?* I know he has his good points but somehow he is so soiled for a woman like her to fancy. Oh! Do please comply with this humble request.'[17]

While not impressed with celebrity alone, Gaskell wrote many letters of pointed admiration and received many in return. She corresponded with an ever-widening circle of literary acquaintances, intentionally cultivating and maintaining an epistolary community with most of the prominent figures in nineteenth-century print culture. These letters she saved and mounted in three autograph albums (now housed in the John Rylands Library), which constitute a dossier of her career and most famous admirers. Her exchanges with Charlotte Brontë, Elizabeth Barrett Browning, Harriet Martineau, Anna Jameson, Harriet Beecher Stowe, and Florence Nightingale provide literary historians with fascinating glimpses into the personal and professional relationships of an emerging cultural formation, the woman writer. Gaskell's letters and her autograph albums exemplify what Benedict Anderson has called an 'imaginary community' of literary women; that is, a 'deep, horizontal comradeship' grounded in their shared professional and gender identities.[18] This sense of community proves essential for Gaskell's self-construction and for her representation of her peers, particularly Brontë, her fellow northerner.

Knutsford and literary tourism

By the mid to late nineteenth century, England's north-country was attracting visitors from both Britain and America. American writers Ralph Waldo Emerson, Henry Wadsworth Longfellow, and Harriet Beecher Stowe (amongst others) all made pilgrimages to the north. Manchester served as the transportation hub for those travelling south to London or north to Edinburgh, Scotland's cultural capital and entry-way to 'Robert Burns Country' and Sir Walter Scott's Abbotsford. In addition to the Lake District, Haworth and Knutsford, conveniently close to Manchester, became regular stops for literary tourists.

Gaskell's home village received many literary pilgrims in the latter half of the nineteenth century, particularly after the publication of *Cranford* in 1853. Popular print media surrounding *Cranford* and Knutsford provide ample evidence of a substantial tourist industry from mid century until the onset of the First World War. G.A. Payne's *Mrs. Gaskell and Knutsford* (1900) boasts, 'Every member of the Gaskell cult, both of Great Britain and the United States, will at one time or another visit Knutsford.'[19] While never as popular a destination as Haworth, the 'Gaskell cult' grew after her death in 1865 and peaked in 1910, during Knutsford's celebration of the centenary of Gaskell's birth. A *Manchester Guardian* article reported in 1898 that 'Knutsford, where Mrs. Gaskell lived most of her unmarried life, is constantly visited by pilgrims far and near.'[20] The reporter assures the reader that new memorial bust of Mrs. Gaskell 'will be gazed at with admiration not only by the natives of "the old ancient place," but by thousands of visitors who flock to Knutsford, more particularly in the summertime, from Manchester and Liverpool, as well as by our "American cousins." ' This transatlantic theme is echoed by Mrs. Ellis Chadwick in her unauthorised biography, *Mrs. Gaskell: Haunts, Homes, and Stories* (1913): 'Pilgrims from different countries, especially America, visit Knutsford as one of the great literary shrines of England, and they admit they are better able to understand the novelist's Knutsford stories.'[21]

All three of these writers deploy the quasi-religious language of pilgrimage and memorial while emphasising an expansive international market in British literary culture. Chadwick emphasises the decidedly commercial nature of this homage by listing the now-familiar trappings of tourism:

> It is impossible to visit this little provincial town without being reminded of Mrs. Gaskell. The shops sell her portraits, and picture

postcards of her early home and that of her uncle, and Miss Matty's tea shop. All the buildings are pointed out, as well as the Honorable Mrs. Jamieson's, the old Vicarage, and Tatton Park. It has been said that Knutsford has helped to make Mrs. Gaskell's reputation as a writer, but if that is so, she has repaid the debt by immortalizing the 'dear little town.'[22]

Chadwick describes Knutsford as a kind of Cranford-land replete with Gaskell memorabilia and attractions. Portraits, postcards, local tours, and souvenir teas draw in the literary tourists and their cash. Knutsford may be the 'original' of *Cranford* and the making of Mrs. Gaskell, but Chadwick argues that Gaskell 'has repaid her debt' by making Knutsford a profitable tourist site. Chadwick's language continues to deploy the metaphor of economic transaction by arguing, 'This small country town supplied [Gaskell] with most of the material for her writing, and it was in those novels which portray Knutsford scenes and characters that she put her best work, and these are her most popular stories.'[23] Through the medium of fiction, Knutsford provided a material context, a 'place' for the literary persona of 'Mrs. Gaskell'. Though dead, Gaskell remains Knutsford's first citizen – its product, producer, and primary attraction.

In both direct and indirect ways, *Cranford* played (and plays) a central role in producing Knutsford as a site of cultural and commercial significance for literary tourism. Numerous illustrated versions, school editions, translations and dramatic adaptations of *Cranford* exemplify the publishing industry's increasingly sophisticated commercial markets. Likewise, the expanding visual materials testify to advancing print technology as well as Cranford's place as a visual metaphor for rural nostalgia in Britain. Later editions of *Cranford* included postcard-like photographs of Knutsford, complete with captions identifying their fictional locations. The conflation between Knutsford and the fictional town of Cranford continues for the virtual literary tourist who can locate a 'Cranford Walk around Knutsford' on the Virtual Knutsford webpage.[24] More recently, BBC adaptations of Gaskell's works, including *Wives and Daughters* (1999), *North and South* (2005) and *The Cranford Chronicles* (2007), may bring even more Anglophiles and Gaskell fans to Knutsford. All of this is good news for book publishers, the Gaskell Society, and the Chambers of Commerce for Knutsford and Manchester, who stand to benefit from those in search of the 'real' Cranford and the 'homes and haunts' of its author. The continuing vitality of this tourist trade is testimony to the way in which *Cranford* was and remains particularly successful at representing the rural remnants of Britain and shoring up the central myths of Britain's national identity.

Throughout the long nineteenth century, women writers on both sides of the Atlantic positioned themselves within the dynamic context of an international literary market. As a Briton, an author and a woman, Gaskell extended the boundaries of British culture even as she brought thousands of visitors to Britain's shores. We should not elevate Elizabeth Gaskell's critical reputation without also acknowledging her significant roles as a consumer, producer, promoter and subject of popular culture.

Notes

1. Nicola J. Watson, *The Literary Tourist: Readers and Places in Romantic and Victorian Britain* (Basingstoke: Palgrave Macmillan, 2006), 5.
2. James Buzard, *The Beaten Path: European Tourism, Literature, and the Ways to Culture, 1800–1918* (New York: Oxford University Press, 1993).
3. Loren Glass, *Authors, Inc.: Literary Celebrity and the Modern United States, 1880–1980* (New York: New York University Press, 2004), 22.
4. Alison Booth, *How to Make It as a Woman: Collective Biographical History from Victoria to the Present* (Chicago: University of Chicago Press, 2004), 19.
5. Thomas Wemyss Reid, *Charlotte Brontë. A Monograph* (New York: Scribner, Armstrong, & Co, 1877), 191.
6. Elizabeth Gaskell, *The Life of Charlotte Brontë*, ed. Alan Shelston (New York: Penguin, 1980), 22.
7. Ibid., 12.
8. Ibid., 13.
9. Chandra Talpade Mohanty, *Feminisms Without Borders: Decolonizing Theory, Practicing Solidarity* (Durham, NC: Duke University Press, 2003), 106.
10. Gaskell, 17.
11. Gaskell to George Smith, 4 June 1855, in *The Letters of Mrs. Gaskell*, ed. J.A.V. Chapple and Arthur Pollard (Cambridge, Mass.: Harvard University Press, 1967), 347.
12. Gaskell to Smith, 347.
13. Gaskell to unknown, 8 March 1849. 73.
14. Gaskell, *The Life of Charlotte Brontë*, 73.
15. William Howitt, *Homes and Haunts of the Most Eminent British Poets* (New York: Harpers & Bros., 1856), 116.
16. Gaskell to Catherine Winkworth, 25 August 1850, 124.
17. Gaskell to George Smith, 2 November 1859, 586.
18. Benedict Anderson, *Imagined Communities: Reflections on the Origin and Spread of Nationalism*. revised edn (London and New York: Verso, 1991), 5–7.
19. George A. Payne, Frontispiece to *Mrs. Gaskell and Knutsford* (Manchester: Clarkson & Griffiths, Ltd., 1900).
20. 'Mrs. Gaskell: Lancashire Admirers of Knutsford,' Manchester Guardian (Manchester, 1898), n.p.

21. Mrs. Ellis Chadwick, *Mrs. Gaskell: Haunts, Homes, and Stories* (London: Pitman & Sons, 1913), 452.
22. Ibid., 452–3.
23. Ibid., 22.
24. Virtual Knutsford, 'A Cranford Walk Around Knutsford,' Marketing Knutsford Ltd., http://www.virtual-knutsford.co.uk/frameset.php?main=/history_cranford_walk.htm (accessed on 13 October 2008).

12
Rambles in Literary London

Nicola J. Watson

In this brief essay I want to consider one way in which the nineteenth century produced and consumed 'literary London' as an unique type of tourist terrain, namely via the literary 'ramble.' Arguably, the invention of 'literary London' represents an extreme instance of the Victorian reader-tourist's aggressive intervention in relation to the literary, or perhaps it would be better to say, an extreme instance of the reader's performance of readership within the topographical. If nineteenth-century grave-visiting and house-visiting tended to be an act of homage to the poet's past materiality and historical verifiability, and if visiting authorial countries such as the Land of Burns, Scott country, or Wessex tended to be a tour scripted by a single author's works, rambling through literary London by contrast unloosed the reader-tourist almost entirely from the dictatorial logic of any single author, text, *oeuvre* or genre, releasing them into a promiscuously sociable saunter through a canonical litter of biographical anecdote and imaginary episode strewing the streets of the city.

It was only in the mid nineteenth-century that London came to be understood as a city steeped in and conditioned by literary anecdote, a city that could be ranged over far and wide by the book-loving Victorian tourist in search of poets' graves and memorials, sites associated with writers' lives, and places and character-types popularised in fiction. It was Victorian culture that bequeathed to moderns a London conceived as a place you might visit in reality or indeed in imagination in order to visit places associated with the dead and their literary works; a city defined not just by topography but by reading, and in particular by the mapping of the latter onto the former. Victorian London could boast the inaugural site of Anglophone literary tourism – Poets' Corner in Westminster Abbey – along with other lesser but well-populated places of permanent residence such as Bunhill Fields, where Defoe and Bunyan lie. It provided the thrill of the odd writer's birthplace – most notably that of Keats at Moorgate. It was dotted with the houses in which some of the greatest British writers had lived, or were still living: Johnson, Keats, Dickens, Carlyle, Thackeray, Conan Doyle. It had provided in itself settings and occasion for a century of bestsellers: *The Life of Samuel Johnson, Villette, Vanity Fair, Oliver Twist, Bleak House, Our Mutual Friend* and *The Adventures of Sherlock Holmes* amongst them. This wealth of incident and association made (and makes) the capital of Britain exceptional amongst literary tourist terrains, but it presented challenges to already existing models of literary tourism, keyed as these were either to author or works by a single author.[1] These difficulties ranged from the emotional to the practical, although they may all be classed as problems in 'reading' (or performing, or writing) literary London.

Because London as a territory exceeds (and always has exceeded) individual writers and individual books, it has never been available to either a pure biographical model or a simple fictive one. London was impossible to make over into a form of visitable biography of any one writer; one could not trace an itinerary, as literary tourists had first learned to do in Stratford-upon-Avon and then in Burns' Ayrshire, moving from the birthplace to the grave via houses and nationalised inspirational landscapes and plucking a flower or leaf as relic-cum-souvenir, because on the one hand it had been and was still home to too many writers, and on the other hand, it was a city, an inorganic, man-made environment. Nor had any one writer managed to patent London as his or her own fictive territory. That cunning exile Joyce may later have succeeded in co-opting Dublin as above all 'his' literary city, leaving all subsequent Irish writers as incidental details half-visible from the route trodden by Leopold Bloom in *Ulysses* and by thousands of tourists every 16 June since. But even Dickens was obliged to share 'his' London with others in the Victorian imagination. Southwark, for example, may be privileged as one of the most prominent settings of *David Copperfield* and *Little Dorrit,* but it was equally important to the Victorian tourist – and is still to the paying customers of the replica Globe – as one of Shakespeare's 'homes and haunts,' never mind the fact that the Marshalsea debtors' prison had been built almost on top of Chaucer's pilgrims' home from home, the Tabard Inn.[2]

One effect of this overcrowdedness of implication and association is that places in London were always liable to shrug off the emotional affect with which the Victorian tourist wished to invest them. Some of the peculiar problematic that this produces for the literary tourist is neatly illustrated by a rather late and consciously belated book, William Kent's *London for Everyman* (1941, 1947), which provides on successive pages maps of 'Shakespeare's London,' 'Pepys' London,' 'Johnson's London,' and 'Dickens's London' – which are all, of course, representations of much the same bit of Town. Although in part these successive maps are designed to take account of incremental changes in London geography, and perform and lament in the later edition the ravages of history both long-gone and recent, the effect is both to prise apart the palimpsest of history laid down over the same place and to suggest the desirability as well as the difficulty of extricating one London from another.

Compounding these impurities and fissures, this overcrowdedness of implication and affect, there was the contemporary difficulty of deciding how to tackle London as a Victorian tourist given its unprecedented size and sprawl, and given, too, the difficulty of finding a way to 'look' at a modern city as a tourist. In response to these assorted difficulties, Victorian writers and tourists came up with a new tourist-model for conceiving literary London, based upon the aesthetic of the nineteenth-century novel, and quite specifically on the aesthetics of the realist novel, as practised by – most especially – Dickens. To illustrate the beginnings of this, I'd like to turn to an interesting and very early example of a book designed to conceive of a Dickensian London. In the words of the preface:

a Dickensian Directory as is now prepared, will be found a valuable practical guide for those ['Metropolitan visitors'] who may desire to visit the haunts and homes of those old friends, whose memory we cannot 'willingly let die'.[3]

This is a book by Robert Allbut, published in 1886, and it is entitled *London Rambles 'En Zig-Zag' with Charles Dickens*. It is one of the earliest examples of a piece of writing for literary tourists – practical guide or memoir – that uses the idea of the 'ramble,' and the first to locate such rambles within the urban.[4] The concept of a ramble 'en zig-zag' is peculiarly urban – what it refers to is the idea of turning arbitrarily left at the first corner, right at the second, and so on. (This method of generating an unpredicted itinerary is of course useless in New York or any other grid-planned North American city, but it can still get you lost in London or Paris with remarkable efficiency.) It is an instructively aimless form of exploration – episodic, even picaresque – and the title accordingly suggests (misleadingly) that London – and its literariness – will naturally 'happen' to the rambler. It implies that we will be in company with the author – imaginary to be sure, but still a unifying narratorial consciousness acting as an authoritative guide who will help the reader navigate the city. Its stated ambition – to provide a way for tourists to visit the metropolis as though they had colourable business there, visiting 'old friends' or rather, visiting 'the haunts and homes' of 'old friends' as a form of *hommage* to them – 'dead' yet fondly and even dutifully remembered – elevates fictional characters into living 'old friends.' The contents page reads in part as follows:

Ramble I

Charing cross to Lincoln's inn fields

> The Golden Cross; Associations with Pickwick and Copperfield – Craven Street; Residence of Mr Brownlow – Charing Cross Terminus – Hungerford Stairs and Market; Lamert's Blacking Manufactory; Micawber's Lodgings; Mr Dick's Bedroom – No. 3 Chandos Street; Blacking Warehouse – Bedfordbury; 'Tom All-Alone's' – Buckingham Street; Copperfield's Chambers – The Adelphi Arches – The Adelphi Hotel; Snodgrass and Emily Wardle – 'The Fox under the Hill;' Martin Chuzzlewit and Mark Tapley – The Residence of Miss La Creevy – Offices of 'Household Words' and 'All the Year Round' – Covent Garden market; Hummums and Tavistock Hotels, associated with 'Great Expectations' etc. – Bow Street – Old Bow Police Court; 'The Artful Dodger' – Covent Garden Theatre – Broad Court; Mr Snevellici – St Martin's Hall; Dickens's First London Readings – Russell Court; Nemo's Burial Place – Clare Court; Copperfield's Dining Rooms – Old Roman Bath, used by Copperfield – Portsmouth Street; 'The Old Curiosity Shop' – The Old George the Fourth; 'The Magpie and Stump' – Portugal Street; 'The horse and Groom;' Mr Tony Weller and His Legal Adviser – Lincoln's Inn Fields; Mr John Forster's House; Residence of Mr Tulkinghorn.

Three things seem worthy of note in this summary of this first 'ramble' which Allbut then goes on to describe in detail. The first is the way that places are described alternately by their real place-names and by their status as fictive settings – 'Hungerford Stairs and Market' sits alongside 'Micawber's Lodgings.' The second is the way that the boundaries between Dickens's various fictive Londons are elided, and his characters cramped into occupying the same terrain; thus in a smallish physical space the rambler is expected mentally to skip between the very varied imaginative spaces of *Pickwick, David Copperfield, Oliver Twist, Great Expectations, Martin Chuzzlewit,* and *Bleak House.* The third is the way that the itinerary slips without apparent strain between the biographical ('Dickens' First London Readings' for example), the fictional, and general urban topography. While at first glance this might look rather like end-of-century 'Scott country' with its mix of biography and multiple narratives, in practice the smallness of London as a terrain produces a very different effect. Scott sits under his monument at the centre of an imaginary literary map which extends not only across different historical periods but across lowlands, highlands, islands, England, and ultimately Europe and India, each variously appropriated for a different poem or novel, as demonstrated by contemporary maps of Scott country.[5] By contrast, Dickens and his characters jostle within the same contemporary urban space.

Allbutt's guide efficiently renders practicable what was already by the 1870s a prevailing way of experiencing Dickensian London as a mix of personal walking experience, biographical information concerning Dickens, and episodes from across the collected works. This format clearly derives from earlier, highly personalised accounts of such rambles actually undertaken, such as Pemberton's *Dickens' London* (1876), which, to take one instance only, describes visiting the Spaniard's Inn on Hampstead Heath in order to imagine Mrs Bardell's tea-party in *Pickwick,* to imagine Dickens imagining the scene, and, co-opting Dickens as a fellow Dickensian literary-tourist, to imagine:

> how, on some subsequent visit, [Dickens] may have smiled as he looked on the 'Spaniards' Tea Gardens,' and thought of them as peopled with those quaint figures and characters of his own creation.[6]

Or again there is John Hassard's *A Pickwickian Pilgrimage* (1871, 1881) which, despite its title, spends a fair amount of its effort on Limehouse, searching out the locations variously of *Our Mutual Friend* and *Bleak House,* culminating in a pub which Hassard identifies as 'The Six Jolly Fellowship Porters.' (This pub, incidentally, the Grapes on Narrow Street, has been busily identifying itself as such ever since.) Hassard is typical in his insistence on simultaneously imagining Dickens' own nocturnal rambles during which he found his inspiration, rambles which form the pretext for Allbutt's conceit of rambling 'with' Dickens. The conflation of this writer's biography with his works is not unprecedented by the 1870s; Dickens' own deployment of autobiographical material, for example in *Great Expectations,* helped to make this the more possible, and so did any number of accounts by his friends Sala, Forster, and Fields of walking the streets of London in company with Dickens himself. But what is striking is the way that this mode of literary apprehension of London seems to be made possible by one particular aspect of the very structure and aesthetic of nineteenth-century fiction.

The nineteenth-century novel as practised by Dickens, his precursor Scott and his rival Thackeray, draws much of its energy from traversing between the apparently unconnected. The Victorian novel, to put it another way, was itself given to rambling en zig-zag. Structured around a set of personages and locations often apparently unrelated until the dénouement proves that they are intimately connected, the focus of the London-centred novel typically switches between the West and East Ends, between the romantic and the comic, the domestic and the feral, the sentimental and the violent. In so doing, Dickens' fiction in particular yokes in sequence wildly disparate and apparently unconnected moods, modes, settings and clutches of characters. This Dickensian grotesque would provide a hospitable model for the experience of being a stranger on the loose and at a loose end in London. Modelling the urban tourist, Dickens's characters frequently wander London – often lost, outcast, or strangers, adrift from the social structure which regularly threatens to appear from their alienated position unrelated and out-of-proportion. More generally, the many obscurely linked subsets of characters, settings, and plot-lines that populate Dickens's fiction and the fiction of his rivals allow for conceiving of the reality of London as a multi-generic text in itself, containing and thriving on difference of topic, subject, mode, characters, period, while offering reassurance that they are all organically interconnected by the material reality of London itself. Thus, a juxtaposition that would normally measurably weaken the sentimental affect of one sort of literary tourist site would for a literary tourist of London simply be an enriching incongruity. This can be illustrated by conjuring up Anne Hathaway's cottage, which for a full 150 years has stood for a Shakespearean idyll, a sentimental rural merriness.[7] Just outside it there is a stone which a hundred years ago was known as 'Dickens' stone' – where Dickens sat down to rest, having just walked out to Shottery from Stratford. The picture of the Victorian urbanite Dickens seated in the foreground of 'Shakespeare country' does less than nothing to strengthen our current versions of the Shakespearean or the Dickensian – intruding into this terrain, Dickens is one literary genius too many. In strong contrast, the knowledge that Dickens as a boy worked in a blacking factory in the City, later fictionalised as the warehouse at Blackfriars where the young David Copperfield is confined – a warehouse which is yards from the site of the only London house Shakespeare ever bought – seems altogether more plausible and powerful as an apprehension; here the two figures mutually reinforce each other. London is a long enough, a large enough, an eclectic enough, an historical enough novel to encompass both episodes.

The notion of London as a novel would prove an expandable model – for where Becky Sharp and Mr Tulkinghorn can co-exist within a literary panorama, there is also plenty of room to add in other spectral literary Londoners within the same epistemological terrain. What connects up this terrain, the aesthetic practice that melds them into the common reality of literary London, is the walk, dictated and coloured by the reader-walker's literary imagination, as it rummages promiscuously along a mental bookshelf. As Laurence Hutton wrote in his *Literary Landmarks of London* (1885), for the well-read it will thus be:

> very easy, in walking with Johnson and Boswell from the club in Gerard Street through Long Acre and Bow Street, to Tom Davies' shop in Russell Street, Covent Garden, to call by the way on Dryden, Wycherley, Waller, Fielding, Charles Lamb and Evelyn; to stop for refreshment at Will's or Burton's or Tom's with Steele, Addison, Colley Cibber, Pepys, Davenant, and Pope; and going a step or two further to utter a silent prayer perhaps in the church of St Paul, Covent Garden, for the repose of the souls of Butler, Wycherley, Mrs Centlivre, and 'Peter Pindar', who sleep within its gates.[8]

While Hutton is here interested solely in biographical ghosts, John Hassard would write at about the same time of the peculiar way in which this habit of mind could come readily to erase the distinction between the fictional and the historical as forms of imagined reality:

> What wonder that an American in London should be haunted by the spectres of the never-to-be-forgotten [Pickwick] Club which have made the names of London streets, and the very aspect of London courts and houses, hardly less familiar to us than our own? To us, the characters in Dickens' earlier books are living personages. I no more doubted that I should discover the footprints of Sam in the Borough, and find the very house of Mrs Gamp in Kingsgate Street, than I questioned that the ghost of Samuel Pepys made 'mighty merry' at the Cock over against Temple Bar ... or that, when I seated myself on one of the ancient wooden benches of The Cheshire Cheese in a dark

little alley off Fleet Street, I should be half-conscious of the presence of Oliver Goldsmith and Dr Johnson in their accustomed corner.[9]

Hassard's evocation for the readers of the *New York Tribune* of the constitutive inability of 'an American in London' to distinguish (or to wish to distinguish) between biography and fiction brings me to the peculiar importance, and to some of the peculiarities, of American writing, visitors, and patronage in the development of literary London.[10] To think both about the ways in which 'literary London' was conceived by and for Americans in the last quarter of the nineteenth century, I might draw on a wealth of materials – American periodical journalism, the papers of James T. Fields, editor of *The Atlantic Monthly* and friend of Dickens, Thackeray and Trollope, or the many guidebooks and travel memoirs written by Americans or conceived principally for the American market. However, I'm going to turn to the best-selling book for adolescent girls, *What Katy Did Next* (1886), written by the American author Sarah Chauncey Woolsey (better known by her pen name 'Susan Coolidge') as a sequel to *What Katy Did* (1872). The book as a whole deals with the European tour taken by Katy as companion to Mrs Ashe and her daughter Amy. Katy begins her travels by taking the boat to 'Storybook England,' travelling down from Liverpool to spend time in London. Although Katy is fictional, her travels were based on Coolidge's own European tour in 1870–1872 (itself influenced by the account of Amy March's travels in Louisa May Alcott's bestselling *Little Women* (1868)), and her vision of literary London is meant to be representative of what an educated American girl would and should think of London, designed as it is for the consumption of American girlhood unavoidably stuck at home with only a pile of books for amusement. *What Katy Did Next* accordingly details with admirable simplicity and speed an itinerary, together with the emotional stances then suitable to a transatlantic enthusiast trying to match (or extend) her reading to the contemporary reality of London.[11] She eats muffins (a disappointing experience, given that 'muffins sound so very good in Dickens, you know', 60), and decides to stay at Batt's Hotel on Dover Street, 'because it was mentioned in Miss Edgeworth's *Patronage*.' ' "It was the place," she explained, "where Godfrey Percy didn't stay when Lord Oldborough sent him the letter." ' (Though, as the narrator comments with some irony, 'It seemed an odd enough reason for going anywhere, that a person in a novel didn't stay there', 70.) En route, she spots Wimpole Street, identifying it as 'the street where Maria Crawford in *Mansfield Park*, you know, "opened one of the best houses" after she had married

Mr. Rushworth' (70). When it comes to planned sightseeing around London, she opts 'like ninety-nine Americans out of a hundred' (73) for Westminster Abbey and Poets' Corner, but subsequently her main guide is 'a quaint elderly American, who had lived for twenty years in London and knew it much better than most Londoners do' (77). With him she:

> visited the Charter-House, where Thackeray went to school, and the Home of the Poor Brothers connected with it, in which Colonel Newcome answered 'Adsum' to the roll-call of the angels. They took a look at the small house in Curzon Street, which is supposed to have been in Thackeray's mind when he described the residence of Becky Sharp; and the other house in Russell Square which is unmistakably that where George Osborne courted Amelia Sedley. They went to service in the delightful old church of St. Mary in the Temple, and thought of Ivanhoe and Brian de Bois-Guilbert and Rebecca the Jewess. From there Mr. Beach took them to Lamb's court, where Pendennis and George Warrington dwelt in chambers together; and to Brick Court, where Oliver Goldsmith passed so much of his life, and the little rooms in which Charles and Mary Lamb passed so many sadly happy years. On another day they drove to Whitefriars, for the sake of Lord Glenvarloch and the old privilege of Sanctuary in *The Fortunes of Nigel;* and took a peep at Bethnal Green, where the Blind Beggar and his 'Pretty Bessee' lived, and at the old Prison of the Marshalsea, made interesting by its associations with *Little Dorrit.* They also went to see Milton's house and St Giles Church, in which he is buried, and stood a long time before St. James' Palace, trying to make out which could have been Miss Burney's windows when she was dresser to Queen Charlotte of bitter memory. And they saw Paternoster Row, and No.5 Cheyne Walk, sacred forevermore to the memory of Thomas Carlyle... and by great good luck had a glimpse of George Eliot getting out of a cab. (78–9)

The itinerary described here assumes that the teenage girl readers to whom it was addressed would be familiar with a bookshelf containing *Patronage, Mansfield Park, Vanity Fair, The Newcomes, Ivanhoe, The Fortunes of Nigel, Little Dorrit,* the biographies of some London-based writers – Thackeray, Carlyle, Fanny Burney, the Lambs – and even Chettle and Day's Jacobean play-of-the-ballad, *The Blind Beggar of Bethnal Green.* Katy's literary itinerary flattens out any hierarchy of authenticity between the biographical and the fictional, and between dead writers and live writers – all are construed as sights to be seen; this London is notable for its eclectic simultaneity, part biography, part fiction, ranging (courtesy of Scott) from the medieval through the Jacobean, the Georgian, and so right through to the contemporary literary scene. Accordingly, Katy effectively reads London as a serialised novel. (She is forced, however, to read it as a novel suitable for girls, and not merely because she demonstrates a bias towards what a less dignified age would term 'chick lit'. Not much Dickens here, for the excellent reason that rambling on foot through the Limehouse slums, or checking out any of the pubs such as the Cheshire Cheese, would have been socially completely impossible even for a fictional girl. She remains confined to a chaperon and a carriage. In this sense, *What Katy Did Next* provides an interesting corrective to those contemporary guidebooks, including Allbut's, which generally inexplicitly assume that the literary tourist is a man, in flat defiance of the actuality of the myriad of American women tourists who flooded into Britain over the next 50 years in search of literary thrills. As such, *What Katy Did Next* might well alert us to the deeply rooted gendering of the literary tourist experience throughout the century.)

Thus far, *What Katy Did Next* echoes and expands the model I have already identified deployed in the roughly contemporaneous books by Allbut and Hassard, although in the more strictly virtual form of fiction and with the addition of a distinctively American insistence that the 'dream or story' London, indeed 'storybook England' as a whole, is more available, more present, to Americans than to natives, which is why her elderly expatriate Yankee guide knows more about London than does the Londoner, and why Katy and her companions typically have more appropriate sentiments and have read more and more thoughtfully than the native. The insistence on the greater sentimental openness of Americans to English heritage lays strong claim to a literary heritage supposedly undervalued or misunderstood by the native English.[12] It also claims that not just literary London but by extension, the whole of Britain is read most accurately and usefully as a historical novel laid out for the well-read rambler.

Notes

1. See Nicola J. Watson, *The Literary Tourist: Readers and Places in Romantic and Victorian Britain* (Houndmills: Palgrave Macmillan, 2006) for a taxonomy of such literary sites as they developed within Britain.
2. On Shakespeare tourism in London see Nicola J. Watson, 'Shakespeare on the Tourist Trail' in Robert Shaughnessy, ed. *The Cambridge Companion to Shakespeare and Popular Culture* (Cambridge: Cambridge University Press, 2007), 199–226, esp. 216–20.

3. Robert Allbut, *London Rambles En Zig-zag with Charles Dickens* (London: Edward Curtice, 1886).
4. For the rural precursor see Archibald R. Adamson, *Rambles through the Land of Burns* (Kilmarnock: Dunlop and Drennan, 1879).
5. For representative maps of Scott country as it had developed by the turn of the century, see Charles S. Olcott, *The Country of Sir Walter Scott* (New York: Houghton Mifflin, 1913).
6. Thomas Edgar Pemberton, *Dickens's London* (London: Samuel Tinsley, 1876), 18.
7. See Watson, 2006, 210–12.
8. Laurence Hutton, *Literary Landmarks of London* (London: T. Fisher Unwin, 1885), 100.
9. John R.G. Hassard, *A Pickwickian Pilgrimage* (Boston: James R. Osgood and Co., 1881), 10.
10. See Westover in this volume for an exploration of this trope of inheritance in relation to American travel-writing and tourist practices.
11. Susan Coolidge, *What Katy Did Next* (Hertfordshire: Wordsworth Classics, 1995). All further references in parenthesis.
12. This recurrent strategy may therefore be added to Foster's and Westover's descriptions of other rhetorical strategies deployed by American tourists in their essays elsewhere in this volume.

13
Time-Travel in Dickens' World

Alison Booth

A restless traveller and travel writer himself, Charles Dickens has done more than his share for commercial and literary travel. Memorials, pilgrimages, festivals and museums have crowded round Dickens with an almost Shakespearean intensity, in spite of his dying wish to have no memorial or monument[1] – and in spite of the absence of a unique, established shrine. The likeness of Dickens is amongst the most recognizable of any author's, while he and his cast of characters seem to walk the earth from the Dickens Universe in Santa Cruz, California, to the Dickens Fellowship in Japan.[2] His persistence is both spatial and temporal. Specific locales have become 'Dickens Country' and thrive on literary tourism.[3] More broadly, much of England's past is 'Dickensian,' a heritage and homeland for the reader-citizen.[4] On the one hand, he is tethered to solid objects and accessible places. Like other nineteenth-century novelists he has registered certain landmarks as the originals of fictional or biographical settings. On the other hand, he is diffused as an adjectival association of ideas of Victorian England. How does an author become both materialized and abstracted as a sort of ubiquitous historical anachronism? In this brief essay I feature certain forms of Dickensian reception associated with objects, houses, and places as well as performances. I wish to bring out the dimensions of time travel in 'homes and haunts' literature and literary tourism, waiving for the moment the distinctions amongst the interrelated pursuits of experts, journalists and tourists. In practice, a mix of these approaches guided my observations during recent visits to the Dickens Museum in London, the Dickens Festival in Rochester, and Dickens World in Chatham.

From its beginnings, literary tourism both calibrates and resists historical time. In what ways does literary tourism serve as time travel? The tourist, according to John Urry, seeks escape from the everyday.[5]

In literary tourism the movements of readerly imagination and travel mimic each other, often entailing a visit to a real-world setting transformed by author and reader into the space-time of characters. Reading 'homes and haunts' narratives, visiting sites or participating in festivals share aspects of virtual reality or being 'lost in a book'[6] – experiments in time. In general these are backward glances, motivated perhaps by nostalgia or homesickness as well as attraction to the uncanny. A literary walk often doubles as a ghost walk, revealing the kinship of cultural and heritage tourism with the Gothic and its sensational historicism. The literary pilgrim or tourist resembles Scrooge in *A Christmas Carol*, conducted on an instructive as well as entertaining quest by a series of representative spectres (sometimes dressed as Dickensian characters). Built attractions especially may introduce ghosts of the future as well; as in science fiction, the time travel is by no means unidirectional. Preserved sites, testimonials of haunting and encounter, and the practices of re-enactment seem to share the common impulse to deter the decay of time, to shore fragments against our ruin.

Of course the recollection and the arrest of time are elusive. A pilgrim never knows when she has arrived just as a collector never acquires the complete set, while the very openness of an author's house to the public is a proof of that author's absence. Yet audiences have claimed to encounter Dickens's characters everywhere, while the franchising of Dickensiana, like the manufacture of saints' bones, swells beyond the scale of the man's biographical boundaries. He anticipated this ubiquity, as if the world were a projection of the brain that had so capaciously re-peopled it. Although he claimed that he never dreamed of his characters – it would 'be like a man's dreaming of meeting himself'[7] – he told his friend the American publisher James T. Fields that 'the children of his brain ... would sometimes turn up ... to look their father in the face. Sometimes he would pull my arm while we were walking together and whisper, "Let us avoid Mr. Pumblechook, who is crossing the street to meet us"; or, "Mr. Micawber is coming"' (235). What is especially uncanny is the undying vitality of the replicas of English people this Frankenstein created. It is the sort of reanimation that underwrites house museums, literary biography and national canons, and it certainly warrants tourism. As in Dickensian Christmas stories, the ghosts ultimately are benevolent, much like our friend the implied author: the Father's Law tempered by Walworth sentiment.

In spite of his evocations of homelessness, wandering, and doomed houses, Dickens became associated with feeling at home and getting to eat the Christmas goose. Tourists came to London, Rochester and other sites to encounter Dickens's characters walking about in the settings of his fiction.[8] As early as *The Pickwick Papers*, Rochester became Dickensian. In the visitor's book of the Bull Hotel in Rochester, a guest wrote a poem in 1877:

> The man who knows his Dickens as he should
> Enjoys a double pleasure in this place;
> He loves to walk its ancient streets, and trace
> The scenes where Dickens' characters have stood. ...
> The gifted writer 'sleeps among our best
> And noblest' in our Minster of the West;
> Yet still he lives in this, his favourite scene
> Which for all time shall keep his memory green.

Reproduced in a 1908 tourism pamphlet of the 'Dickens Associations' of Rochester, this is followed by an advertisement for 'Arts and Crafts,' a shop opposite the museum, 'The Best House for Dickens Souvenirs and Post Cards.'[9] Perhaps it is a comfort to see that it is far too late to protest Disney-fication.

In *The Dickens Country*, a fashionable form of bio-geography in 1905 (revised edition in 1911), Frederick G. Kitton tracks down sites associated with Dickens (person and works). The documentary illustrations have something akin to contemporary photographs of fairies, as the subject of the image is often what has disappeared or what the viewer imagines as in the photographs captioned 'Lant Street, Borough. Showing the older residential tenements. The actual house in which Dickens lived [when working at the blacking warehouse] is now demolished' and 'The Sun Inn, Canterbury. "It was a little inn where Mr. Micawber put up, and he occupied a little room in it" ("David Copperfield").'[10] Kitton's friend B.W. Matz pursued a similarly wilful delusion in *The Inns and Taverns of Pickwick* (1921), and a sequel, *Dickensian Inns and Taverns* (1922).[11] Matz combs through each novel, collating characters to be encountered and accommodations to be enjoyed at each site. He ties the *oeuvre* to national economic history: 'For a brief period...it seemed that even so great a British institution as the old English inn, and its first cousin the tavern, were doomed to pass away' due to the railways, but the 'invention of the motor-car' restored them to 'that atmosphere of friendly hospitality and utility...which is so faithfully reflected in every book of Dickens' (15–16). Better than a museum, where nothing on display may be touched or eaten, the hospitality of Dickens' books continues on offer.

These turn-of-the-century Dickensians were emulating Dickens's own conceits. Aware of the precedents of Scott, Wordsworth, and others, Dickens established a home in a setting of personal and literary associations, rehearsing and repeating the sensation of haunting. Anticipating that his renown would infuse where he lived, he created a prophetic ghost story about the inevitability of his literary inheritance of Gad's Hill House, to be repeated by later pilgrims and biographers. In the famous encounter with 'a very queer small boy' in *The Uncommercial Traveller*, Dickens underlines the Shakespearean and autobiographical endorsement of the place: 'where Falstaff went out to rob those travellers' and where his father promised, 'If you were to be very persevering and were to work hard, you might some day come to live.'[12] Like the historic Restoration House adapted to the embittered 'Satis House' of Miss Havisham (Kitton, 217), Gad's Hill appears associated with the aspirations of Dickens's boyhood double and even with some sort of theft that goes unpunished. But the house in 'the very heart of Dickens land' (Kitton, 205) was open to literary visitors as a display of happy domesticity. Dickens performed as host rather as he impersonated characters in his public readings, to invoke the spirits of novels past. Later descriptions seem assured that they have seen documentary sources for the apparitions, as in a picnic excursion to the graveyard in Cooling, the site of chapter one of *Great Expectations* (Fields, 224–6).

Everyone is invited to follow in the author's and his characters' footsteps through open-air haunts right into the home and the inner sanctum of creation. Accordingly, homes and haunts essays and literary biographies and museums privilege the study and its artefacts: desk, chair, pen, memorabilia of other authors. Curiously Dickens had two studies at Gad's Hill, one a neatly detachable metonymy of authorship. The prefab Swiss Chalet given to him by the French actor Fechter in 1865 became the summer study in which he was writing *Edwin Drood* the day before he died (the desk from the Chalet is displayed in the Dickens Museum in London). Fields' elegiac *Yesterdays with Authors* of 1871 recalls, 'Once more...we reclined in the cool chalet in the afternoon, and watched the vessels going and coming upon the ever-moving river. Suddenly all has vanished. ... We have all drifted down the river of Time, and one has already sailed out into the illimitable ocean' (228). A later American pilgrim, Theodore F. Wolfe, seems to sit with Dickens in the mirror-lined Chalet to intone a similar pastoral elegy: 'Here the master wrought through the golden hours of his last day of conscious life ... and ... let fall his pen. ... [Here] we behold the view which delighted the heart of Dickens, ... the fields of waving corn, the green expanse of meadows, the sail-dotted river.'[13] The Chalet, vessel of the author's transmigrating spirit, is at the same time perfectly tangible,[14] preserved at Eastgate House, a spreading brick mansion featured in *Edwin Drood*.

The Dickens House Museum in London has much less claim to be haunted, though it houses generations of collected Dickensiana. Number 48 Doughty Street, 'the only London home of Charles Dickens which survives intact structurally,' received 'a long-delayed tribute' (Kitton, 57) in a London County Council plaque, designed in 1903.[15] The Dickens House was about to be destroyed when it was bought by the Dickens Fellowship and opened to the public in 1925. In coffee-table literary bio-tours as in materials provided to visitors, the London house is the site of Dickens's early success, thriving family life, and entertainment of famous people such as his portraitist Maclise, the actor Macready, or Carlyle (whose names add to the aura of the house). A touch of Gothic is added by narratives of Mary Hogarth's on-site death, and I would argue, by the redundant images of the author and his characters, such as a portrait of Mr. Micawber by E. Sherard Kennedy (1873). R.W. Buss's famous unfinished painting, *Dickens's Dream*, a sort of mise-en-abîme of the Gad's Hill study hung in the 'study' at the Dickens Museum, shades into spiritualism on one hand and madness on the other, as the author sits under a cloud of miniature escapees from the illustrated pages of his books, not unlike the alarming spirits of 'The Chimes' (another time-travelling Christmas story). This and many other images of Dickens amongst his creations strive to turn obsession into a dream of comic plenitude, of surrogate intimacy with the author. Yet the effect is closely related to the posthumous painting, Fildes's *The Empty Chair*, an image of Dickens's study at Gad's Hill without the author – not unlike the empty carriages or riderless horse at a funeral.

Like many house museums, the Dickens Museum is more collection than reconstruction: a curiosity shop of metonymies of the writing and reading experience and relics of the author and his associates. Furnishings from later residences have been arranged according to probable former functions of the rooms, but only the drawing room has been redecorated, and purposes of exhibition overwhelm domestic function except in the basement, where the wine cellar and scullery demonstrate the labouring conditions in middle-class Victorian households. The former kitchen is now a library for Fellowship events, lined with editions of Dickens's works on glass-enclosed shelves. Throughout the house, walls and display cases assemble an extraordinary amount of evidence of celebrity, literary reception and spin-offs. Dickens gave the cue for capturing everyday objects as tokens of meaningfulness: the little wooden midshipman described in *Dombey and Son*[16] – over-read as more than a shop sign – becomes an artefact preserved here. In keeping with the meaning of 'Dickensian,' the museum's uppermost floor offers rotating exhibits that mesh Gothic entertainment and historical instruction: in 2003, 'Gore of Yore,' a recreation of Dickens's *A Child's History of England* with such displays as an executioner in a prison cell: 'It will take you on a journey into the unknown past; explore Dickens's sensational and gory rewriting of history!'[17] In 2007 it was 'Ignorance and Want,' an exhibit on Victorian social conditions with a running reference to Dickens. Altogether the historical aims of the museum mesh with the biographical and memorial, combining many methods of resisting oblivion.

The note of unpleasantness in the exhibits confirms the familiar dark connotations that have accrued to the term 'Dickensian.' But I think there is more to it. Some have suggested that tourists seek contact with back spaces, and that tourist sites resemble stage sets to display scenes of production and reproduction usually hidden from view;[18] an author's study is one example. Further, like pilgrimage, tourism often hopes to cross a temporal threshold, to transcend ordinary existence, and hence the journeys to shrines, graves, or other memorials. The traveller's departure from the everyday may be a controlled experiment with mortality. Today's dark tourism or thanatourism – attraction to sites of the Holocaust or other genocide, natural disaster, slavery – I would argue emerges from the brush-with-death time travel underlying tourism of various aims. In limited and lighter ways, these motives may be detected behind some of the sights in Rochester and Chatham at the beginning of June, 2007.

Many long-deceased authors lose their hold on pilgrimage, but Dickens remains magnetic. The longstanding biannual Dickens Festival in Rochester (in its 29th year) and the brand new Dickens World (opened 25 May 2007) draw a largely British audience who might not wish to retrace specific itineraries of Pickwick or David Copperfield or Pip, but who recall Dickens' novels and engage in the pleasure of cultural tourism. The Dickens Festival is a cornerstone of the local economy, involving many costumed fans, professional actors and event staff. Eastgate House features a flower exhibit and readings of Dickens by skilled performers. The historic area from Eastgate and High Street to the esplanade above the River Medway doubles as an open-air museum and commercial district, with shops such as Little Dorrit Revival offering ethnic clothing and body piercing. I witnessed the first parade (1 June); elderly Brits, local families, and French school groups lined the thoroughfare to watch, alerted by a comic town crier who resembled Ben Franklin. About 120 well-groomed people, from children to the elderly, marched in costumes of varying styles circa 1830–1870. A few played musical instruments. Some carried tall signs to make clear which Dickens character they represented; some of the older men were instantly recognizable as Scrooge or Pickwick. Unlike the paid first-person interpreters, the amateur participants exchanged jolly humour with tourists taking their pictures. Although scheduled performers bring out the Dickensian themes of poverty and squalor, the parade reduces signs of class difference, dirt, or distress in confirmation of Victorian gentility – very different from Dickens World nearby. Over three days there are many free events, from the five parades to wrestling and costume competitions. Ticketed events include dramatic readings, music halls, and a grand ball. On both a paddle steamboat cruise and Mr Pickwick's Special Train to and from London, Victoria, costumed passengers become part of the exhibit. A full schedule of street performers, fairground rides and booths selling crafts and treats turn this segment of Rochester into an amusement park for all ages. Thelma Grove of the Dickens Fellowship judges the best children's costume recreating a Dickens character. It is gratifying heritage tourism, aided by the historical authenticity of the buildings and the consensus that Dickens is a shared memory.

Dickens World has its element of heritage – the author lived in Chatham as a boy and his father used to work at the Historic Dockyards – but it is an invented attraction like the Great Exhibition, or more proximately, the Millennium Dome. Privately funded, the £62m project joins in the effort of the Southeast England Development Agency.[19] At a nuclear cleanup site desolated by the closing of the naval shipyards, a computer-animation-style set of Dickensian London has been constructed inside a 71,000 sq ft warehouse flanked by a shopping mall and a multiplex cinema. The amusement is designed to instruct as well; in a subtly patriotic tone, the marketing appeals to British parents who will spend £12.50 per adult and £7.50 per child to introduce their children to dark, squalid Victorian times. Images of Oliver Twist/Little Nell-like children in the promotional materials suggest that it is dazzling fun. The site is what is known as a tourist 'bubble,' a non-sequitur from the devastation of post-industrial Chatham.

The 'New Themed Entertainment Visitor Attraction Based Upon the Life, Times, Books and Characters of Our Most Famous and Enduring Author' drew, on the sixth day of its opening, a more prosperous sector of the population than I saw at the grimy downtown bus terminal – intent on an outing, but not happy with the hour-and-a-half wait to buy tickets.

Occasionally we were distracted by one of the 50 'actors' or first-person interpreters. The Artful Dodger delightfully 'stole' my camera. Past the Old Curiosity Shoppe with its souvenir mugs and Victorian toys, we could see the entrance dominated by a clock suspended in outstretched hands captioned 'The Time of Their Lives.' The lobby is inscribed with Sleary's desperate motto of entertainment in *Hard Times*: 'People mutht be amuthed, thomehow; they can't be alwayth a working, nor yet they can't be alwayth a learning. Make the betht of uth; not the wurtht.' It is unclear whether 'us' is the management or the populace, and the working and learning were perhaps better put out of mind.

The 'experience' is supposed to be an immersion in sights, sounds, and smells of an evening in Victorian London, itself the atmosphere of Dickens's novels; no white parasols here. Like other visitors, I was predisposed to be amuthd for my money. Perhaps this is not incompatible with the site's themes of suffering children, crime, industrial poverty, prisons, and graveyards – as I suggest, Dickens may draw some of the customers for dark tourism. The dimly lit town square surrounded by grotesque buildings is effectively menacing. You have to discover the unidentified attractions approached from the square through hallways of smoky plaster, distressed bricks, mechanically roughened 'beams,' and smoke detectors: Newgate Prison, Britannia Music Hall, the Great Expectations Boat Ride, the Haunted House of 1859, Dotheboys Hall (a classroom with strict discipline and computer terminals), Fagin's Den (a play area for little kids), and Peggotty's Boathouse. In the latter, almost the only direct recognition of the author appears in a clever and informative 4D HD animated movie about Dickens, his near death experiences and his travels and travel writing. At every new home, the wiry author magically rearranges furniture, as a desk, chair, pen and paper fly from all directions to assemble a new scene of writing. In the square, the interpreters mingle, not yet at ease in their roles, mostly interacting with the youngsters in such hearty games as gambling and kidnapping. Many of the costumed women are what the media has called 'wenches,' though I didn't witness their reported soliciting. The Rat Catcher pretended to be very suspicious of me as I took notes.

Perhaps Dickensian London was a boring queue rather than a crime-ridden thrill. Waiting in a dank hallway to get on the boat ride, I gradually deciphered under the talk of the crowd a recorded monologue of Little Dorrit describing the Marshalsea. A local woman said, 'Not a lot happening is there. They could have more going on about the history.' Passengers don plastic-hooded outer-garments advertising the

Kent Messenger, 'We've Got You Covered,' and sit in boats resembling a log-flume ride at Six Flags. The water is supposed to be dyed brown to signify a sewer, with animatronic rats and other things a-swim in it; like the promised Victorian smells, these effects were not functioning and I can't say I'm sorry. The ride passes the gravestones (five lozenges) of the Pirrip family at Cooling, a grave marked 'Scrooge,' a large 'stone' angel, and some lugubrious but unanimated mannequins. The boat, ostensibly to recall Magwitch's attempted escape on the Thames, rises on its tracks to rooftops resembling a set for *Oliver Twist*, plunges backwards with a splash that wets everyone's arms and feet, and glides to its end. The Haunted House looks promising: on the outside a ruined castle, on the inside the realistic vestibule of a ruined mansion. But upstairs it becomes a dark unfurnished corridor like an aquarium, as the crowd slowly passes a sequence of display windows, each with a colour 3-D video projected on angled plexiglas: an accelerated, badly acted version of *Christmas Carol*; a pantomime of Dickensian characters like figures on an old town hall clock, as the voice of Dickens, perhaps, talks about his favourite creations. Dickens World may be strange, but it is not uncanny – in contrast to the similar indoor attraction, the Bram Stoker Dracula Experience in Dublin, the only time cultural tourism has ever made me scream.

I was almost at the head of the queue for the so-called Haunted House when an angry woman leaving the exhibit came up and asked if I was a reporter. 'I wish you were. This place is dreadful. Not worth the 40 quid.' Yet some visitors appeared to be having a good time. I stood near a trio of female relatives, perhaps grandmother, mother and daughter. The youngest one obviously liked the whole effect of the historical past; she remarked that going to the toilet was 'coming back out of it.' 'I don't think you'd want to go to the loo the way they had it then,' said the middle-aged woman. Some minutes later, the oldest: 'I didn't like *Pickwick Papers*. That's his first book.' Youngest: 'We only did part of *Great Expectations* in school' – I think she said they performed it – 'but I want to read the rest of it. And we did *Christmas Carol*.' Middle-aged: 'We didn't do any Dickens in my school, we did Hardy.' The attraction's composite memory of reading is as dim as the lighting, and no refresher seems called for. On the wall by the entrance to the show about Dickens and his travels, I found a series of small biographical posters, the only extensive verbal text in the place.

Gerald Dickens, the great-great-grandson, is quoted in support: 'I don't think it is a case of doing a Disney on Dickens...he was a show-man who wanted to entertain people and today he would have been blogging on the Internet.'[20] An appeal to authorial intention endorses the venture again and again: Dickens would have done this if he could. The managing director Kevin Christie defends the park as interpretation of Dickens, and cites the planning participation of Thelma Grove of the Dickens Fellowship (she who judges costumes in Rochester).[21] It does seem to reify the 'Dickensian' in a sort of clean-up archaeological dig of present-day Chatham. This attraction has decided that time travel sufficiently changes the subject from current economics. But there is something to be said for this as a continuation of Victorian entertainment, and as paraliterary criticism of what Dickens means in popular culture since the neo-Victorian Maggie Thatcher. The site is no far cry from the Dickensian pursuits of Kitton and Matz a hundred years ago, or from the earliest Pickwickians who sojourned in Rochester before them. The visitors in their own way collaborate in textual production, and turn the day's outing into the best or worst of times of their lives.

Dickens World suggests that literary tourism seeks to negate the contemporary space that it ineluctably inhabits. The visitor is to forget the scenes around the Pentagon Centre terminal in Chatham, a cross between a steel town in upstate New York in the 1970s and the set for a post-apocalyptic film like *Children of Men*, its cast of scruffy teenagers, the depressed, the disabled, the elderly, all with more or less of the regional blight on hair, teeth, skin. Instead, one takes a voluntary trip into aestheticised 'history,' the Victorian slums. Portions of Rochester offer a different model of time travel with similar purpose: more like Stratford, Haworth, or Colonial Williamsburg, Virginia, the city can claim authentic buildings and rename its commercial enterprises. Dickensians dress as characters from Dickens novels, perform scenes in Eastgate House, and in general recreate the seasonal festival that projects a hazy Victorian conviviality into a few days of the twenty-first century. The teachers or parents who bring children to either site in the spirit of improvement seem to subscribe to the assumption that history is only absorbed through re-enactment. Children must be excited, and 'gore of yore' excites. At the Dickens Festival, the actor Oliver Naylor performs 'Charlie, the Victorian Shoe Shine Boy,' one of his 'interactive history shows,' 'Steps in Time,' designed for 'the Key Stage 2 National Curriculum': 'bringing history to life without a textbook in sight.'[22]

The tourist may seek authenticity and immersion in virtual 'back spaces' – 'Discover Dickens's Kent' – but may also value palpable artifice and conscious anachronism, signs of human manipulation of time and place. Attendance at the museum, festival or attraction has the comforting quality of repetition with a voluntary difference. No one needs to be an expert on the originals, Dickens's life or novels (though Dickens Fellowship members may know them better than any scholar). Most practically, literary tourism sponsors preservation of the marked region, town or house against the homogeneity of globalisation, and it is a growth industry. Similarly, cultural tourism may hypostatise 'history' as simpler olden days to counteract the presentism of contemporary media and post-modern culture. For a few days and hours, an immersion in the Dickensian (Victorian) may heighten the sense of the time of our lives in an entertaining brush with an undead past, a shared memory of a time when the children of the nation ostensibly knew Dickens, their minds and their everyday walks peopled with characters conjured from the pages of his books. At the end of the tour, it's always nice to come back home.

Notes

1. S.C. Hall, *A Book of Memories of Great Men and Women of the Age, from Personal Acquaintance* (London: Virtue, 1871), 450.
2. Mitsuharu Matsuoka of Nagoya University manages an important website on Dickens affiliated with the Japan Dickens Fellowship: 'The Dickens Page', http://www.lang.nagoya-u.ac.jp/~matsuoka/Dickens.html (accessed 3 January 2008). The University of Kent at Canterbury reports a conference called Literary Medway, cosponsored by the School of English and the Medway Council, coinciding with the issue of Monica North's *Dickens Country: A Literary Guide to the Medway Area* and a performance by Gerald Dickens (University of Kent at Canterbury, 'Research and Enterprise Report 2001/2002', http://www.kent.ac.uk/research/reports/ [accessed 3 January 2008]). Amongst countless commercial ventures see TeaAntiques.com: in a Christmas issue of its 'Tea Clipper' newsletter, 'Charles Dickens and Teaantiques Home Town of Portsmouth, Hampshire, England', an Illustrated description of the museum in Dickens's birthplace ('Tea Clipper', 14 [2001]), http:///www.teaantiques.com/teaclipper/teaclipper200112.htm, (accessed 3 January 2008). See Portsmouth City Council, 'Charles Dickens' Birthplace Museum', http://www.charlesdickensbirthplace.co.uk/ (accessed 3 January 2008). The Talking Tour Company offers audio for iPod or CD player, 'Shakespeare and Dickens Tour', http://www.talking-tours.co.uk/shakespeare. htm (accessed 3 January 2008). Travel journalism abounds, for example Karen Kenyon, 'For Dickens It Was a Not-So-Bleak House', *Christian Science Monitor,* 1 December 2004, http://www.csmonitor.com/ (accessed 3 January 2008). The BBC sponsors a low-tech online game, 'Survive Dickens' London', in which a little boy prospers or fares ill according to Dickensian locations and characters encountered (BBC Arts, http://www.bbc.co.uk/ [accessed 3 January 2008]). Various web auctions feature Dickensian cigarette cards including 'Historic Places from Dickens Classics' published by Spinet House, R. and J. Hill, Ltd., in 1926.

3. The private 'Bleak House Museum' occupies Fort House, where Dickens spent summers in Broadstairs, and there are miscellaneous plaques at other locations. On the Dickens Country Protection Society in Kent, see Sharon Whitley Larsen, 'Following in Charles Dickens' Footsteps', *Copley News Service* (2 November 2007).

4. For the 'Dickensian' as both suffering children and serialised epic narrative see the HBO series *The Wire*: Alessandra Stanley, 'No Happy Ending in Dickensian Baltimore', *New York Times* (6 January 2008), AR1, 12. In particular, see Murray Baumgarten, 'Urban Labyrinths: Dickens and the Pleasures of Place' in Peter Brown and Michael Irwin, eds, *Literature and Place: 1800–2000* (Oxford: Peter Lang, 2006), 69–85.

5. Dean MacCannell cites Urry, *The Tourist Gaze* (London: Sage, 1990) as one model for commercial tourism as 'ego-mimetic' (27), certain of its own subjectivity and the adequacy of perception; MacCannell insists that this gaze is accompanied by a less deterministic gaze that is not escapist and that knows 'seeing is not believing' (36). MacCannell, 'Tourist Agency', *Tourist Studies* 1: 1 (2001): 23–37. On literary tourism, see especially Nicola J. Watson, *The Literary Tourist* (Houndmills: Palgrave Macmillan, 2006), and James Buzard, *The Beaten Track* (Oxford: Clarendon Press, 1993).

6. Marie-Laure Ryan, *Narrative as Virtual Reality* (Baltimore: Johns Hopkins University Press, 2001), 93–5.

7. James T. Fields, *Yesterdays with Authors*, 1871 (Boston: Houghton Mifflin, 1900), 235. Further citations in parenthesis.

8. Hubbard Elbert, *Little Journeys to the Homes of Good Men and Great* (New York: Putnam's, 1895), 267. In 1905, B.W. Matz (1865–1925) devised a walking tour, retracing Dickens' and his characters' steps in East London. EastLondonHistory.com,   http://www.eastlondonhistory.com/matz.htm (accessed 18 December 2007). Matz launched *The Dickensian* in 1905, having helped to establish the Dickens Fellowship in 1902.

9. Edwin Harris, a printer in Rochester, self-published a series (beginning in 1897) of 25 illustrated tourist pamphlets, *Old Rochester*, bound in one volume after 1926. The 'Extract from the Visitors' Book of the Bull Hotel, written by Mr. J.J. Dean, of Bishop Auckland, 18th September 1877' appears on the back page of number 22, 'The "Bull Hotel", Rochester, and its Dickens Associations' (1908). In number 7 (1916), Harris notes, 'Charles Dickens has rendered [the Bull Hotel] famous throughout the world by his celebrated "Pickwick Papers" ... for a fuller description ... consult "A Week's Tramp in Dickens' Land," by William R. Hughes, F.L.S., a book which every lover of Dickens should possess' (7).

10. Frederick G. Kitton, *The Dickens Country*, 1905. Rpt. 1911 (n.p.: Folcroft Library Editions, 1979), facing p. 7; facing p. 200. Further references appear in the text.

11. This form of collecting has been updated by Reg Edmondson and Ron Cook, *Eating Out with Charles Dickens*, on a website of the same title: 'Trying to Unearth All the Inns and Taverns in Britain Where Dickens Stayed or Where He Sent His Characters.' http://www.eatingwithdickens.com/thebook.asp (accessed 18 December 2007).

12. Kitton, *The Dickens Country*, 184–5, 204. Fields quotes the same anecdote (212), replacing 'amazed' with 'annoyed.' The Dickens Fellowship's website

for Gad's Hill reinforces Dickens's proud possession of a Shakespearean site. Dickens commissioned an illuminated document by Owen Jones, to hang at Gad's Hill Place: 'This House/Gad's Hill Place/Stands on the Summit/ of/Shakespeare's/Gadshill/Ever memorable for its association in his noble fancy/with/Sir John Falstaff/ ...' It serves now as a sort of indoor 'blue plaque' at the Charles Dickens Museum.

13. Theodore Wolfe, *A Literary Pilgrimage among the Haunts of Famous British Authors* (Philadelphia: Lippincott, 1897), 55.

14. The chalet now stands in Eastgate Gardens, but it can be owned in 5.5 inch replica. The 'starter set of two,' priced $65, includes 'Dickens' Writing' – presumably the model of a bearded man in the chair beside the chalet, but as punctuated, it implies that you could buy his writing. Alpine Village Series Accessories 2007, item number 56.58488, 'Dickens' Gad's Hill Chalet', http://www.dept-56.org/Masterlist.txt (accessed 4 June 2008).

15. The Doughty Street plaque was amongst the first since the London County Council took over in 1901 from the Royal Society of Arts. Kitton notes that the Portsmouth Town Council had rescued Dickens's birthplace in 1903 (3). See L.M. Palis, *The Blue Plaques of London* (Wellingborough, England: Equation/Thorsons, 1989).

16. Michael Hardwick and Mollie Hardwick, *Writers' Houses: A Literary Journey in England* (London: Phoenix, 1968), 12.

17. *The Dickens House Museum* (Banbury: Classic Cheney Press, n.d.), brochure at the museum in 2003. The exhibit ran 29 April to 31 October 2003. Argonaut Productions advertises at the museum and on the web the one-man show (in its seventeenth year), 'A Friendly Encounter with Charles Dickens, the Sparkler of Albion', Dee Hart, dir., with Lloyd Lee as Charles Dickens, http://homepages.tesco.net/argodickens/Index.html (accessed 5 June 2008). Brochure in 2007: 'The Friends of the Charles Dickens Museum' carries portraits and first-person statements of Lucinda Hawksley (great-great-great granddaughter) and Cedric Charles Dickens (great grandson); the website, 'The Charles Dickens Museum, London', www.dickensmuseum.com (accessed 8 January 2008), promises an evening of wine with Dickens descendants. See also the brochure sold at the museum in 2007 with text by Michael Slater, *The Charles Dickens Museum Souvenir Guide* (n.p.: Dickens Fellowship, n.d.).

18. Dean MacCannell, *The Tourist*, rev. edn (Berkeley: University of California Press, 1999), 100–2.

19. The late theme-park developer Gerry O'Sullivan-Beare initiated the idea of a Dickens park in the 1970s. It was designed by RMA of Pinewood Studios (Sarah Balmond, 'RMA/O'Sullivan-Beare Theme for Dickens World', *Design Week* 21 April 2005, http://www.lexisnexis.com/us/lnacademic/ (accessed 18 December 2007) for the Continuum Company ('Dickens World: Not-So-Great Expectations', *The Independent* 24 May 2007, http://news. independent.co.uk/uk/this_britain/article2578476.ece (accessed 17 December 2007).

20. Quoted by Bloomberg [no first name], 'Please, sir, I want decor; The Dickens World theme park opens in England. Hey kids, come quick and meet Uriah Heep!' *National Post* (Canada), 28 May 2007: ARTS & LIFE; AVENUE; Pg. AL7.

21. cf. Finlo Rohrer, 'Great Expectations?' *BBC News UK Magazine* http://news.bbc.co.uk/go/pr/fr/-/2/hi/uk_news/magazine/6559197.stm   (accessed   17 December 2007).

22. 'A fast-paced journey through a day in the life of Charlie…. From orange sellers to psychics, con-men to toyshop owners, you'll meet them all in this comical interactive show' ('Steps in Time' flyer distributed at Dickens Festival 1 June 2007).

14
Wessex, Literary Pilgrims, and Thomas Hardy

Sara Haslam

Poet and Oxford Professor of Poetry, Edmund Blunden, is a key figure in the history of Thomas Hardy's reception. He kept the Hardy tradition alive between the world wars.[1] He was a pilgrim to 'Wessex' too, led there at first in 1922 by Siegfried Sassoon. Blunden later explored what was compelling about 'Wessex,' arguing that, in *Return of the Native*, Hardy discovered how the 'important aspects of his writing could be linked together;'[2] 'the harmony of the whole', Blunden concluded, 'came from Hardy's Wessex scenes and seasons.' Harmony, of various kinds, is central to much of the comment on and experience of Wessex (by Hardy and others), and it forms an organising concept in this essay.[3] But discordant notes are present too, including a deeply felt and always active ambivalence in Hardy towards the whole Wessex project. This ambivalence had its roots in the tensions between Hardy's ambitions, literary and otherwise, and his background. It was perfectly illustrated, as I will argue here, in the national debate (in which he took part through his will) about where his body belonged after his death. In this essay, then, I assess to what extent Hardy was the happy creator of 'Wessex,' himself hooked, along with increasing numbers of reader-pilgrims, by the country the reviewers always said he should not leave.[4] I also consider to what extent, and in what ways, he became its victim too.

Hardy makes a bold claim for his conception and use of Wessex in the famous preface to *Far from the Madding Crowd* (1895): 'I believe I am correct,' he wrote, 'in stating that, until the existence of this contemporaneous Wessex in place of the usual counties was announced in the present story [...] it had never been heard of in fiction and current speech.' The claim is too bold, and Michael Millgate corrects it in a biography, referring it back to the work of Dorset preacher and poet, William Barnes.[5] Hardy's elision of this debt is odd, because Barnes is the one contemporary (and friend) he is generally happy to acknowledge as an influence.[6] It is possible Hardy did not make the debt explicit in this instance because even from the beginning he was aiming for a bigger stage than Barnes (according to the *Oxford Companion to English Literature* (1989) a 'quaint provincial versifier'), but at this point in time, more particularly, Hardy was also immersed in the business of constructing his own claim for fiction in the area.[7]

Peter Ackroyd has used the notion of the 'territorial imperative', the ways in which the geographical characteristics of an area may 'bind and determine the nature' of those who grow up there, in relation to Shakespeare.[8] Barnes and Hardy both exhibit symptoms of being bound and determined by place, and the continuity with Barnes' localised devotion is made plain in Simon Gatrell's important essay on the later writer, 'Wessex'.[9] But Gatrell also argues that Hardy had a decision to make about the status of Wessex as he wrote the 1895 preface to *Far from the Madding Crowd* (and I agree with Gatrell about the momentousness of this decision for Hardy while, as we shall see, differing in my understanding of its effects). This decision meant reflecting on the way he was bound and determined by place, and also on the image he projected of it. It meant a debate about exchanging a more private relationship with Wessex for a more public one; about exchanging the implicit inspiration of the heath, say, for a consciously acknowledged debt to a Wessex landmass, and about exchanging Wessex as what Gatrell calls a 'process of vision and interpretation' for a place that could be drawn as a map.[10] As he made that decision in the early 1890s, Hardy came to the understanding that Wessex should indeed be presented as a 'homogenous historical object' and re-wrote aspects of his novels as they were re-published accordingly.[11] Such editing signified Hardy's adoption of a role as an historian and recorder of life in Wessex that was disappearing, and the development of his understanding of its emotional and commercial potential abroad. An essay by J.M. Barrie – 'Thomas Hardy: the Historian of Wessex' (1889) – should have encouraged him. Here, Barrie uses the word 'Wessex' liberally to describe what Hardy does well, writes that he 'loses himself' when he 'wanders beyond Wessex', and claims that when he takes for his subjects London society and professional life 'he fails absolutely' (*Critical Heritage*, 157–9). The reading public agreed, and the pilgrimage habit (what Blunden called the 'incidental reward of the "definite" novelist') gathered pace as Wessex took shape through the collected works. 'From London to the heart of Wessex, the land of Hardy's novels – of "Bathsheba Everdene", "Clym Yeobright" and "Giles Winterbourne" – seems far away enough, but it is only five hours from Waterloo' opens one 1890 article on Hardy's work.[12]

Where did the pilgrims think the five hours travelled from London would get them? The answer lies in a unique combination of factors, all of which can be related to the concept of harmony, as sociological or cultural construct. A defining feature of Hardy's rural world, was, as Gatrell puts it, 'the resilient abiding community of mutual interest' (20). The communal note is also sounded by reviewers.[13] Writing in 1941, Edmund Blunden was able to achieve a longer perspective on this idea, observing that 'a remarkable interest in rural affairs and village communities was stirring in England at the time when Hardy was forming his series of Wessex novels, and it touched him closely' (52). This interest was itself part of a contemporary national debate about Englishness, and attendant theories of urban degeneration – by the end of the nineteenth century polarised perceptions of England as either 'workshop' or 'shire' were increasingly common in literature.[14] The 'shire' was imaginatively important for regenerative purposes, as a refuge from urban chaos, and for relocating and revisiting the past. As such it may have attracted some of those persuaded of the degeneracy of the nineteenth-century city. Hardy's primary theme, though, was not a nostalgic response to the encroachment of the city, and this is what set him apart from other later writers in this vein – H.V. Morton, J.B. Priestley, and Tolkien, for example.[15] The community around him was not simply a corrective to the London whirl that he also knew at first hand, but was itself capable of rendering all of life. As such it was important macrocosmically, but microcosmically as well of course – a typical Victorian perspective. In Wessex he believed he had the whole of nineteenth-century life and history at his fingertips: 'There is more within a mile of me than I shall ever comprehend,' he wrote to Edmund Gosse in 1913.[16]

Hardy's ambition was to record as much of what surrounded him as he could and to pass it on. '[His] picture of Wessex is the most elaborate study of landscape in English letters,' combining the 'botanist's microscope' with the 'astronomer's telescope,' wrote David Cecil in 1942, pre-empting G.K. Chesterton's less admiring formulation that Hardy 'went down to botanise in the swamps.'[17] The intense detail drove Wessex hunters to visit exact scenes, painted, or photographed – the microscope is a realist's tool – as they seemed to be, from life.[18] The 'astronomer's telescope' took in the long view too. Cecil was making particular reference to Hardy's philosophical ambition as manifested in *The Dynasts*, but that telescope was also necessary to Hardy's broader, partly historical, and equally complete vision of his landscape – in calling Max

Gate the 'watch tower of Wessex' (61), Blunden also managed to convey the custodial element of Hardy's vigilance. There was, in any event, a great deal for him to see. Wessex is rich in visible signs of its history (the monuments, the earthworks, the Roman remains), many of which Hardy employs more than once, and it boasts great geographical variety within its 'borders.' J.H. Bettey has called this variety its 'outstanding physical characteristic;' tracing, in his study, the chalk downland, clay vales, hilly country, moorland and heathland of Wessex.[19] Coastline both domesticated and untamed are both in evidence too. Hardy uses such variety to the full; it was important to him to show his knowledge of all parts of Wessex, and to exploit dramatic tensions originating (or creatively imagined to originate) in each one. He had his own understanding of the territorial imperative.[20]

This combination of microscopic and generous vision, based as it was in a uniquely varied landscape setting, meant that Hardy seemed to be projecting an all-inclusive world to those who read him, and then tried to visit him, in Wessex. It was a world of which he was master, and his masterfulness was both attractive and motivational. Such effects might be attributed to Hardy's keen instinct for cathartic potential – he himself maps Wessex onto Greece when he considers his dramatic heritage;[21] it was also just to do with a particularised knowledge, and how much of it he seemed to have. 'There is none who reigns over a territory quite as Hardy reigns over Wessex,' wrote C.H. Sisson in 1978.[22] As early as 1918, Edmund Gosse conjured with the idea of 'wizard' Hardy: 'with the passage of years, observing everything in the little world of Wessex, and forgetting nothing, [he] has become almost preternaturally wise, and "knowing", with a sort of magic.'[23] Havelock Ellis, visiting in the 1890s, did not find magic, but was not disappointed with the 'genius' he found – and, crucially, such experience was common to more than merely 'literary types.'[24] W.T. Stead's contemporaneous project to promote socially-mixed pilgrimages to sites including Wessex, and the visit of the hundred members of the Whitefriars Club in 1901, as well as the numerous accounts of the individuals who hunted Hardy in Wessex, testify to the wide but intense appeal of what he had to say.[25]

Wessex, then, conceived as geographically (and, by extension, emotionally) varied yet 'complete', and dominated by the authorial mastery of Hardy, was a powerful package that achieved one kind of realisation in the first – projected – collected edition of his works. This series, published from 1895 by Osgood, McIlvaine, is not as significant as the later Macmillan edition of 1912. However, it was launched with the kind of marketing boost most writers would envy: to the aesthetic harmony and authorial mastery already projected by Wessex, Hardy managed to add sex and scandal with the publication of *Tess of the D'Urbervilles* (1891) and *Jude the Obscure* (1895). R.G. Cox points out that the sales of both were 'far higher' than those of previous novels; *Tess*, in addition, 'did more than any other novel to widen Hardy's reputation' (*Critical Heritage*, xxviii, xxxii). With the publication of *Jude*, Hardy also stretched the boundaries of Wessex north to Oxford (thus, in the opinion of some, spoiling its harmony and weakening its power[26]). As we have seen, he began to reassess Wessex in other ways too, reconstructing it in the new prefaces to individual novels. He ceased looking forward, in other words, and experimenting with what could be done with fiction – partly of course as a response to having to censor these late novels for magazine publication, and to the more extreme critical reactions – and began to find out how much more could be done with already completed work, with the Wessex that was making his name.

First of all, he decided to show readers something more of where Wessex was located. Each of the *Wessex Novels* came now with a map. In the preface to *Far from the Madding Crowd* (1895), he acknowledged that his work had already generated 'explorers;' it is hard to avoid seeing this addition as an aid (though not an exact one) for pilgrims.[27] His maps[28] may well also have been prompted by books like Annie MacDonell's *Thomas Hardy* (1894), which itself contained a map, as well as suggestions for a Wessex tour.[29] We certainly know from Hardy's letters that he maintained a hawk-like, self-interested view of such competing developments, and the 1895 map was in part a defensive gesture (*Letters*, iii, 15–16). This map also – whatever limitations Hardy ascribed to it – symbolised a few final harmonies: topography and story, fiction and reality were openly allied; it was simultaneous proof of the value of 'writing what you know' and his mastery of it; it showed the extent of his commitment to the place his readers wanted him to be (and it provided him with more money and more fame). One of his rewards was that Wessex was made 'so real that it is constantly and seriously spoken of as though it was English geography' (*Critical Heritage*, 400). Another, surely, was the boost it gave to the 'Thomas Hardy' being constructed as what Peter Widdowson terms the 'poet of Wessex', a 'component of the national culture.'[30] But for Gatrell, the new definite status of Wessex (to return to Blunden's word) was final in another sense: it killed the novel-writing instinct in Hardy (32).

This is true, but not quite in the way Gatrell means it – and here I turn from the harmonies of Wessex to its more discordant notes. The experience of his pilgrims now began in key ways to diverge from Hardy's own. With an irony worthy of Hardy – and unique to Hardy – the maps that confirmed his success and quickly became ubiquitous also pointed the way to a creative constraint that could only intensify as his readership grew. For the maps were not just a visual representation of the life of his stories, they were a visual representation of his own life: the realities of his biography were all here to be found and interpreted too. There were good reasons – considering the combination of the facts of his late pretensions to mastery, and that he was writing in nineteenth-century England – why Hardy himself did not want to be found.

It mostly comes down to snobbery. However hard he worked to educate himself – and like Jude, he worked hard – he could not, according to Cecil, get within sight of 'that intuitive good taste, that instinctive grasp of the laws of literature, which is the native heritage of one bred from childhood in the atmosphere of high culture' (*Hardy the Novelist*, 146).[31] To this way of thinking, the more important pre-condition of the work is how, and more particularly where, Hardy was 'bred'.

Hardy knew it. On 16 July, 1899, he wrote to the publishers of Chambers' *Encyclopaedia*, to ask if he might correct some errors in the Hardy entry (1895 edition). Millgate writes that the 'identification of his birthplace as "Upper *Bog*hampton" ' [my italics] was 'doubtless a source of particular irritation' (*Public Voice*, 163). What was on one level a humorous mistake would indeed have irritated Hardy, because of serious concerns he had about his public persona. It does after all tie in neatly with Chesterton's critical location of Hardy 'in the swamps.' Chesterton was comparing Hardy to Meredith: while Hardy was busy botanising on this lowest rung of the Darwinian ladder of authors, Meredith, according to the writer of the exquisitely urban *The Napoleon of Notting Hill* (1904), was climbing 'towards the sun.'[32] This is not simply a case of parochial rivalry. When he could have been grieving privately for the death of his mother in April 1904, Hardy instead spent time writing to a variety of publications challenging their representation of her, her house, and its poverty (*Public Voice*, 204–6). Any concealment provided by 'Wessex' as it had been (when it was less definite, and pilgrims and interviewers were fewer) no longer worked; indeed, it had been strategically abandoned, and Hardy often found himself regretting its loss.

In these early years of the twentieth century, then, when Hardy thought a great deal about Wessex autobiographically, harmony seems increasingly absent. In 1902 he turned down the opportunity of writing for a new Dorchester guidebook. He felt that those who came to the region because of anything he had written – or would write – did so invasively, in the attempt to 'penetrate a disguise' (*Letters*, iii, 17). A few years later he wrote to a journalist friend, James Milne, alleging that the mystifications regarding reality and place in his 'earlier Wessex books' were a deliberate disguise that became useless, and so were removed (*Public Voice*, 255). Some very real part of him could not afford to let them go: in the interim, his painful exchanges with Hermann Lea over depictions of his birthplace can be interpreted in part as slightly pathetic and, because of his success, always doomed, attempts to re-instate them. (Hardy first tried to steer Lea away from views of the cottage at Upper Bockhampton when Lea was compiling his guide in 1904 – because of 'trippers' with 'Kodaks' (*Letters*, iii, 145–6). The same subject came up when Lea was completing the fully-fledged study, *Thomas Hardy's Wessex*. On 11 July 1913 Hardy wrote that he should 'prefer the view of the house to be omitted' (*Letters*, iv, 286). Six days later he relented, and asked Lea to consider substituting a sketch he had made of it. Hardy's sketch does appear, and has the effect of making the house a little more like Clement Shorter's 1910 description of it as a 'hall' than the real thing.[33]) Far from being a playful game of cat and mouse with a benign public, or a conscious experiment with fiction versus reality, we can begin to see the cost of Wessex to Hardy, measured in different terms from its material and artistic benefits. Hardy needed a readership, of course, and even the pilgrims, but, problematically, he wanted to control the view of him that readership had.[34] The balance of power was not in his favour. Edmund Blunden intuited that Hardy's need for mastery was in part a response to his sense of (certainly historical) social inferiority in comparison with many of his readers. Hardy came from the country, Blunden wrote, 'of an ancient or tardy manner into the centre of things'. He was writing with the awareness that 'his readers were generally there before he was' (208). When they, in turn, came to find him, Hardy often felt they would not let him forget the difference in their points of origin.

The sense of vulnerability that this exposure caused in Hardy, at the same time as it was providing his income, symbolises the fractured relationship with Wessex that prevailed post-1895. Gatrell paints a positive picture of that relationship as Hardy moved into the second phase of his creative life, replacing the 'mire and blood' of the valleys in the fiction with the liberty of 'Wessex Heights' (33). But the social and psychological nerves that were set jangling by his decision to deliver up Wessex to the market, and to become 'Hardy, the poet of Wessex,' can be discerned for the rest of Hardy's life. On one level it was both a level-headed response to the 'constant inquiries of readers for the actual places',[35] and a conscious and even cynical retort to the critics and moralists who had tried to sideline him as distasteful. On another, he was plagued by the sense that it was him, Hardy, who was being judged (or hunted), and thus marketed – and ultimately was found wanting.[36] Wessex suffered too, until a defender, of a kind, appeared.

Sydney Cockerell became an important figure in the last years of Hardy's life. A Cambridge-educated, senior public servant – Director of the Fitzwilliam Museum – he signifies important aspects of Hardy's relationship with Wessex after he ceased writing fiction. He was admitted to Hardy's confidence astonishingly quickly after his first visit to him in September 1911. He came to see Hardy then because he wanted to organise him into distributing his prose manuscripts to a range of museums. Cockerell evidently knew the value of these papers, and was seeking to preserve them, but his interactions with Hardy (at exactly the time Macmillan was producing the *Wessex Edition*), are striking mainly because of the way they indicate Hardy's perplexity as to that same value, and reveal Cockerell's inability to persuade him of it. To one contemporary, Hardy expressed himself bamboozled by Cockerell ('He told me how Cockerell had asked him for an MS, and when he suggested that C. should choose, C. contrived to carry away *all* the MSS'); on the other hand Hardy himself said he didn't regard the value of the manuscripts,[37] and wrote to Cockerell just six days after first meeting him that he would be 'very glad' to send the 'whole lot' of his manuscripts to him 'to dispose of' (*Letters*, iv, 178). Hardy's letters to Cockerell on the subject of the redistribution of his manuscripts are heart-rending. Hardy doesn't really know, or care, where they are headed for (wherever Cockerell thinks best is his constant refrain), and sounds pathetically grateful only for the fact that his manuscript cupboard is bare, thus leaving him free of responsibility. He discusses his 'temerity' in presenting 'these old MSS' to museums, and, in a reprise of Martin Henchard's will, wants Cockerell's name to be prominent on the labelling, as opposed to his own. Hardy is at this point in his seventies, and the need to be free of some of his affairs is perhaps understandable (until we place this image of an aging country-man alongside that of the poet who had not yet written the *Poems of 1912–13*). But his self-belittlement is at odds with the harmony that Wessex could have provided, and at one stage did provide – and with what should have been his understanding of his reputation.[38] He confessed to Edmund Blunden in the early 1920s that it was a 'convenience' to allot his manuscripts to public libraries, as Cockerell suggested, because, he said 'I have no descendants, and short shrift may be allowed any leavings of mine' (*Thomas Hardy*, 138).

Perhaps Cockerell can be forgiven for his decision to override Hardy's request in his will to be buried at one with Wessex (and Emma), at Stinsford. Fulfilment of this wish would have done much, if only symbolically, to ameliorate the anxieties of the previous 30 years. But maybe, in the end, what happened is more brutally true to the overall effect of Wessex on Hardy's life. Claire Tomalin writes that Cockerell's 'intentions were good', and, after all, when he ensured a burial at the Abbey,[39] he proved he knew Hardy's national worth, and the value of Wessex, better than Hardy himself (despite, and because of, the pilgrims) often did. So he orchestrated the butchery of Hardy's body; his ashes were taken to Westminster Abbey, while his heart went to the local churchyard. To me, another Hardy pilgrim, the churchyard is the poorer for it, and so is Wessex. The Abbey's gains, meanwhile, seem limited by comparison: who goes to the Abbey to find Hardy, or even 'Hardy'?

At Stinsford, Hardy's words as well as his wishes are passed over; he was right to anticipate 'short shrift.' The inscription he drafted for his own tomb ('Here rests also Thomas Hardy...') have been replaced by Cockerell's ('Here lies the heart of Thomas Hardy...').[40] The 'heart,' alone, stands out – along with that change in verb. Edmund Blunden, with his eye on harmony, records Hardy's desire that his body be 'laid amongst his people in Stinsford Churchyard,' because it was Wessex, the 'kingdom he had well won' (178). The winning might not be better signified by his body, but there's a harrowed and discordant air created by its absence that the words, 'his ashes rest in Poets Corner Westminster Abbey', do nothing to dispel.

Notes

1. See Michael Thorpe, *The Poetry of Edmund Blunden* (Chatham: Bridge Books, 1971), 11.
2. Edmund Blunden, *Thomas Hardy* (Macmillan: London, 1941), 44.
3. See Havelock Ellis (1883) and Coventry Patmore (1887) in *Thomas Hardy: the Critical Heritage*, ed. R.G. Cox (London: Routledge and Kegan Paul, 1970), 120, 148; also Andrew Enstice, *Thomas Hardy: Landscapes of the Mind* (London: Macmillan, 1979), x, 1.
4. See unsigned review of *Two on a Tower* (1882), and comments by J.M. Barrie (1889), Edmund Gosse (1890 and 1896), John Buchan (1904) reprinted in *Critical Heritage*.
5. See Millgate's *Thomas Hardy: His Career as a Novelist* (London: The Bodley Head, 1971), 127–8.
6. See Samuel Hynes, *The Pattern of Hardy's Poetry* (Chapel Hill, NC: The University of North Carolina Press, 1961), 23.
7. See also ibid., 24; Millgate, 128.

8. Peter Ackroyd, *Shakespeare: the Biography* (London: Vintage Books, 2006), 7–8.

9. See also Claire Tomalin's biography, *Thomas Hardy: the Time-Torn Man* (London: Viking, 2006), 33.

10. 'Wessex' in *The Cambridge Companion to Thomas Hardy*, ed. Dale Kramer (Cambridge: Cambridge University Press, 1999), 29.

11. See W.J. Keith, 'Thomas Hardy and the Literary Pilgrims', *Nineteenth-Century Fiction* 24 (June, 1969): 80–92.

12. Blunden, 61. Havelock Ellis had been ahead of the game by touring Dorset in preparation for his long essay on Hardy, printed in the *Westminster Review* in April 1883.

13. See *Critical Heritage*, 13, 83–4.

14. On Englishness see my introduction to Ford Madox Ford's *England and the English* (Manchester: Carcanet, 2003), Alun Howkins' 'The Discovery of Rural England' in *Englishness: Politics and Culture 1880–1920*, eds Robert Colls and Philip Dodd (London: Croom Helm, 1986) and Martin Weiner's *English Culture and the Decline of the Industrial Spirit* (Cambridge: Cambridge University Press, 1981).

15. *In Search of England* was published in 1927, *English Journey* in 1933, *The Hobbit* in 1937.

16. 5 October 1913. The *Collected Letters of Thomas Hardy*, ed. R.L. Purdy and Michael Millgate, (Oxford: Clarendon Press, 1984), vol. iv, 1909–1913, 306 – henceforth *Letters*.

17. David Cecil, *Hardy the Novelist* (London: Constable and Co, 1942), 69–73; Chesterton quoted (*Victorian Age in Literature*, 1913) by Blunden, 95.

18. For reviews admiring Hardy's 'graphic pictures of rustic life' see *Critical Heritage*, 9, 21. The Royal Academy exhibited paintings of Wessex scenes in 1893 and a gallery in Bond Street showed 35 of Frederick Whitehead's 'Wessex paintings' in 1895.

19. J.H. Bettey, *Rural Life in Wessex 1500–1900* (Gloucester: Alan Sutton Publishing, 1987), 7–8.

20. See the way in which later versions of the map of Wessex give novel titles in the distinct and particular areas where the action occurred. Nicola J. Watson reprints an example, by J.H. Field, in *Literary Tourism: Readers & Places in Romantic and Victorian Britain* (Houndmills: Palgrave Macmillan, 2006), 200.

21. See the General Preface to the Wessex Edition in 1912.

22. Introduction to *Jude the Obscure* (Harmondsworth, Middlesex: Penguin, 1985 [1896]), 21. See also Horace Moule in 1874 and R.H. Hutton in 1887 (*Critical Heritage*, 11, 145).

23. *Critical Heritage*, 451. For similar pilgrim sentiments on the parts of Gissing, Charles Hind, Hermann Lea, William Lloyd Phelps, see Jim Gibson, *Thomas Hardy: Interviews and Recollections* (London: Macmillan, 1999), 49, 52–3, 55, 63–4.

24. For Ellis, see Gibson, 18–19.

25. For Stead's project and the visit of the Whitefriars Club see Millgate, *Thomas Hardy's Public Voice: the Essays, Speeches, and Miscellaneous Prose* (Oxford: Clarendon, 2001), 128, 165. W.J. Keith testifies to the 'hosts of Hardy readers who undertook a Wessex pilgrimage' from the mid 1890s, 88.

26. See Gosse quoted in Blunden, 87.
27. Keith calls it a 'stimulus' – in contrast to his more common argument that Hardy was bullied into provision of this kind by his topographically obsessed readers (80, 90).
28. He produced more than one map, over time, in keeping with the idea that Wessex became more and more 'definite.' A letter to Macmillan in October 1911 describes, and offers, a 'fuller and larger' version than that currently in circulation in the *Wessex Novels* (*Letters*, iv, 182).
29. See Watson, *The Literary Tourist*, 182–3 and Keith, 81, 84 on the earliest mapped version in 1891.
30. Peter Widdowson, *Hardy in History: a Study in Literary Sociology* (London: Routledge, 1989), 55.
31. For similar views, see Hynes, 88, 21.
32. For Gissing's analogous view see Gibson, 49–50.
33. Millgate calls Shorter's description, written to challenge the popular view of Hardy's birthplace as a 'humble cottage', 'an absurdity' (*Public Voice*, 309).
34. For Hardy's desire for control over his public persona, see Gibson, 19.
35. *Letters*, iv, 137.
36. Hardy's letters testify to the exhausting ambiguities in his sense of his own worth (see, for an example, *Letters*, iii, 235).
37. Gibson, 106.
38. The first of his honorary degrees was conferred by the University of Aberdeen in 1905; Edward, Prince of Wales, visited Max Gate on 23 July 1923.
39. Tomalin, 370. In the end Hardy had to be cremated instead of buried – also always the intention of Hardy and his family – because of a lack of space.
40. *Public Voice*, Appendix: 'Hardy as Memorialist', 477–8. Millgate says the words on the tomb are 'probably' Cockerell's.

15
Americans and Anti-Tourism
Shirley Foster

Tourists and the literary tradition

By the mid nineteenth century a steady stream (later to become a torrent) of Americans was crossing the Atlantic to visit the Old World a trip which had often been dreamt of and planned long before. Continental Europe had its powerful attractions, especially in Italy, but it was the 'homeland' – England and Scotland in the main – that exerted the greatest pull. This was the land of forefathers, the progenitor of the new, democratic nation now emerging in the United States. It was, as importantly, also a land already familiarised and sanctified by literary associations and culturally generated preconception. These associations in large part determined the American tourist's itinerary: Stratford for Shakespeare, the Lakes for Wordsworth and Scotland for Burns and Scott.

The notion of Britain as a site of 'hallowed shrines' was pre-eminently established for Americans by Washington Irving, whose rendition of it as 'a place full of storied and poetical associations'[1] (he is talking of Windsor Castle here) was perhaps most responsible for the subsequent hordes of Americans seeking the romantic experience of literary encounter. Furthermore, sites which were already sanctified by their links with revered writers had their iconic status codified and reinforced by the accounts of subsequent visitors and thus became essential elements in the American tourist's cultural pilgrimage. Many of these visitors found what they sought and were unhesitatingly enthusiastic about the objects of their veneration. Exemplary in this respect is Grace Greenwood (the pen name of Sarah Jane Clarke), poet and journalist, who visited Britain mid century and fulsomely recorded her experiences in her *Haps and Mishaps of a Tour in Europe* (1853). The archetypal 'sentimental tourist,' Greenwood weeps when she first sees a red rose in

England, and feels in Edinburgh 'a charm for my heart and a power over my imagination peculiar and pre-eminent' because of its associations with Scott and Burns.² Even for visitors as self-dramatisingly enthusiastic as Greenwood, however, there were moments when the experience itself and their part in it became questionable and problematic in various respects. First, actuality – the encountered reality – proved not always commensurate with expectation – the idealised preconceptions, built up from textual and anecdotal pre-knowledge. This discordance had to be negotiated so as to enable the tourist to come to terms with the disillusion it produced. One way of doing this was to ignore the deficiencies, continuing to offer unqualified veneration at hallowed sites. Another response, while acknowledging the constructed and codified nature of such cultural sanctification, sought to accommodate to its demands by using the imagination to create an alternative vision that enhanced reality with a degree of fictionalisation.

The experience of discordance also raises questions of authorisation and authenticity, implicit in the observer's own awareness of his or her role as both consumer and – as is the case with all the subjects discussed here, who were already established writers when they came to England – recorder. Perceptive American tourists recognised that, as 'pilgrims,' they were themselves as much the object of commercial and cultural exploitation as the sites they visited. In order to resist the stereotype of 'sentimental tourist,' and to show themselves as so doing, they implemented discursive strategies enabling them to establish their own agency and to challenge or subvert the domination of literary cultism and the commodification of an inherited aesthetic. Through ironic textual self-representation such tourists reveal themselves as 'knowing' visitors who have not relinquished their republican independence. Foregrounding their willing accession to the myths offered them, they both acknowledge the seductiveness of literary pilgrimage and establish their own separation from it; by showing themselves as (temporarily) sentient cultural dupes, they also speak cogently for a pro-American position, which, while recognising the importance of the European literary tradition, sees too the need for the alternative native aesthetic being urged by figures such as Emerson, Thoreau and Whitman. Although, as Henry James notes in his *Hawthorne* (1879), America may seem sadly deficient in cultural riches, for these visitors knowledge of such limitations must not automatically lead to blind canonisation of Old World idols.

These varying responses are, of course, neither discrete nor exclusive to individual tourists. All the visitors discussed here, as will be shown, at some time indulged in self-defensive fantasising in order to enhance their foreign experience. They were also capable of acknowledging their own complicity in the cultural codification of literary tourism. In examining how these positions overlap and interlink, this paper will focus mainly on approaches to the three most 'visited' figures, Scott, Burns and Shakespeare, paying particular attention to the last, since of all of these, the accretion of mythology pertaining to the Bard made for the most complex responses.

Fantasies

In order to align the realities of the contemporary location with the treasured preconception, tourists used various imaginative strategies to create a more desirable picture. These range from fanciful elaboration to inventive transformation, seeking to sustain the cultural heritage of an idealized homeland and thus reinforcing the kind of literary colonialism which, as has been indicated, writers of the American Renaissance were challenging. All such attempts to redeem an unwelcome or deficient actuality were usually conscious strategy. James acknowledges this when, commenting on how the appearance of Charlecote Park (near Stratford-upon-Avon) in the 1870s must be changed from Shakespeare's day, he notes wryly: 'the traveller does his best to believe [it] unaltered.'[3] Irving, too, avowedly visiting Stratford 'on a poetical pilgrimage' (326) in the 1820s, is (as will be shown) prepared to accept the absurdly false mythologies associated with the place in the interests of his own status as knowingly susceptible tourist:

> I am always of easy faith in such matters, and am ever willing to be deceived, where the deceit is pleasant and costs nothing...and would advise all travelers who travel for that gratification to be the same...There is nothing like resolute good-humored credulity in such matters. (328)

He thus acknowledges both the degree to which literary tourism depends on a Coleridgean willing suspension of disbelief and his own overt complicity in the process.

A frequent mode of imaginative enhancement is the dramatic completion of an iconic landscape or scene by inserting the relevant literary figure into the picture. Thus Greenwood, as she wanders along the banks of the River Doon, is 'half-cheated by excited fancy' that she might actually see Burns himself leaning over the bridge or walking in the countryside (118). The excitement generated by this fantasy is, however, heightened by Greenwood's recognition that this is a knowing act of self-deception. In the same way, Sophia Hawthorne, travelling in Scotland with her family in the 1850s, consciously increases her enjoyment by imagining Scott standing in the 'peculiarly enchanted' realm of Ellen's Isle, with his 'magic wand;'[4] likewise, at Newstead Abbey ('poetical ground'), she sits where Byron used to sit and tries to visualise him looking out on to the pictorial landscape (89).

Unsurprisingly, Stratford and its environs are most subjected to this imaginative treatment. Irving, noting that 'the whole country about here [around Stratford] is poetic ground; everything is associated with the idea of Shakespeare' (337), creates an image of the young Shakespeare composing poetry under the trees beside the Avon, fully conscious that his own tourist experience is enriched by such inventive reproduction – 'I like to deck out pictures for my own entertainment' (345). Harriet Beecher Stowe, visiting Britain in 1853, is particularly aware of the part that imagination has to play in the fulfilment of the literary tourist's agenda, nowhere more crucially than at Stratford. In Shakespeare's house, constructing a vision of 'a bright-eyed, curly-headed boy creeping up those stairs, zealous to explore the mysteries of that dark garret' and 'fanc[ying]' the disapproval of his elderly female relatives at his unruly behaviour,[5] she foregrounds the value of her own speculative processes for the production of pleasure. Stowe also calls attention to the transforming function of the imagination in the sanctification of literary sites. Like Greenwood, who would like Stratford to remain as it was in Shakespeare's time, 'wrapped forever in a charmed sleep', as if in a fairy tale (19), she is aware of the need for inventive creativity in the maintenance of ideality. In the coarse Elizabethan age, Shakespeare can have come by his 'deep heart-knowledge of pure womanhood' only from his mother, she argues, so she clings to her 'vision of one of those women whom the world knows not of, silent, deep-hearted, loving...who yet have a sacred power, like that of the spirit of peace' (I, 203). Interestingly, the desire to protect the sanctity of the literary idol by linking it to the female spirit is also seen in Sophia Hawthorne's re-enactment of her visit to Burns' cottage at Mossgiel. Appalled by the dirt and disorder she finds there (a common reaction of visitors), she feels compelled to create a more congenial environment for the poet: 'I only hope and believe that his mother, who was a woman of remarkable piety and sense, was also unusually neat for a Scotchwoman, and that she and her daughters kept everything clean and sweet' (134). In both these cases, the discordances of historical actuality (itself of course a construct) are resolved by a more agreeable version of history, dependent upon an idealised maternity.

Tourism as resistance

As has already been suggested, almost all percipient American tourists at one time or another sought to separate themselves from the pervasive power of literary cultism, in order to assert both individual and national identity and to challenge the codifying voices of Old World cultural authority. By overtly presenting themselves as gullible enthusiasts and worshippers, they were able to foreground the self-constructedness and performativity of the tourist's role, acceding to it and subverting it. Catherine Sedgwick, landing in England for the first time in 1839, well represents this subversiveness as she records her initial reaction:

> When I touched English ground I could have fallen on my knees and kissed it; but a wharf is not quite the *locale* for such a demonstration ... so I contented myself with a mental salutation of the home of my fathers.[6]

Here Sedgwick positions herself within a framework of exaggeratedly conventional response then ironically deflates it to show its ludicrousness. In a similar vein, Greenwood sends up her fanciful vision of 'jolly friars, faithful esquires and stout men-at-arms' (14) at the entry to Warwick Castle:

> I could almost see the waving of banners and plumes, the flash of shields and arms, and gorgeous vesture, as the glory of feudal power and the flush of courtly beauty swept by. Alas for wasted sentiment! I all too soon ascertained that this rocky pass was constructed by the late earl, the castle having formerly had a different approach. (15)

The deliberate shift in linguistic register, from florid poeticism to blunt matter-of-factness, highlights self-ridicule of her own status as naïve observer.

As has been suggested, intrinsic to this kind of response is an ironically evaluative awareness of the part that the observer's imagination plays in the construction of literary or historical icons. The note of self-mockery, evident in Sedgwick's and Greenwood's subversiveness also raises issues of identity imbricated within the literary tourist's experience; paradoxically, it is an indicator both of anxiety about the visitor's ability to read and reproduce a site already canonised within an aesthetic heritage, and of self-confidence in an individual and comprehending apprehension of what is viewed. So James Fenimore

Cooper, recalling his haste to view the ruins of Carisbrooke Castle in the Isle of Wight, mockingly foregrounds the process by which his own fancy necessarily transforms the scene: 'There was literally nothing but a very small fragment of a blind wall, but with these materials we went to work with the imagination, and soon completed the whole edifice.'[7] The observer thus turns his own naivety into creative empowerment. Stowe – foreshadowing Mark Twain later in the century – offers the most notable example of knowing iconoclasm, ironizing her own complicity with the cultural packaging offered to American visitors. This confident self-authorisation – textual exploitation of tourist naivety – valorizes the traveller/writer's subject position, though it does not preclude recognition of the complex machinery by which literary cultism is established. For Stowe, as for Cooper, the ironic discrepancy between expectation and actuality becomes the opportunity for comic self-deflation as well as enjoyment. Recounting her delight at walking on Bothwell bridge, immortalised by Scott in *Old Mortality*, she adds with amusement that she was 'rather mortified, after we had all our associations comfortably located upon it, to be told that it was not the same bridge – it had been newly built, widened, and otherwise made more comfortable and convenient' (I, 65). She employs a similar strategy of self-deflation when she describes her planned visit to the churchyard in which Gray wrote his famous 'Elegy.' Having discovered an ancient ivy-covered church, 'all perfect as could be', she recites the 'Elegy' and gives herself up to melancholy, only to find out later that it was the wrong church and the wrong place. Self-dramatisation gives way to confidently humorous manipulation of the absurdity of her touristic expectations and posturing: 'However...we could...console ourselves with the reflection that the emotion was admirable, and wanted only the right place to make it the most appropriate in the world' (II, 49–50).

Once again, the most frequent occurrences of such deconstructive tourist positioning are found in American responses to Shakespeare and the region associated with him. This is not only because in the nineteenth century, as now, Stratford was probably the most visited literary site in Britain, and its 'son' the most venerated figure, but also because here the tourist position was most problematised: any adulation was merely the echo of thousands before, and enthusiasm became ventriloquy, mimicry of stale convention. Interestingly, of all the American visitors at this time, Nathaniel Hawthorne most firmly resisted the cult of Shakespeare worship, refusing even the delights of self-mockery. Disillusioned, for example, by the shabbiness and dinginess of Shakespeare's house, 'such as the most poetical imagination would find it difficult to idealise', and finding its smallness 'more difficult to accept...than any other disenchanting particular of a mistaken ideal,'[8] he is unable to brighten the picture with consciously fanciful embellishment. Unlike many other visitors, he cannot – or will not – play the part of compliant tourist:

> I was conscious of not the slightest emotion while viewing it, nor any quickening of the imagination...Whatever pretty and apposite reflections I may have made upon the subject had either occurred to me before I ever saw Stratford, or have been elaborated since. (I, 163)

Hawthorne's response is sceptical, soberly rational and grimly uncompromising: even his wry concluding remarks on leaving Stratford – 'we had now done one of the things that an American proposes to himself as necessarily and chiefly to be done, on coming to England'[9] – show little of the delight in self-ridicule exhibited by other commentators.

For most other observers, as has been indicated, self-referential humour is pivotal in their chosen roles as 'anti-tourists.' Irving, his enthusiasm in no way diminished by his recognition of the industry of gulling tourists at Stratford, presents a comedic rendition of his experiences, indicating both his enjoyment and his sense of superior apprehension: 'There was ample supply...of Shakespeare's mulberry tree, which seems to have as extraordinary powers of self-multiplication as the wood of the true cross; of which there is enough extant to build a ship of the line' (327). Stowe similarly selects the Shakespeare industry as an arena in which to humorously exploit her role as sentimental tourist, knowingly complicit with its enticements. In her comic account of her Stratford experiences (including staying at a hotel whose rooms, somewhat ominously, are named after Shakespearian tragic heroes), she describes how she and her party, having reverentially visited and meditated upon Shakespeare's house, and seen his mulberry tree – in other words, 'having conscientiously performed every jot and tittle of the duty of good pilgrims' – are then informed that 'Shakespeare's house...wasn't his house, and...his mulberry...wasn't his mulberry.' She is 'quite ready', however, to turn the tables on herself, and 'to allow the foolishness of the thing, and join the laugh at [my] expense' (I, 214).

Several decades later, when visiting Stratford in July 1873, Twain also seized on the same material on which to work his sharp wit. Noting how much money 'Shakespeare' takes in each year, he records in his journal:

> Shakespeare's mulberry tree has been cut [down] by that thieving monster [the Reverend Francis Gastrell, in 1756]. Yet plenty of wood left. Man in Warwick furnishes any amount of these trinkets [made from this tree]...The man's lumberyard covers 13 acres of this mulberry tree.[10]

This is Twain's familiar voice, his disingenuous amazement asserting his resistance to the tricksy world of tourist exploitation yet also expressing his relish for its absurdity. The impact of this particular item of cultural commercialism must have been particularly striking, since in England Twain is generally far less iconoclastic than he is in Europe; not only does he show more reverence for tradition and history here, but he produced no work about England comparable to *The Innocents Abroad* or *The New Pilgrim's Progress*.

In the same decade as Twain, James also visited Stratford. Writing of his visit to Warwickshire in 1877, he too takes an ironic, albeit milder and more distanced, look at 'the American tourist [who] usually comes straight to this quarter of England – chiefly for the purpose of paying his respects to the birthplace of Shakespeare' (120). In a typical instance of self-reflectivity, he notes that 'the sentimental tourist' (of whom of course he is one) '[i]nevitably...has a great deal to say to himself about this being Shakespeare's county' (122). Yet part of the irony is that James does not in fact say much about the dramatist or his birthplace, realising that it has all been told endlessly before. Instead, he describes Stratford from a more peripheral topographical viewpoint, presenting it as 'a stage set for one of Shakespeare's comedies,' in which the sheep in the landscape themselves become complicit in the tableau: 'they were poetic, historic, romantic sheep; they were not there for their weight or their wool, they were their for their presence and their compositional value, and they visibly knew it' (123). Here, the literary site has become a dramatic location in which the tourist observer delightfully calls attention to its artifice by including the non-human 'extras' in his appreciation. As ever, James shows himself the most self-conscious, as well as the most perceptive, of American tourists.

These American visitors, then, discovered that their encounters with a much-anticipated reality demanded a greater complexity of response than they could have foreseen. As eager tourists, they were part of an industry demanding participation in its workings. As writers, they had to find ways of representing their experience and their engagement with it which would be both truthful and self-respecting. As Americans, they wanted to pay due homage to an Old World aesthetic heritage while at the same time upholding their own and their readers' sense of national independence. Their accounts reveal the strategies by which they negotiated these complexities, extending the parameters of apprehension of well-known sites and showing how the practice of literary tourism could be both canonical and subversive, precedential and original. Out of such awareness they produced works that are historically illuminating and entertaining.

Notes

1. Washington Irving, *The Sketchbook of Geoffrey Crayon, Gent.* (1848) (Tarrytown, New York: Sleepy Hollow Press, 1981), 105.
2. Grace Greenwood, *Haps and Mishaps of a Tour in Europe* (Boston: Ticknor, Reed, and Fields, 1854), 132.
3. Henry James, *English Hours* (1905) (Oxford: Oxford University Press: 1981), 122.
4. Sophia Hawthorne, *Notes in England and Italy* (London: s.n., 1869), 181.
5. Harriet Beecher Stowe, *Sunny Memories of Foreign Lands* (1854), 2 vols (Boston: Phillips, Sampson, and Company, 1856), I, 202. For a wider discussion of Stowe's personal and literary relations with Europe, see Denise Kohn, Sarah Meer and Emily B. Todd eds., *Transatlantic Stowe: Harriet Beecher Stowe and European Culture* (Iowa City: University of Iowa Press, 2006).
6. Catherine Sedgwick, *Letters from Abroad to Kindred at Home* (1841), 2 vols (New York: Harper & Brothers, 1855), I, 13.
7. James Fenimore Cooper, *Gleanings in Europe* (1837), Robert E. Spiller ed., 2 vols (New York: Oxford University Press, 1928; Kraus reprint, New York, 1970), I, 30.
8. Nathaniel Hawthorne, *Our Old Home* (1863), 2 vols (London: Chatto and Windus, 1890), I, 158, 159.
9. Nathaniel Hawthorne, *English Notebooks,* Thomas Woodson and Bill Ellis, eds, *The Centenary Edition of the Works of Nathaniel Hawthorne*, Vols. XXI, XXII (Columbus: Ohio State University Press, 1997), I, 203.
10. Mark Twain, *Notebooks and Journals*, eds Frederick Anderson, Michael B. Frank, Kenneth M. Sanderson, Vol. I (Berkeley: University of California Press, 1975), 563–4. c.1880–1882, Twain wrote a humorous 12-page letter to the *New York Evening Post* about a cutting from the mulberry tree which he had been given. The MS was never published; though Twain apparently later suggested it for inclusion in his book of sketches, *The Stolen White Elephant* (1882), W.D. Howells suggested to the publisher, Osgood, that this piece be omitted.

16

How America 'Inherited' Literary Tourism

Paul Westover

Many nineteenth-century Americans took it for granted that the literatures of Great Britain and the United States should be read together, and literary tourism had a powerful role in constructing 'English' in those transatlantic terms. An Anglo-American canon of authors and associated tourist sites took root through a process of 'quotation' – allusion, citation, and imitation – by which American authors, and tourists, proclaimed themselves heirs to the English tradition.

The genesis of American literary tourism came about in the context of debates concerning America's proper relationship to British culture. George Henry Calvert, recalling his first visit to Britain in the 1820s, wrote:

> [The American in Britain] is like a wealthy heir, sent from home a bantling, come back at twenty-one to take possession…. His rights are so deep that they are inalienable; for they descend to him though the books he has read, and the plays he has seen, and the history he has learnt, and the language he speaks…and the imaginations he has fondled.[1]

Like other writers of his generation, Calvert argues that Americans have claims on Britain because of the language and culture they have inherited. Yet Calvert's use of the word *bantling* is suggestive. While the word generally means 'small child,' in his time it could also mean 'bastard.' Calvert thus reminds us that an important question in America's early national period was whether or not Americans were *legitimate* heirs to British culture, and especially to British writers. This concern distinguished American tourists in Britain from other visiting foreigners. Indeed, the fact that many Americans claimed a British inheritance in their writings – or, conversely, spent energy repudiating it – betrayed their anxiety on the subject. A good deal, in literature as well as in politics, depended on whether Americans were extending a tradition or creating one. While many insisted that American culture should strike out independently, even the most nationalistic Americans could acknowledge the force of Europe's tradition and speak in terms of inheritance, claiming, in Whitman's words, that 'its action [had] descended to the stalwart and well-shaped heir who [approached].'[2]

That tradition-conscious Anglo-Americans would turn culture tourists in Britain makes sense. Many whose parents or grandparents were British had never seen the Old Country themselves. Some sought out ancestral home towns and graves, while almost all visited the monuments of shared culture at such places as Westminster Abbey and Stratford-upon-Avon. This habit – linked with talk of inheritance – persisted for decades. Near mid century, Nathaniel Hawthorne asserted, 'An American has a right to be proud of Westminster Abbey; for most of the men, who sleep in it, are our great men, as well as theirs.'[3] In claiming the British dead, Hawthorne was speaking in terms employed by many American travel writers.

Britain remained an imaginary possession for many nineteenth-century Americans because they felt they knew it through literature. They grew up largely on British books. One might say that, to literate Americans, Britain *was* a book, 'a perpetual volume of reference,' as Washington Irving put it.[4] The leading literary shrines were known to them through standard texts and through engravings in periodicals like the *Gentleman's Magazine*. The familiarity of landmarks only grew as the years passed and the volume of travel accounts (both British and American) increased. Thus, Hawthorne's reaction to Westminster Abbey, recorded in the *English Notebooks* (1855), was typical:

> Poets' corner has never seemed like a strange place to me; it has been familiar from the very first; – at all events, I cannot now recollect the previous conception, of which the reality has taken the place. I always seem to have known that somewhat dim corner...[5]

Hawthorne's sense of *déjà vu* is also a sense of *déjà lu*: it occurs because the Abbey is the setting of favourite writings – he mentions Addison's famous 'Reflections in Westminster Abbey' – and the abode of 'friendly presences' (329). Poets' Corner is a place that underlines the feeling, common to many American travellers, that their trip to Britain is a homecoming. Hawthorne claims Westminster Abbey and so might be said metonymically to claim Britain as a whole – Britain imagined as a vast burial ground, haunted with the friendly ghosts of reading. Here we see what I call the necromantic equation: Britain=library, museum, ancestral graveyard, and cultural homeland. (It is telling that Hawthorne later called his revised notebooks *Our Old Home*.) This equation makes nationality less important than shared cultural knowledge.

It is in the light of constructing a common Anglo-American identity and literary tradition that I read passages like this one from Harriet Beecher Stowe's *Sunny Memories of Foreign Lands* (1854):

> Say what we will, an American, particularly a New Englander, can never approach the old country without a kind of thrill and pulsation of kindred. Its history for two centuries was our history. Its literature, laws, and language are our literature, laws, and language. Spenser, Shakespeare, Bacon, Milton, were a glorious inheritance, which we share in common. Our very life-blood is English life-blood.[6]

For Stowe, consanguinity consists largely in books: the English canon itself flows in a New Englander's veins. George Calvert, too, applies the terms of blood to literary culture:

> Englishmen and Americans cannot put into words, cannot grasp in thought, their obligation to Shakespeare. Through the possession, the ever closer possession, for many generations, of his high think-ing, his subtle insight, his clear, infallible intuition, these have come to be absorbed into the tissue of our race, congenitally immixed in our blood…. At birth we are stronger and better than we otherwise would have been, because…of Shakespeare.[7]

Calvert's claim is similar to British Romantic assertions (as in Godwin's *Essay on Sepulchres* or Shelley's *Defence of Poetry*) that all people, even those who have not read Shakespeare, have benefited from the Bard's influence. But in Calvert, the argument is explicitly trans-nationalised and racialised: Shakespeare has been 'absorbed into the tissue of our race.' Similar locutions appear throughout the corpus of Anglo-American travel writing, reminding us that the mid nineteenth century redefined the term 'Anglo-Saxon' as a racial marker.[8] Nevertheless, the writings of former slaves like Frederick Douglass and William Wells Brown dem-onstrated that Americans without acknowledged biological inherit-ance from Britain could also lay claim to Britain's political and cultural birthright. In doing so, they denied claims that literary tradition could be transmitted in the blood. Their books sharpened the insight of books like Irving's *Sketch-Book* and later efforts in its tradition – namely, that to inherit the British legacy one had to claim it through reading and quoting.

Douglass's 1845 *Narrative* helps makes the point with its famous argument – turning on the author's watershed encounter with *The Columbian Orator* – that 'education and slavery [are] incompatible with each other.' William Wells Brown amplifies Douglass' emphasis on literacy's power by foregrounding his own familiarity with English literature. He does this most fully in *Three Years in Europe; or Places I Have Seen and People I Have Met* (1852), his contribution to the transatlantic tour genre.[9] His work, less familiar than Douglass's to most readers, may require a brief introduction: Brown went to Britain in 1849 and remained in Europe until 1854, detained by the passage of the Fugitive Slave Law. Setting out to extend the work of Charles Lenox Remond and of Douglass, who had previously toured Britain delivering lectures, he presented himself not only as an emissary of the Abolition movement, but also as a professional man of letters, supporting himself through literary labour. His *Three Years in Europe* shows him rubbing shoulders with literary lions and commenting deftly upon Britain's literary tourist itinerary. In fact, early reviews of his book show that contemporary readers understood Brown's argument; a black man, contrary to doctrines of racial inferiority, could claim literary culture as his own.

Enforcing his claim to self-culture, Brown shows mastery of his genre from the start, beginning with an epigraph from 'Childe Harold's Good-Night.' The Byronic lines of farewell, often quoted in Americans' tour books, become the first occasion for Brown to route racial politics through English literature – a former slave's farewell to America, he explains, must differ in its emotional colour from a white man's farewell.[10] This is the first of many quotations, several of which appear in connection with Brown's visits to literary shrines. The pattern emerges early in Brown's account, even before he reaches Liverpool. When he visits the Irish birthplace of Thomas Moore during a brief stopover, Brown recalls Moore's verse: 'Where is the slave so lowly/Condemned to chains unholy,/Who, could he burst/His bonds at first/Would pine beneath them slowly?' In Brown's hands, Moore becomes an abolitionist, praiseworthy not only for poetic genius, but also for 'the support which his pen has given to civil and religious liberty throughout the world.'[11] Apparently, Brown knows Moore's verse by heart. He can claim ownership in Britain for the same reason Anglo-Americans can do so; he has absorbed British books.

Brown also takes pains to show himself an active literary student, and it is in this context that he most explicitly addresses the question of cultural inheritance. Reporting that he has stayed up until 2 a.m. reading, he explains:

> He who escapes from slavery at the age of twenty years, without any education, as did the writer of this, must read when others are asleep, if he would catch up with the rest of the world.... The son may take possession of the father's goods at his death, but he cannot inherit with the property the father's cultivated mind.... Property may be bequeathed, but knowledge cannot. Then let him who would be useful in his day and generation be up and doing. (132)

Brown argues that culture cannot be inherited biologically, but that it must be claimed through labour. Brown has performed, is performing, the necessary work, yet American law denies his claims, not merely to cultural ownership, but to property of any kind, even in himself. It is perhaps worth noting that Brown, like Frederick Douglass, had a white father, so that he might (perversely) have claimed cultural inheritance on biological grounds. However, he rejected that option – one fraught with its own spectres of illegitimacy; his claim was for the law of books rather than the law of blood. Thus, Brown's thesis could be expressed in the terms of Calvert: 'My literacy, dramatised by both my itinerary and my writing, proves that I am a true heir to British culture'; or, in the words of a reviewer for the *Glasgow Examiner*: 'The author of [this book] is not a man in America, but a chattel, ... but in Europe, he is an author, and a successful one, too.'[12] Brown's modern editor errs when he omits several sections from his reprint on the ground that 'they include extended descriptions of landscapes, museum interiors, grave sites, and assorted monuments' and so are 'less central to the 'argument' of the book.'[13] It may be true that Brown's visits to Westminster Abbey, Abbotsford, and Newstead Abbey – all omitted from this edition – are 'less interesting to the modern reader,' but for a nineteenth-century audience, they formed the book's essential argument.

As Brown demonstrates, once writers remove blood from the conversation, replacing biological metaphors with cultural logic, the question of literary inheritance reveals itself as an expression of the broader 'dialectics of authenticity' – that is, of general concern (fundamental to tourism) over what is genuine or legitimate and what is not.[14] A case study appears in Washington Irving's 'Stratford-upon-Avon' sketch, when his alter-ego, Geoffrey Crayon, encounters a character who figures in several American tourists' accounts: the resident guide at Shakespeare's birthplace. This is no doubt a Mrs. Hornsby, who made her living by showing the house and its relics and peddling copies of her own lack-lustre dramatic works. Crayon says he is willing to believe that this 'poetical cicerone' is, as she claims, a direct descendant of the Bard – at least until he looks at one of her plays, 'which set all belief in her consanguinity at defiance.'[15] Note that although Irving employs the language of blood here, his 'consanguinity' is mainly an affair of kindred genius. Literary paternity – like biological parentage prior to genetic testing – is a matter of faith: it cannot be proved, though it may be suggested by parental traits showing up in offspring. The *Sketch-Book* is the record of Irving succeeding where Mrs. Hornsby fails, establishing his claim as a descendent of Shakespeare. As a child of an English mother and a Scottish father, Irving too could conceivably stake a biological claim to British culture; and in fact, the *Sketch-Book* toys with that concept occasionally, as if Irving could possess the sort of blood-borne Shakespearean-ness described by Calvert and others. Nonetheless, Irving always returns to a literary, citational logic. By demonstrating canonical mastery, he seeks the faith of readers on both sides of the Atlantic and asserts a right to inherit a place in the 'English' tradition. He keeps quoting his way to legitimacy, as if to prove that books can be absorbed in the blood like an acquired DNA.

American writers working in the tradition of Irving's *Sketch-Book* used the same 'quotation' techniques to enter the canon and then the tourist itinerary. They helped create a touristic United States, modelled on literary Britain. It was not an easy task. Even for American writers working in the 1850s, a U.S.A. saturated with historical and literary associations seemed like a fantasy. Harriet Beecher Stowe wrote, 'I wonder how many authors it will take to enchant our country from Maine to New Orleans, as every foot of ground is enchanted here in Scotland.'[16] In a necromantic age, Americans sometimes lamented that they seemed to have so few native materials – so few ruins, great books, and canonical dead people.[17] To the extent that they succeeded in creating their own 'classic ground,' they could imagine their achievement as a heroic transcendence of historical disadvantage.

Washington Irving holds the honour of defining the transatlantic journey genre for future American writers, and it is he who suggests how an American itinerary of British, and by analogy American, tourist sites might be established. The impact of his *Sketch-Book of Geoffrey Crayon, Gent.* (1819–1820) on tourism can hardly be overstated: future travellers sought out the Red Horse Inn in Stratford-upon-Avon for Geoffrey Crayon's sake. When Emerson went to England in 1847, he went on a packet ship called the *Washington Irving*. Throughout the century, Americans showed extraordinary consistency in their British itineraries and in their atavistic, relentlessly citational manner of writing about them, precisely because they had thoroughly absorbed the lessons of the *Sketch-Book*. It was Irving who ensured that the problem of inheritance remained central to the tour genre.

Part of what makes Irving such a good model is his conscious promotion of a paradox: *citational originality*. The concept goes to the heart of Romantic authorship, with all its claims to novelty, and colours especially what it means to be an American literary tourist and writer. There is no such thing as an original tourist – that is commonplace – but Irving rather suggests that there are no original writers either. Just two months before the *Sketch-Book* appeared in England, Sydney Smith posed his famous question: 'In the four quarters of the globe, who reads an American book?' The implied answer, of course, was *nobody*, not even Americans. Yet people on both sides of the water did read the *Sketch-Book*, and in *The Spirit of the Age*, Hazlitt accounted for Irving's popularity by citing his clever appropriations of British books:

> [Irving] is by birth an American, and has, as it were, *skimmed the cream*, and taken off patterns with great skill and cleverness, from our best known and happiest writers, so that their thoughts and almost their reputation are indirectly transferred to his page, and smile upon us from another hemisphere ...: he succeeds to our admiration and our sympathy by a sort of prescriptive title and traditional privilege.[18]

This was more than the hackneyed accusation that American literature was derivative; it was an argument that Irving, expressing the Zeitgeist, had succeeded by claiming 'traditional privilege' – by quoting or imitating with genius. Hazlitt had read the *Sketch-Book* on its own terms, finding the case for citational originality in Irving's burlesques. Some readers (falling into terms proleptically mocked by Irving, especially in the sketch called 'The Art of Book-Making') might accuse Irving of poaching; nevertheless, Hazlitt contended that Irving had implicitly bolstered the English canon by absorbing it; and the key point, as time would prove, was that Irving had entered the canon himself. He had shown that the literary tradition inhabited a transatlantic common land, not a national hunting preserve: it was an 'English' tradition in the sense that moderns speak of English departments, defined by language (and a shared tradition of recycling), not nationality.

Irving gained canonical status by stepping into places traditionally occupied by British writers. It was something like George Washington (Irving's namesake) replacing George III on the tavern sign in 'Rip Van Winkle.' In fact, a similar exchange materialised briefly in the twentieth century, when Stratford's Red Horse Inn was renamed the Washington Irving.[19] In the 1800s, Irving was called an 'English writer' and adopted as a model of English prose style by both European and American textbooks. He was quoted as a leading authority on Stratford and other locales in British guidebooks for tourists.

Through such quotations and replications, Washington Irving became a sort of New York Sir Walter Scott. Here, arguably, begins the story of America's deliberate importation of literary homes, haunts, and graves. The Irving-Scott relationship publicly began when Scott, a fan of Irving's *History of New York*, received the young American at Abbotsford in 1817. Later, Scott convinced Murray to publish Irving's *Sketch-Book*. The association between the two writers continued even after Scott's death, when Irving published (in 1835) *Abbotsford*, an affectionate account of his visit to Scott's home, and when (in 1848) he added a new preface to the *Sketch-Book*, gratefully acknowledging Scott's early patronage.[20] However, in keeping with the *Sketch-Book's* status as the *summum genus* of literary tour books – Irving's self re-creation as the American Scott[21] occurred most powerfully within its pages. Consider 'Rip Van Winkle,' one of the book's signature pieces: Irving's story (a 'posthumous' work of Dietrich Knickerbocker, Irving's antiquarian alter-ego, who here resembles Walter Scott's Dr. Dryasdust) works up a German legend first pointed out to him by Scott, and summoning New York's Dutch and Native American ghosts, it converts the Catskills into a haunted, quasi-gothic landscape like Scott's Scottish Highlands. In light of this sort of transatlantic translation, it was no coincidence that early admirers of the *Sketch-Book* speculated that Scott was its author. But Irving's achievement, though analogous to Scott's, was new: establishing classic ground in his native country, weaving literary associations into its landscape and even preparing it for export. Irving had created a literary America – an America of interest to literary tourists.

The citational process of canonisation culminated during Irving's final years at Sunnyside, his New York clone of Scott's Abbotsford.[22] Irving understood Abbotsford House's role in situating Scott as a national bard and tourist attraction. Like Abbotsford, Sunnyside struck contemporaries as a romance made material – an externalisation of the author's imagination and an entry to the world of his books. It was, in fact, a palpable mix of Irvingism and Scottism: an unusual 'blend of Dutch colonial history [the realm of Diedrich Knickerbocker] and Gothic Revival architecture.'[23] Irving followed Scott's lead even in details: much as Scott incorporated building materials from Melrose Abbey in Abbotsford, Irving imported ivy clippings from Melrose to plant on Sunnyside's walls. Sunnyside, the physical sign that, for the first time, an American author was a tourist draw, was literally adorned with transplantation from the Scottish Borders.[24]

While labouring on his last work, the *Life of Washington*, Irving enjoyed a kind of posthumous existence as a tourist attraction at Sunnyside, welcoming travellers just as Walter Scott had once received him. Four years after Irving's death, as if to eternally link him with the Author of Waverley, artist Christian Schussele painted *Washington Irving and His Literary Friends at Sunnyside*, a group portrait that featured Irving amongst Hawthorne, Longfellow, Emerson and other American writers.[25] An intriguing conversation piece in its own right, it is also a quotation piece: it mimics an 1849 work by Thomas Faed, *Sir Walter Scott and His Literary Friends at Abbotsford*. In the earlier painting, Walter Scott joins the dead-or-nearly-dead likes of Jeffrey, Campbell, Crabbe, and Wordsworth, all grouped before the bow window of Abbotsford's library. In Schussele's painting, the window is replaced by a bookcase still framed by parted curtains, as if to make books the light source. A bust of Shakespeare presides in the upper right-hand corner, reinforcing the link between Geoffrey Crayon and the Bard, but also recalling that Scott had such a bust. By placing Irving on a level with Scott and perhaps, by extension, dignifying all American writers, this image makes visible the canonisation Irving worked for in life. In fact, Robert Spiller reports that Irving owned a copy of Faed's Walter Scott painting and made it a showpiece:

> When Irving, then an old man, was living in retirement at Sunnyside, a New York reporter visited him and found an engraving of Thomas Faed's Scott and His Literary Friends on the wall of his parlor. 'I knew every man of them but three,' said Irving, 'and now they are all gone!'[26]

In this 'extempore effusion' scene, Irving confirms his status as a writer worthy to mingle with the immortal great of Anglophone letters. He joins the luminous company in offering his blessing to a rising generation of reader-tourists.

Similar canonisation stories can be told of Hawthorne, Stowe, and others who now have permanent homes on the tourist itinerary. One might describe Hawthorne's achievement as doing for Salem what Irving did for the Hudson River Valley. Travellers can still visit literary Salem, including Hawthorne's birthplace and the adjacent House of the Seven Gables; they can also see Uncle Tom's (actually, Josiah Henson's) Cabin and the Harriet Beecher Stowe House in Hartford, or the house where Stowe lived in Cincinnati. Tourist boards sponsor celebrations of both authors – recently, the bicentennial of Hawthorne's birth (July 4, 2004) and the Stowe Festival of Cincinnati, marking the 150-year anniversary of *Uncle Tom's Cabin* (2003). The Stowe Festival, punctuated by the commission of a new Stowe bust and a musical called *Harriet*, uncannily mimicked the Stratford Jubilee, of which all author-inspired festivals are echoes. In sum, the canonisation of all these authors can be shown to follow the pattern of quotation. I single out Irving because his remarkable success set the stage for later literary Americans.

The movement via Irving from British to American tourist sites extends even to the graveyard. In 1855, a cemetery called Sleepy Hollow opened in Concord, Massachusetts. In time, it gathered together Thoreau, Hawthorne, Emerson, the Alcotts, and others on a hill known as Authors' Ridge. Not long after, the Tarrytown, New York cemetery where Washington Irving was interred in 1859 was renamed 'Sleepy Hollow,' honouring the area's literary associations and Irving's own request. In effect, Irving had been buried in the ground of his own ghost story – and Concord's literati surely recalled that story when naming their new cemetery.[27] It seems fitting that so many of America's literary dead should be buried in Sleepy Hollow(s), as if to eternally witness to Irving's impact on American letters and to the power of his model of transplantation.

Nonetheless, notable literary graves are missing from Sleepy Hollow – and from all the touristic destinations for which I take it as an emblem. Amongst graves that inspire few pilgrimages is that of William Wells Brown, who, like Hawthorne and Stowe, chased the ghost of Irving and laid claim to Britain's literary patrimony. He died not far away from Concord's Sleepy Hollow, yet his unmarked grave in Boston, identified only by a number, stands as a silent acknowledgment that the nineteenth-century could not easily canonise him. (Arguably, it was blood that kept him out of Sleepy Hollow in the end.) Perhaps, because Brown had no place in America that he could claim as his own, his emplacement could be only literary or historical – and there his place was equally tenuous. Irving could install himself in Sleepy Hollow Country, Hawthorne in Salem, and so on, but Brown was (and is) a man without a landmark.

Notes

1. George Henry Calvert, *First Years in Europe* (Boston: William V. Spencer, 1866), 16.
2. Walt Whitman, 'Preface,' *Leaves of Grass*, 150th Anniversary Edition. ed. David S. Reynolds. (Oxford: Oxford University Press, 2005), iii.
3. Nathaniel Hawthorne, *The English Notebooks* (Centenary Edition of the Works of Nathaniel Hawthorne, vol. xxi, ed. Thomas Woodson and Bill Ellis [Columbus: Ohio State University Press, 1997]), 321.
4. Washington Irving, *The Sketch Book of Geoffrey Crayon, Gent.*, ed. William L. Hedges (New York: Penguin, 1988), 9.
5. Hawthorne, 373.
6. Harriet Beecher Stowe, *Sunny Memories of Foreign Lands*, vol. 1 (Boston: Phillips, Sampson, 1854), 18.
7. Calvert, 232.
8. See *Anglo-Saxon*, definition III in the *OED*: ' Used rhetorically for English in its wider or ethnological sense...; thus applied to (1) all persons of Teutonic descent (or who reckon themselves such) in Britain, whether of English, Scotch, or Irish birth; (2) all of this descent in the world, whether subjects of Great Britain or of the United States.' This usage develops in the 1800s, in part via texts such as those discussed in this essay.
9. *Three Years in Europe* was the title of the book's first edition, published in London (1852). The American edition (Boston, 1855) was called *The American Fugitive in Europe: Sketches of Places and People Abroad*. The American title placed the work in the tradition of Irving's *Sketch-Book* while pointing out Brown's position of forced exile.
10. Byron's lines from *Childe Harold's Pilgrimage* (Canto 1, stanza 13) read, 'Adieu, adieu! – my native shore/Fades o'er the waters blue;/The night winds sigh, the breakers roar,/And shrieks the wild sea-mew./Yon sun that sets upon the sea/We follow in his flight;/Farewell awhile to him and thee!/My native land, good-night!'
11. Paul Jefferson, ed., *The Travels of William Wells Brown* (New York: Markus Wiener, 1991), 103.
12. William Wells Brown, *The Rising Son: Or, the Antecedents and Advancement of the Colored Race* (1882), 18.
13. Jefferson, 15.
14. I borrow this term from Dean MacCannellís *The Tourist: A New Theory of the Leisure Class* (New York: Schocken Books, 1976), 145.
15. Irving, 211.
16. Stowe, I, 48.
17. Obviously, this common point of view required discounting many 'native materials.' Native Americans and their relics troubled Anglo-centric national imaginings.
18. William Hazlitt, *The Spirit of the Age* (London: Colburn, 1825), 409–10.

19. Christopher Mulvey, *Anglo-American Landscapes: a Study of Nineteenth-Century Anglo-American Travel Literature* (Cambridge University Press, 1983), 78.

20. Washington Irving, 'Abbotsford,' in *The Crayon Miscellany* (The Complete Works of Washington Irving, vol. 22, ed. Dahlia Kirby Terrell [Boston: Twayne Publishers, 1979]), 125–168.

21. James Fenimore Cooper, too, was sometimes called an 'American Scott.' Part of the transmission of literary inheritance is the conferral of symbolic genealogies. On this point, see Jane Spencer, *Literary Relations: Kinship and the Canon* (Oxford University Press, 2005).

22. Abbotsford, in turn, can be thought of as Walter Scott's version of Horace Walpole's Strawberry Hill. My aim is not to privilege Scott as Irving's 'original,' but rather to show that an American writer could learn quotation from a British master of the art.

23. Adam W. Sweeting, *Reading Houses and Building Books: Andrew Jackson Downing and the Architecture of Popular Antebellum Literature, 1835–1855* (Hanover: University Press of New England, 1996), 137.

24. Ibid., 135.

25. I was first alerted to the existence of this painting by Alison Booth.

26. Robert E. Spiller, *The American in England During the First Half Century of Independence* (New York: Henry Holt, 1926), 285.

27. The literati were deeply involved; at the cemetery's dedication, Emerson spoke and Channing recited an original poem.

17
Harriet Beecher Stowe and Florida Tourism

Diane Roberts

Before Cinderella's Castle, there was Mrs. Stowe's Cottage. A hundred years before Disney World, Duval County boasted one of nineteenth-century Florida's premier tourist attractions, conveniently located on a bluff above the St. Johns River. In the 1870s and 1880s, punters paid 75 cents to board the *Mary Draper* or some other steamer out of Jacksonville, 'guaranteeing' them a good gander at her orange groves and a glimpse of America's most famous writer in her chair under the great oak tree which had been built into their veranda, reading or composing or perhaps watching the great blue herons wading in the shallows. Less orderly visitors – often New England fans of *Uncle Tom's Cabin* – would invade her gardens and groves and, as Harriet Beecher Stowe's son tells it, 'pick flowers, peer into the house through the windows and doors, and act with that disregard of all the proprieties of life which character-ises ill-bred people when on a journey'.[1]

Stowe herself was at once notorious and celebrated, the scourge of the South come to live amongst ex-Confederates who had declared undy-ing enmity for her and ex-slaves who had been the beneficiaries (or the victims) of her magisterial novel. Her move south to what had been, in 1860, the fastest-growing slave state in the nation, made good copy. New York and Boston periodicals publicised Stowe's winter retreat; Florida steamboat companies, hotels and other businesses directed at Northern travellers advertised her presence. Stowe advertised herself as a new Floridian, wearing orange blossom in her hair; she publicised citrus from her orchards, shipping it in crates stamped 'Oranges from Harriet Beecher Stowe, Mandarin, Florida.' She wrote boosterish dis-patches for Northern periodicals touting the beauty, warm weather, and economic opportunities of the St. Johns country, trying to lure visi-tors down from their cold cities in the hope that they would decide to relocate to Florida. Indeed, Stowe, the 'little lady who made the great war,' also 'invented the Florida tourist industry,' as historian and journalist Jeff Klinkenberg puts it.[2] She became the grandmother of Florida attractions from the mermaids of Weeki Wachee Springs to the talking Mouse of the Magic Kingdom, the largely unacknowledged genetrix of Florida's four billion dollar tourist economy.[3] During the seventeen years she spent at Mandarin, Stowe's house was a destination; she was an attraction. Yet she was also an instigator, selling Florida as a place that would fulfil the dreams and fantasies of Northerners ready to soak up the sun down in the chastised, seductive, transgressive South. For Stowe, Florida was not just a retreat, it was a political project: using tourism as a catalyst for colonisation which would, in turn, cleanse the old Confederate states of their racism.

It didn't work. Slavery was replaced by sharecropping, Jim Crow, poll taxes and vigilante enforcement of segregation. It took a hundred years beyond Appomattox before African Americans were accorded civil rights under the law and even longer before society in Florida caught up with the United States Constitution.[4] Stowe left Mandarin in 1884. A series of disastrous freezes had decimated the orange crop, her husband was dead and she was suffering from dementia. Her son Charley Stowe was supposed to be taking care of the groves, but he wasn't really interested and let the whole property slide into disrepair. Mandarin, the village she put on the map, has been subsumed into the city of Jacksonville, the groves are suburbs, and there's not so much as a brick or a board left of Stowe's cracker cottage. It was pulled down in 1902, the fittings and lumber given away to anyone who wanted them. Mary Graff reported in that in the 1950s around Mandarin 'Many Negro cabins were embellished with decorative trimmings from the Stowe cottage.'[5]

There had been one attempt to restore the house and recover Stowe as a tourist attraction. In the late 1930s, a couple called Nicholl opened the Stowe Lodge, a restaurant, in a rebuilt house next to the famous oak tree. The place survived long enough to appear on some postcards and souvenir plates of Jacksonville, but the venture failed during World War II – gas rationing made it hard for customers to drive there.

These days few traces of Stowe's Mandarin sojourn remain. The Mandarin Museum has some relics and old photographs of the Stowes on their porch, though the sinking of the *Maple Leaf*, a paddlewheeler-turned-Union supply ship torpedoed in the St. Johns in 1864, gets more exhibition space. The Mandarin Community Club boasts a modern (and splendidly romanticised) portrait of her, wearing a claret coloured dress. Outside, there's a 'Harriet Beecher Stowe Garden' with some of the crops and ornamental plants she writes about in *Palmetto Leaves,* her 1873 paean to the St. Johns country. Recently the Community Club hosted a 'Stowe impersonator,' University of Florida Victorian literature student Lindsay Schwieterman. She appears in period costume and performs a monologue based on Stowe's writings for a few faithful pilgrims and schoolchildren whose teachers have bussed them in.[6]

The Florida homes of later writers Marjorie Kinnan Rawlings, Zora Neale Hurston, and Ernest Hemingway remain bona fide tourist draws. Cross Creek, immortalised in Rawlings' *The Yearling* (1938) and other books, is now a state park. The town of Eatonville, Hurston's birthplace and setting of much of her 1937 novel *Their Eyes Were Watching God,* holds a festival in her honour every summer. Key West puts on 'Hemingway Days,' commemorating 'Papa's' twelve-year sojourn on Whitehead Street. There's a look-alike pageant and a 'Bad Hemingway' prose contest. All year round visitors queue up to pay $12 to get into Hemingway's elegantly crumbling antebellum house and its tropical gardens, permanently festooned with six-toed cats.[7]

Perhaps all this would have happened anyway; perhaps Florida would have become a place of admission-charging cultural monuments, roadside reptile farms, theme parks, wildlife preserves, freak shows, resorts and beaches no matter what. But I don't think it unreasonable to connect Harriet Beecher Stowe's dogged promotion of Florida as an antidote to the frigid North, a flowery, damp Eden in which the world might yet be reinvented for the better, with the Florida the state tourist board still sells today. Stowe did not invent the paradisal image of Florida; William Bartram beat her to it by a hundred years, calling Florida 'Elysium,' depicting it in his 1773 *Travels* as a 'blissful garden,' a 'blessed unviolated spot of Earth.' In 1513, Juan Ponce de Leon, credited as the first European to explore the peninsula, was so taken by the spring blossoms, he named it after the festival of Easter flowers, 'Pascua Florida'.[8] Nevertheless, her representation of Florida's salutary warmth, beauty, fecundity and sheer amusement value, reached many thousands of Americans who'd never heard of the Spanish conquistador or the English botanist. Stowe sold Florida as the locus of pleasure to a nation weary of war, sectionalism and guilt.

Uncle Tom's Cabin, Harriet Beecher Stowe's mighty jeremiad, was the publishing phenomenon of the nineteenth century. Only the Bible could beat it for market coverage and saturation: appropriate since Stowe often suggested that God had written the novel through her. In any case, *Uncle Tom* changed the world. Serialised in *The National Era* in 1851, and brought out as a two-volume novel in 1852, it made Stowe an international superstar, mobbed on her European book tour and feted by the rich and powerful. She was important enough to be insulted by Matthew Arnold as 'a Gorgon' and dismissed as a 'religious middle-class person,' and to be taken up by the Duchess of Sutherland and Lady Byron.[9]

The only place Stowe and her bestseller were not officially celebrated was the American South, including Florida. *Uncle Tom's Cabin* was widely reviewed by Southern newspapers and journals and just as widely reviled. Pro-slavery commentators accused Stowe of being a 'Cincinnati schoolmistress' with a dirty mind, a free love-touting New England radical who had never spent time in the South and consequently didn't know what she was talking about.[10] Louisa McCord, like Arnold, attacked Stowe on class grounds, disdaining 'Mrs. Stowe's store-clerk brother' and assuming, with great distaste, that Stowe must have 'associated much with negroes, mulattoes and abolitionists.' Stowe was called 'masculine,' 'deformed;' an anonymous writer in *the Southern Literary Messenger* charged that Stowe was 'instigated by the devil'.[11]

It was not easy to get hold of a copy of *Uncle Tom* in the slave states. A bookseller in Mobile, Alabama who had the temerity to stock the novel was run out of town and his shop torched. Various state legislators declared that should Harriet Beecher Stowe ever show her face below Mr. Mason's and Mr. Dixon's line, she should be arrested for sedition.[12] Nevertheless, the planter class read *Uncle Tom's Cabin,* some of them obsessively. The South Carolinian diarist Mary Boykin Chesnut recorded her constant readings of it during the American Civil War, as if to crack some sort of mystifying code. Susan Bradford Eppes of Pine Hill Plantation in Florida notes in her journal that a family friend gave her father a copy of the novel. He read it then threw it on the fire: 'I wanted to read that book myself, but it must have been a bad book for Father, who loves books, to have treated it in that way.'[13]

The planter class understood that abolitionist fiction, from its titillating beginnings in the Tragic Mulatta novels of the 1830s to *Uncle Tom's* devastating critique not merely of the South but of American democracy, was a powerful challenge to their hegemony, an existential attack. Obviously, the best way to fight a good anti-slavery story was with a good pro-slavery story. Beginning in 1852, 'answers' to Stowe sprung up like dandelions. They had titles such as *Aunt Phillis' Cabin, North and South, or, Slavery As It Is, The Sword and Distaff* and *The Planter's Northern Bride.*[14] None came close to selling like *Uncle Tom.* Even popular pro-slavery writers such as William Gilmore Simms found that his South Carolina romances, with their graceful heroines, knightly heroes, grand estates and loyal servants, could not win the argument when faced with Stowe's cruel belles, sexual menace, hellish plantations and desperate human chattel. Refusing to concede defeat, Southern apologists wrangled with Stowe well into the twentieth century: Margaret Mitchell considered *Gone With the Wind* (1936) to be, amongst other things, a 'refutation' of *Uncle Tom's Cabin*.[15]

Yet only two years after the end of the bloodiest, most devastating, bitterest war in American history, the South's *bête noir* went to live in the South. She put, as it were, her money where her text was. Stowe did not regard the burnt-out, bankrupt, defeated South as deserving of God's terrible swift sword or the vintage of the grapes of wrath, as it says in the 'Battle Hymn of the Republic.' She did not descend on the exhausted Old Confederacy in triumph. Quite the contrary, as befitted a member of America's most famous clerical family, she was on a mission.

Stowe's son Frederick was wounded at Gettysburg in 1863 and had been suffering from depression and alcoholism ever since. Stowe decided he needed something to do and someplace nice and warm in which to do it. Postbellum Florida looked like a good idea. In 1864, her brother James Beecher had been stationed with the Union Army in 'the American Italy,' the St. Johns River country, and gave a positive report of it. Invalids' handbooks of the time declared Florida a positive tonic for the sick, with its pine forests exhaling 'delicious terebinthine odours' which 'not only purify the atmosphere but impart a healing, soothing, and peculiarly invigorating quality.'[16] In 1865, she rented Laurel Grove, a plantation across the river from Mandarin, and sent Frederick down to plant cotton. Things did not go well. The rain came at the wrong time. His first two hundred acres were eaten by worms. Stowe had invested $10,000 in the venture, and Laurel Grove's total yield in 1866 was two bales of cotton.[17] Early in 1867 Stowe decided to come see the place herself. Arriving with a load of furnishings and 'treats' to make the house more comfortable, she swiftly developed a new business plan, not only for Laurel Grove but for Florida and eventually the whole of the South.

The irony inherent in Harriet Beecher Stowe's living at a plantation – indeed, since former slaves still worked the cotton fields, colluding in the remnants of the very system she argued so passionately against – hardly needs underlining. Moreover, the history of Laurel Grove was as lurid as anything Stowe had concocted for *Uncle Tom's Cabin*. The proprietor had once been Zephaniah Kingsley, a big-time Florida slave trader and landowner, a strange hybrid of Simon Legree and Augustine St. Clair. While Florida was still under Spanish rule, he had 'married' one of his slaves, a thirteen-year-old Senegalese named Anna Madgigaine Jai.

Kingsley owned a huge house on Fort George Island and kept a string of slave women in establishments of their own nearby, following the French *plaçage* system, yet he also bequeathed property to Anna and their children when he died. Stowe would have surely been put in mind of her own wronged or endangered slave women, Eliza, Emmeline or the cultivated *plaçee* Cassy, who eventually gets the better of the monstrous Legree by 'haunting' him to near madness.

Nonetheless, Stowe loved the place. She declared that the moment she arrived in Florida she felt 'quite young and frisky'.[18] Moreover, she was convinced the South was progressing. She wrote to her brother, the Reverend Charles Beecher, that she wished to establish 'a line of churches' in East Florida to educate ignorant whites and blacks equally. Plus they would inculcate socially progressive religion. She told her Beecher siblings she intended to 'found a colony' in Florida; she would alter the retrograde culture of the South by exposing it to the bracing intellectual and moral rigor of New England egalitarianism.[19] By 1868, Stowe had decided that Florida was not just a good spiritual investment but a good financial investment, too. She asked her husband to send her $5000. She had found a bargain, thirty acres of orange groves at Mandarin on the St. Johns River and wanted to buy it fast since she had noticed that property prices, even in the wreckage of the South, were rising. Writing to George Eliot in the late 1860s, Stowe casts Mandarin as some sort of Thoreauvian Eden, Walden in the sub-tropics:

> I found a hut built close to a great live-oak 25 feet in girth...we threw out a wide veranda all around, for in these regions the veranda is the living room of the house. Ours had to be built around the trunk of the tree, so that our cottage has a peculiar air, and seems as if it were half tree or something that has grown out of the tree.[20]

Stowe did not originate the idea of colonising the South in order to cleanse it of its racist sins. As revealed by John T. Foster, Jr. and Sarah Whitmer Foster in their excellent history *Beechers, Stowes and Yankee Strangers*, Harrison Reed of Massachusetts, who became governor of Florida under the Reconstruction regime in 1868, presided over a soft invasion of Yankee social reformers. He actually created a new cabinet post, Commissioner of Immigration, to attract right-thinking Northern compatriots to the state. Chloe Merrick, who eventually married Reed, arrived in Florida from New York as a volunteer in the National Freedman's Relief Association. She founded an integrated orphanage in Fernandina, north of Jacksonville on the Atlantic. Another Northern pilgrim, the Reverend John Swaim, worked tirelessly to promote Florida as a new and promising frontier, singing the praises of warm winters, cheap land and the chance to raise a benighted populace.[21]

Swaim was the master theorist of reforming Florida through tourism. He maintained ties with newspapers such as the Newark *Sentinel of Freedom* and others back in New Jersey, encouraging them to come to the 'New South.' Trinity Methodist, his church in Jacksonville, was situated near the city's most posh hotel. Visitors to East Florida in the late 1860s were mostly involved in federal Reconstruction work or invalids hoping that heat would cure them, but if they ventured to Sunday services, chances were good that they'd be evangelised to take trips down the St. Johns or Oklawaha rivers then invest in land nearby. When former Florida Governor David Shelby Walker commented bitterly that he'd rather be with his comrades in their 'honourable graves' than living under the Reconstruction's 'oppressive government' (in which landowning whites like Walker were disenfranchised), Swaim essentially said *good riddance*: 'The best way and the only way to fix those fellows is to settle 'em out – settle 'em out! Come Kansas and Nebraska over them.'[22]

The idea was to overwhelm recalcitrant Southern partisans with right-thinking New Englanders so that within a generation the plantation mentality would be wiped out. The advent of Harriet Beecher Stowe was a boon to the promotion of Florida. Indeed, she was an enthusiastic participant in Swaim's project. She wrote to one potential investor: 'We are very anxious for New England men to come amongst us. Ours is a sort of colony where six or eight young men have come in and are trying experiments in agriculture.'[23]

Reed and Swaim were the brains behind this ideological colonisation, but Stowe soon eclipsed them. They were mere political figures; Stowe was a mega-star. Though hated by most of the old slaveholding classes, she had tried to be fair to the South in *Uncle Tom*, casting a New Englander as the chief villain and depicting Tom's old Kentucky plantation home as a rose-covered ideal. For her part, Stowe knew she had a responsibility to the South, having helped create the national will to force it to give up slavery and change its undemocratic and unchristian ways. She was particularly committed to bettering the lives of former slaves: 'My heart is with that poor people whose cause in words I have tried to plead, and who now, ignorant and docile, are just in that formative stage in which whoever seizes has them.'[24]

The Beechers and the Stowes were sophisticated propagandists, though they occasionally had their own public relations difficulties.

The Reverend Charles Beecher originally came to Florida with Harriet to recover his mental and physical health after three of his children died within one year (his son was killed out west, two daughters drowned in a boating accident). As if that weren't bad enough, he had been put on trial by his denomination for heresy: he dabbled in Transcendentalism and Spiritualism and believed that souls had multiple existences. Within a few months of arriving, he had bought a little house at Newport, south of Tallahassee, the state capital, and joined Gov. Harrison Reed's administration as education chief. In 1870, Stowe herself landed at the centre of a scandal over her book *Lady Byron Vindicated*, a polemic in defence of the widow of the notorious poet, who charged him with abuse, viciousness and incest with his half-sister Augusta.

John T. Foster and Sarah Whitmer Foster suggest that the outcry over *Lady Byron* (Stowe was accused of putting before the public the 'disgusting secrets' of a certifiably Great Man) caused her to downplay her connection to the rich and famous and advocate 'colonising' Florida more subtly than she otherwise might have done.[25] In any case, Stowe backed off full-scale lobbying of rich Yankees and began to write sketches of Florida life for *The Christian Union*, a newspaper owned by her brother, the Reverend Henry Ward Beecher, later notorious as the villain in a nasty divorce case. Her pieces on the glories of magnolias, the beauty of the Oklawaha and St. Johns rivers, what to grow in Florida and how to buy land there, became enormously influential. *Palmetto Leaves*, the 1872 collected volume, proved to be a signally important intervention in the re-imagining of Florida as a place where the fondest dreams of shivering Northerners would come true, a gold-plated tourist destination.

Stowe had not, however, reckoned on being a tourist destination herself; at least, not at first. But the furnishings had hardly been moved into the gabled house before she, and it, became the highlight of any Florida tour. Articles about her new Southern home (often called a 'plantation') appeared in the Northern press: the Newark *Sentinel of Freedom* featured Mandarin in 1873. A Southern railroad company commissioned Georgia poet Sidney Lanier to write an enticing 'Handbook and Guide' to the area its trains passed through. Boating down the St. Johns River, Lanier describes the place of pilgrimage rather more coolly than most. He was, after all, a former Confederate soldier:

On the left is Mandarin, a small but long-settled village. Here, in the early Indian wars, occurred a dreadful massacre. It is now most noted as the residence of Mrs. Harriet Beecher Stowe. Her house is a brown cottage, near the shore, nearly obscured by foliage. It is not nearly so imposing as her tree ....[26]

Edward King's large and handsome picture book, *The Southern States of North America* (1874), a compilation of articles written for *Scribner's Magazine* in the early 1870s, features an elaborate frontispiece of the Oklawaha River as described in *Palmetto Leaves*, complete with the Florida signifiers of alligator, Spanish moss, swamp and exotic birds. *The Southern States* also features an illustration of Mandarin, capturing its odd combination of gothic and gingerbread, with a tiny, engraved Harriet Beecher Stowe on the porch. He chooses to be annoyed on her behalf, sniffing that she is 'besieged by hundreds of visitors who do not seem to understand she is not an exhibition'.[27]

Of course Stowe *was* an exhibition, and she knew it. Rumours that the Stowes got a cut of the profits from steamship tours or even charged passengers embarking at their wharf 25 cents to enter their gardens, remain persistent but unsubstantiated. Nonetheless, the Stowes did not protest when steamer companies out of Jacksonville advertised day trips to Mandarin to see the 'famous authoress.' A brochure from the late 1870s for the DeBary-Baya Merchants' Line advertises Mandarin as one of its 'sights' and includes the by-now familiar engraving of the Stowe house and its enormous oak tree. C.E. Stowe and Lyman Beecher Stowe deny that their mother profited in any way: 'An enterprising steamboat company in Jacksonville advertised excursions to Mandarin and Mrs. Stowe's orange grove – so much for the round trip – without consulting her or offering her consideration of any sort for being made a public spectacle.'[28] Charles Edward Stowe recounts how his father became 'distracted by these migratory bipeds' when:

one of them broke a branch from an orange tree directly before his eyes, and was bearing it off in triumph with all its load of golden fruit [and] he leaped from his chair, and addressed the astonished individual on those fundamental principles of common honesty, which he deemed outraged by this act. The address was vigorous and truthful, but of a kind which will not bear repeating. 'Why,' said the horror-stricken culprit, 'I thought this was Mrs. Stowe's place!' 'You thought it was Mrs. Stowe's place!' Then, in a voice of thunder, 'I would have you understand, sir, that I am the proprietor and protector of Mrs. Stowe and of this place, and if you commit any more such shameful depredations I will have you punished as you deserve!' Thus this predatory Yankee was taught to realize there is a God in Israel.[29]

The Stowes had become real Floridians, sounding just like residents of contemporary Orlando or Miami, constantly complaining about pushy tourists. The Stowes had also become savvy about their own value as ambassadors for a renewed South. They didn't put up fences. They did not fall back on some caste or class system, which would have been associated with the plantation South. They appealed to higher morality. The 'Yankee' tourist in this case got away with his oranges. And many more followed him to Florida: not just to visit but to set up businesses and buy properties. By 1873, 50,000 visitors were coming to East Florida alone; the permanent population in 1865 was around 45,000; fifteen years later it had nearly tripled.[30]

By now, it will have occurred to the reader that the woman many white Southerners blamed for the Civil War and its devastating aftermath got a curiously easy ride in the land of the Lost Cause. White Southerners from the land-owning classes, defeated and disenfranchised but still possessed of a strong sense of grievance and pride, did not bother to object to Stowe, lording it over her own mini-plantation. It's not that there was no resistance to 'Black Republican' rule in Florida. Harrison Reed's gubernatorial term was hampered by fights between opportunistic capitalist Republicans and social reformist Republicans. Moreover, the old Bourbon aristocracy still wielded considerable local power as enablers of domestic terrorism. Recalcitrant Confederates joined the Ku Klux Klan and the so-called Young Men's Democratic Club, and regularly harassed freed slaves and Northerners who had come South to teach or preach. In the area around Mandarin, John Dickison, an ex-Confederate officer turned vigilante, threatened any black person who dared to try to vote.[31] Billing himself as the Swamp Fox of Florida (after Francis Marion, the South Carolina guerilla of the American Revolution), Dickison and his gang did their best to disrupt Reconstruction.

So why didn't Stowe have to put up with Night Riders, crosses burning on her lawn, or at least a rotten tomato or two tossed her way? Certainly, Stowe was not 'received' by ladies of the old plantation elite. The Broward family of East Florida, a land-owning tribe fallen on hard times after the War, do not refer to Stowe in their letters, even though she lived in their midst. Others of their kind continued to harbour deep resentment of *Uncle Tom's Cabin*.

Yet Stowe was mobbed by well-wishers when she toured Southern cities. In Tallahassee, a plantation centre, Florida's capital and locus of Lost Cause piety, she was cheered by blacks and whites alike at the railroad station and honoured at a reception. The Florida Archives have a photograph of her with various dignitaries taken on the steps of the capitol: the very place from which slaves had once been sold, the very spot from which Florida's secession from the Union had been declared in 1861. Perhaps Stowe was simply too famous. In nineteenth-century America, as now, celebrity provided a kind of impermeable shield. Stowe was the brightest literary star the nation had to offer, hotter than Mark Twain, hotter than William Dean Howells, hotter than Whitman. It's clear a substantial number of formerly pro-Confederate white Floridians had decided to be proud of the world famous author who had chosen to live in their state. One finessed the vexed question of *Uncle Tom* thus:

> I am sure I have been told that Mrs. Stowe is sorry she wrote *Uncle Tom's Cabin*. She is a good, kind-hearted woman, and I believe she would have cut off her right hand rather than write that book if she could have foreseen all the misery she was to cause by it.[32]

Perhaps white Floridians chose to be magnanimous because of the way Stowe depicted Florida as a form of Paradise, only with fewer rules. Perhaps they were prescient, somehow intuiting that a few years after Stowe became a tourist attraction at Mandarin, Gilded Age moguls such as Henry Plant and Henry Flagler would transform Florida from a great, wet wilderness to a chic destination for the nouveau riche.

Again, Stowe was not the innovator, not the first to 'Edenize' Florida. The eighteenth-century naturalist William Bartram had described Florida as 'a glorious apartment in the sovereign palace of the Creator'.[33] But, using her unmatched celebrity, she publicised the beauties of the place in her book *Palmetto Leaves*, praising the luxury of flowers in January, declaring 'the yellow jessamine itself, in its wild grace, its violet-scented breath, its profuse abundance, is more than a substitute for the anemones of Italy.' And, twenty years before Henry Flagler opened his grand hotels in St. Augustine, she laid the groundwork for him, describing the old city as like being in Europe but without the bother of an Atlantic crossing:

> Here you see the shovel-hats and black gowns of priests; the convent, with gliding figures of nuns; and in the narrow, crooked streets

meet dark-browed people with great Spanish eyes and coal-black hair. The current of life here has the indolent, dreamy stillness that characterized life in Old Spain.[34]

It is not an enormous leap in sensibility from Stowe's romantic Florida to Disney's Magic Kingdom, with its ersatz 'international pavilions' (like being in Old Spain or Old England or Old France without the irritations of actually being on another continent) and well-groomed nature to boot. Stowe invoked wood spirits and bountiful harvests; now Florida offers Tinkerbell and all-you-can-eat buffets. She even prefigured Florida's eco-tourism industry with her many injunctions against bird- and alligator-shooting and her lush encomium to the Oklawaha: 'long, swaying draperies of gray moss interpose everywhere their wavering outlines and pearl tints amid the brightness and bloom of the forest, giving to its deep recesses the mystery of grottoes hung with fanciful vegetable stalactites.' When disobliging people such as the doctor who published a newspaper account of Florida as malarial, colder than advertised and 'nine-tenths water and the other tenth swamp,' she sprang to the state's defence, insisting that you could get malaria in New York City and besides, 'we never pretended that Florida was the Kingdom of Heaven or the land where they shall no more say, "I am sick" '.[35]

Stowe's move to Florida in 1867 follows the pattern of the majority of Florida's population today: come as a tourist for a short, 'therapeutic' visit, end up buying property and staying. Indeed, the publicity around her move to the state suggested the possibility of making a new life in the 'New South' for thousands. They came, armed with a little capital and a copy of *Palmetto Leaves*. Many, like the 'Yankee strangers' who flooded into Florida in the 1870s and 1880s, intended to better the place but ended up lulled out of their ambitions . It was cheap and charming down South, not like the 'real life' of the urbanising, industrialising North.

The punchline here (if that is the right word) is that Stowe's social revolution stalled when she was herself seduced by the warmth and high standard of living (if you were white and well-off) of Southern life. Florida offered no snow to shovel, no chilblains to soothe. There were neighbours such as Governor Reed's very rich sister Martha Reed Mitchell, always generous with their hospitality; and black servants could be had for cheap. Edward King warned his readers: 'This is the South – slumbrous, voluptuous, round and graceful. Here beauty peeps from every door-yard. Mere existence is a pleasure; exertion is a bore.'[36]

By the late 1870s, Stowe's reformist activities had slowed to a near halt. She was getting older, true, but life at Mandarin was just too pleasant to expend energy on protest. Following the disputed – probably stolen – presidential election of 1876, in which Florida played a major role (what happened in 2000 was hardly unprecedented), federal troops withdrew from the South. White Southerners called this 'Redemption,' and proceeded to legislate neo-slavery under the guise of Jim Crow laws and poll taxes. Lynching increased; night riders harassed blacks who dared register to vote. The tourists kept coming, oblivious. And Stowe, who had exposed the racial fault-line in American democracy so powerfully, seemed oblivious as well. In 1877, she wrote that 'Florida is all serene in politics as in nature'.[37] The sweet air of Mandarin, promising pleasure and ease, had done its work. Florida thrived, but it would be nearly another hundred years before Uncle Tom's children would attain full citizenship.

Notes

1. Charles Edward Stowe, *The Life of Harriet Beecher Stowe, Compiled from Her Letters and Journals* (New York: Houghton Mifflin, 1890), 277.
2. Jeff Klinkenberg, 'Mrs. Stowe's Florida,' *St. Petersburg Times*, 19 November 2006, sec. B1.
3. Abraham Lincoln was supposed to have said this to Stowe when he met her, but the story is probably apocryphal. See Joan D. Hedrick, *Harriet Beecher Stowe: A Life* (Oxford University Press, 1994), 232ff. Tourism revenue figures are based on 2005–2006 figures published by the State of Florida.
4. There are those who would argue Florida was still mired in Jim Crow all the way into the twenty-first century, what with the corrupt voting systems of 2000 which famously disenfranchised so many African American voters. See Jeffrey Toobin, *Too Close to Call* (New York: Random House, 2001).
5. Mary B. Graff, *Mandarin on the St. Johns* (Gainesville: University Press of Florida, 1953), 143.
6. June Weltman, 'UF Student Brings Author Harriet Beecher Stowe to Life,' *Mandarin Sun*, 24 January 2008, sec. B4.
7. See Anne E. Rowe, *The Idea of Florida in the American Literary Imagination* (Gainesville: University Press of Florida, 1993), 92–112.
8. William Bartram, *Travels*, ed. Mark Van Doren (New York: Dover, 1928), 78, 90.
9. H. Milford ed., *The Letters of Matthew Arnold* (Oxford University Press, 1932), Arnold to A.H. Clough, 2 March 1853, 197.
10. Hedrick, 232 ff.
11. Louisa McCord, 'Review of *Uncle Tom's Cabin*,' *Southern Literary Quarterly* 23 (Jan. 1853), 83. 'Review of *Uncle Tom's Cabin*,' *Southern Literary Messenger*, March 1853, 22.
12. Diane Roberts, *The Myth of Aunt Jemima* (London: Routledge, 1994), ch. 2.

13. C. Vann Woodward ed., *Mary Chesnut's Civil War* (New Haven: Yale University Press, 1981), 314. Susan Bradford Eppes, *Through Some Eventful Years* (Georgia: J.W. Burke, 1926), 101.
14. Mary E. Eastman, *Aunt Phillis' Cabin* (Philadelphia: Lippincott, 1852); Caroline Rush, *North and South* (Philadelphia: Crissy and Markley, 1854); William Gilmore Simms, *The Sword and the Distaff* (Philadelphia: Lippincott, 1853); and Caroline Lee Hentz, *The Planter's Northern Bride* (Philadelphia: T.B. Peterson & Bros, 1854). See Roberts, 55ff. on pro-slavery responses to Stowe.
15. Gerald Wood, 'From *The Clansman* and *Birth of a Nation* to *Gone With the Wind*: The Loss of American Innocence,' in Darden Asbury Pyron, ed., *Recasting: Gone With the Wind in American Culture* (Gainesville: University Press of Florida, 1983), 134.
16. *Appleton's Illustrated Hand-Book of American Winter Resorts for Tourists and Invalids* (n.p.: New York, 1891), 17.
17. John T. Foster, Jr. and Sarah Whitmer Foster, *Beechers, Stowes and Yankee Strangers* (Gainesville: University Press of Florida, 1999), 46ff.
18. Hedrick, 330.
19. Hedrick, (letter to Charles Beecher, 29 May 1867) 340–41.
20. Quoted in C.E. Stowe and Lyman Beecher Stowe, *Harriet Beecher Stowe: The Story of Her Life* (New York, 1911), 221.
21. Foster and Foster, 40–59. I am indebted to their work throughout this essay.
22. Ibid., 57.
23. Ibid., 48–9.
24. Harriet Beecher Stowe, *Palmetto Leaves*, ed. Mary B. Graff (Gainesville: University Press of Florida, 1999), x.
25. Foster and Foster, 51.
26. Sidney Lanier, *Florida: Its Scenery, Climate and History with an Account of Charleston, Savannah, Augusta, Aiken and a Chapter for Consumptives* (Philadelphia: Lippincott, 1875), 122.
27. Foster and Foster, 98; Edward King, *The Southern States of North America* (Harper: New York, 1874), 385–6.
28. C.E. Stowe and Lyman Beecher Stowe, 234–40.
29. Ibid., 277–8.
30. Raymond A. Mohl and Gary R. Mormino, 'The Big Change in the Sunshine State: A Social History of Modern Florida,' and Jerrell H. Shofner, 'Reconstruction and Renewal, 1865–1877' in Michael Gannon ed., *The New History of Florida* (Gainesville: University Press of Florida, 1996), 418–46; 249–65.
31. Diane Roberts, *Dream State* (Florida: University of Florida Press, 2004), 137.
32. C.E. Stowe and Lyman Beecher Stowe, 234.
33. Bartram, 15.
34. Stowe, *Palmetto Leaves*, 16, 100, 213.
35. Stowe, *Palmetto Leaves*, 249, 120.
36. King, 9.
37. Foster and Foster, 108.

18

On the Trail of Rider Haggard in South Africa

Lindy Stiebel

This paper has as its focus the recent development of the Rider Haggard literary trail, a trail dedicated to this nineteenth-century British writer's time in South Africa spent intermittently over the years 1875 to 1916. The concept of the literary trail is a recent one in South Africa and may in a sense be seen as encouraging a kind of 'new literacy' in the postcolonial world generally, but particularly so in a developing country such as South Africa. As Mike Robinson has written on this score:

> Indeed, literary tourism is now part of a 'new' literacy. As tourists, the public now access and encounter writers and their works through guided tours, literary museums, heritage centres, festivals, theme parks, hotels with literary allusions, and a vast range of related merchandise. In these popular arenas of literary encounter, new audiences for creative writings are being forged, arguably reflecting new ways of storytelling and a shift, not back to the oral traditions whose passing was mourned by Benjamin and Ong, but forward to a genesis of multi-media, hyper-sensory 'traditions.'[1]

Considered thus, it is worthwhile to conjecture how a Victorian writer such as Rider Haggard, a product of a different age and different country, can nevertheless be made to speak to new audiences in challenging ways. The development of the Rider Haggard self-guided trail can be considered as part of such a drive to speak afresh to a new age. But before I turn to the Rider Haggard trail proper, I will briefly consider the concept of the literary trail, secondly, describe the context within which this trail was developed; and then proceed to describe the Haggard trail in some detail.

Literary trails as pilgrimage

Literary pilgrimages, understood loosely as journeys of homage, were from their inception literary trails. To follow a literary trail is to link one-self to the writer by seeing the same places s/he saw, or to recapture a moment from the book, to 'find' oneself perhaps by reconnecting with an early childhood reading experience. The literary trail can link specific sites such as the writer's birthplace or home with whole areas created by the writer or linked to the writer's life. For the literary pilgrim, it can therefore usefully join the biographical and the fictional. Viewing the private spaces of writers conceived as the literal origins of a text – the home, the study, the chair, the bed, the clothes – presented as 'authenti-cally' as possible, so as 'to convey the 'atmosphere' in which the writer lived'[2] is combined with the experience of standing overlooking a view that was central to the writer whose book describing the same scene you hold in your hand. The trail additionally offers a way of accessing and making sense of geographic areas described within books as 'set-ting' or whole areas which become identified with a writer – such as Wordsworth's Lake District, or the Yorkshire moors of the Brontës, or L.M. Montgomery's Prince Edward Island. William Faulkner's Yoknapatawa county and Thomas Hardy's Wessex have the additional complication of being fictional areas, yet based on known locations in their home lands of Mississippi and Dorset respectively. In such cases literary pilgrims have the double task of superimposing the fictional versions both in name and altered locations onto the real landscape they visit. South Africa has its own examples of literary 'worlds' or extended settings, including Herman Charles Bosman's Groot Marico district, Richard Rive's District Six in Cape Town, the Sophiatown of the *Drum* writers' era (though neither District Six or Sophiatown survived the Group Areas Act of the apartheid era) and Soweto in Johannesburg. Though no literary trails exist as yet in these areas, the potential exists to identify spaces linked to writers who have written about these places. Identifying such links is all part of the potential of a 'new literacy'.

Constructing literary trails in KwaZulu-Natal

The three trails that have been constructed thus far – featuring Rider Haggard, Alan Paton and writers of the Grey Street area in Durban – have all been developed under the auspices of the Literary Tourism in KwaZulu-Natal research project funded by the National Research Foundation. This is a five year project started in 2002 which is part of an umbrella niche research area entitled 'Constructions of identity through cultural and heritage tourism.' The bulk of the project funding has been earmarked for student bursaries, whilst the rest has gone towards constructing resources to foster literary tourism: notably a Literary Map of KwaZulu-Natal featuring fifty writers linked to the province (see www.literature.kzn.org), a website hosting academic papers drawn from workshops held by the project (see www.literarytourism. co.za), documentary films made of selected writers, and guides to literary trails which can be downloaded from the website.

KwaZulu-Natal is a particularly rich province culturally speaking, offering a wide range of writers both black and white, male and female, writing in English and Zulu predominantly – Alan Paton, Roy Campbell, Mazisi Kunene, Ronnie Govender, Gcina Mhlophe, Daphne Rooke to name but a few. Efforts by scholars to encourage literary tourism in this area inevitably lead one to the development of a research agenda. Within the Literary Tourism in KwaZulu-Natal project this has a threefold purpose involving, firstly, the creation of a literary archive of local writers both past and present; secondly, the recording of selected writers and their works on film, and thirdly, the establishment for locals and visitors alike of routes which bring together writers and the places about which they write – effectively producing a literary map of the region. Such a research agenda carries with it complex questions: how to define a 'local' writer? how to understand the uses a writer makes of place? who should be featured and why? what is the interface between literary tourist and writer? How do the issues of authenticity and commodification make themselves evident in literary tourism? These issues I have addressed elsewhere.[3] Suffice it to say here, however, that these issues also arise in relation to the construction of the literary trails made by the project to which I will now turn.

Before looking at the trails in any detail, three issues need consideration. The first to consider is the choice of subject: why, for example, create a Rider Haggard trail, an Alan Paton Pietermaritzburg trail and a Grey Street writers' trail which are the three trails the project has seen fit to develop thus far? The reason for choosing to produce trails on Haggard and Paton was primarily the tourist potential of these two writers given their close links with particular KwaZulu-Natal places. Paton is one of South Africa's best known writers following his success with his classic novel *Cry, the Beloved Country* (1948). Rider Haggard's popularity in his day as a bestselling writer of exotic African romances has continued into the present – *King Solomon's Mines* (1885) has never been out of print and today in the academic world postcolonial scholarship on Haggard is thriving (see Chrisman 2001, 2003, Monsman 2006). His links to the Anglo-Zulu battlefields of Isandlwana and Rorke's Drift – which feature in his novels *The Witch's Head* (1884), *Black Heart and White Heart* (1896) and *Finished* (1917) – both important sites for cultural tourism in KwaZulu-Natal, allow for 'spill-over' tourism, as opposed perhaps to dedicated literary pilgrims' visits. A few, disconnected efforts by tour operators (some poorly informed) to capitalise on 'Haggard links' also meant there were already some existing sites which could be authentically linked together. That there has been in the past interest in visiting 'Haggard's South Africa' expressed by the Rider Haggard Society in England also contributed to the initiative to construct this literary pilgrimage. Expertise was also available to compile trails for these two writers: the Haggard trail was constructed by myself and Stephen Coan both of whom had published a book on Haggard in Africa;[4] whilst the Paton Pietermaritzburg trail was compiled by Jewel Koopman of the Alan Paton Centre and Struggle Archive based at the University of KwaZulu-Natal Pietermaritzburg campus.

The Grey Street Writers trail, recently completed and launched under the direction of Niall McNulty, research assistant to the project, is the first to feature an area common to a number of published writers both during and after the apartheid era. Reasons for choosing to do a trail on this area speak to the project's desire not only to promote 'standalone' writers but to foster awareness of less well known local writers. The Grey Street area already has a tourist presence in terms of various 'cultural' tours which visit its markets and mosque. It seemed very possible that existing tourists would be interested in the literary trail as an additional feature. The Haggard and Paton trails would attract literary pilgrims who already know and respond to these writers' works; by contrast the Grey Street trail hopes to develop a literary interest in lesser known writers.

The second issue to consider is the constructed nature of these trails, true of all literary trails. In effect, with this trail we have created a narrative of our own which gives a circularity and neatness to Haggard's time in KwaZulu-Natal, a continuity to Paton's life in Pietermaritzburg, and a linkage between writers' lives in Grey Street, which is not strictly true of the actuality of these assembled lives and their trajectories. The trails create a sequence designed to be in the interest of the tourist who is taken on a more or less convenient circular route around the province, city and area respectively, stopping off at places with a 'Haggard link,' or a 'Paton link' or a 'Grey Street writers link.'

The third issue is to do with the dangers of exoticising such trails. Stephen Robins, in a paper on how city sites in the Western Cape have been commodified and marketed to tourists, describes how 'urban planners use tradition to privilege the 'exotic' rather than the more recent and very traumatic events in the country's history. Tradition is placed in a safe past that can be made into 'heritage;' it operates as escape and as containment.'[5] This is certainly true of the way certain sites in KwaZulu-Natal, and indeed the whole province, are marketed as the 'Kingdom of the Zulu' with nostalgic overtones of a glorious warrior-like past familiar to Rider Haggard readers, which completely masks the current impoverished reality of the majority of the province's population. The establishment and marketing of literary trails needs to be sensitively done – where the trails lead to communities, caution needs to be exercised against the tendency to exoticise a 'traditional' past in an effort to paper over the cracks of the past and present.

What, in summary, would the literary pilgrim find on each of these trails? Each trail begins with a short biographical note about the writer or the area to be visited. Then the would-be tourist is taken through a series of places to visit connected to the writer/s with short quotations from relevant texts accompanying the places. A map and photographs illustrate the pamphlet and contact details are provided for the various stops along the way. All three trails developed thus far are designed to be self-guided, though potential exists to train guides to add to the visitor's experience, and feed back into the community.

The Rider Haggard literary trail

The trail pamphlet starts with a short biographical note situating Haggard in South Africa. In summary you can read that Haggard visited South Africa three times on British government business. Most notably, he spent a long time in KwaZulu-Natal on his first visit to South Africa from 1875 to 1881. During this first visit, Haggard stayed in Durban and Pietermaritzburg where he met Theophilus Shepstone, Secretary for Native Affairs, who became his friend and mentor. It is this period that provided the information and inspiration for his subsequent bestseller 'African' texts (such as *King Solomon's Mines* (1885), *She* (1886), *Alan Quatermain* (1887) and *Nada the Lily* (1892)). However, lesser known details about Haggard's life – such as his meeting in 1914 on the occasion of his second visit with John Dube, first president of the African National Congress, and their discussion of the plight of the Zulus – provide another angle on this writer famous for his adventure stories set in a romanticised African landscape. Haggard at this time was part of the Royal Dominions Commission touring Australia, New

Zealand and South Africa. His third and last visit to South Africa was undertaken as part of a tour to investigate the possible settlement of servicemen overseas at the end of the First World War.

The trail starts in Durban, the port town and obvious beginning for Haggard arriving by sea in 1875, for modern tourists arriving by air, or Durban locals keen to try this out. We dispel the myth of the Rider Haggard house on the Berea beloved of estate agents (he did not own property in Durban) and point out it was Allan Quatermain, Haggard's fictional hero, who was said to keep a house on the Berea. From this starting point the route leads to Pietermaritzburg, the administrative capital of the region in 1875 where Haggard, as an employee of Sir Henry Bulwer, stayed at Government House (now part of UNISA). The location footage for the 1937 film version of *King Solomon's Mines* starring Paul Robeson was shot at Otto's Bluff just outside Pietermaritzburg. (As we note, the stars did not come to South Africa and stand-ins were used.)

From there we proceed to Estcourt where one of several pairs of Sheba's breasts can be seen – we use the word 'allegedly' to indicate doubt on this issue – and then on to Fort Durnford where in the Museum there is a photograph of Haggard. The caption incorrectly states he once lived in Albert Street. Newcastle is a natural night stopover as Haggard's farmhouse Hilldrop is maintained as a B&B establishment displaying Haggard memorabilia. This house is now renamed Mooifontein, referring to Haggard's novel *Jess* (1887), and was a place of marital happiness as it was here that his only son Jock was born.

> It was a delightful spot. At the back of the stead was the steep boulder-strewn face of the flat-topped hill that curved round on each side, embosoming a great slope of green, in the lap of which the house was placed.[6]

From the homestead, Haggard could hear the battle of Majuba being fought and it was in this house that the peace terms of the First Anglo-Boer War were negotiated and signed, the house having been rented from the Haggards for this purpose. Fort Amiel Museum on the outskirts of Newcastle has a Haggard display, including an axe that belonged to Mhlophekazi, a Zulu warrior who was the inspiration for the fierce character Umslopagaas in Haggard's fiction.

The next day sees the traveller moving on to the battlefield of Isandlwana, featured in some of Haggard's novels and a popular tourist attraction in its own right. At Isandlwana, Haggard was awed – as are visitors today, by the 'strange, abrupt, lion-like mount,' and he recorded walking the battlefield as the sun was setting in his diary entry of 27 April 1914:

> It was sad for me to stand by the piles of stones which cover all that is left of so many whom I once knew: Durnford and Pulleine and many other officers of the 24th, George Shepstone and the rest...
>
> When I had gone some way I turned and looked back at this lonesome, formidable hill standing there, a fit monument for the multitude of dead; immemorially ancient, stern and grand.[7]

The stop at Mkuze where Tshaneni or Ghost Mountain, featured in *Nada the Lily*, is found, highlights the constructed nature of the trail plus the power of the creative imagination – as powerful as Haggard's description of the mountain and surrounding terrain is, he never actually visited the area. The local hotel Ghost Mountain Inn will not be pleased to have this pointed out as they make much of the association with Haggard as a visitor to the region, whereas here, in fact, is an example of a writer creating an environment in his mind, presumably reconstructed from accounts he had heard during his young adult days in Natal. He only visited Zululand at all in 1914, some years after writing his novels about the area. The good news for this hotel, however, is that it makes a good overnight stop on the route, with the third day bringing the constructed loop to a close in Durban, via Eshowe – featured in *Finished*, the final volume of his Zulu trilogy.

We have, as I point out above, been at pains in the information gathered for this trail to correct popular misconceptions. If one of the aims of literary tourism in South Africa is to foster a 'new literacy' for a new generation of readers, then it is important that the information gathered and disseminated is accurate. With a nineteenth-century writer like Rider Haggard – so remote in time from today and one so linked to an imperialist ideology in reputation – it is particularly important to provide a nuanced and well-informed view. The importance of Rider Haggard today in South Africa as a literary figure is that he provides an opportunity not only to understand (and unpack) the enduring 'image of Africa' his books created – the now obsolete sun-drenched British schoolboys' playground – but also to explore his unexpected opinions on the plight of the Zulus, expressed forcefully to Gladstone after his little-known meeting with John Dube. Haggard speculated thus after this meeting during which they discussed the Native Land Act:

> Seven million of black folk, I think that is about the number including the population of the protectorates, cannot be permanently

neglected (or is oppressed the word?) by one million and a quarter whites. Compressed steam will escape somehow and somewhere. Probably, as Mr Dube says, it will not be by way of war unless a great national leader should arise or the discordant should be tied together by some new faith such as Mohamedanism. The effects of moral pressure exercised by a sullen and discontented multitude robbed of their inheritance are perhaps more to be dreaded.[8]

Prescient words indeed and ones that give the contemporary reader pause, so removed do they seem from the superficially jingoist mood of his African fiction. In the twenty-first century in South Africa, this is the side of Rider Haggard that would be interesting for contemporary tourists engaging with the 'new South Africa', in addition to what they have historically expected of Haggard, the creator of far-fetched adventure stories.

The reception thus far of the Haggard trail from the public has been positive. One newspaper noted that: 'Following the Rider Haggard trail is a fantastic alternative approach to exploring the province and its history.'[9] Such a response substantiates Robinson and Andersen's earlier claim that literary tourism can foster a 'new literacy' – certainly for this reviewer, a 'new history' is opened up. All of the places mentioned in the trail above are not primarily known for their literary connections with Haggard – part of the aim of such a trail is to raise awareness in visitors that such cultural links exist, to offer new ways of seeing familiar places.

Conclusion

But how about widening the subject beyond the dead white male category, especially in twenty-first century South Africa? This is where 'constructing' trails becomes especially significant because part of a trailmaker's brief in KZN might be to foster a tourism interest where one doesn't seem 'obviously' to reside, as previously mentioned: instead of working on 'famous' standalone writers who are few and far between, and inevitably so given that in South Africa during apartheid those who had access to educational and publishing opportunities were few, how about selecting an area where a number of linked (or not) writers might have lived, live or write about? This was the motivation behind the construction of the Grey Street trail. Featuring writers such as Aziz Hassim (*Lotus People*), Dr Goonam (*Coolie Doctor*), Phyllis Naidoo (*Footprints in Grey Street*) and Imraan Coovadia (*The Wedding*), this trail is a walkabout in an area once a hotbed of political dissent during the apartheid years.

Grey Street is tied to the history of the Indian population in Durban. First brought to South Africa by the British in the 1860s to work the sugarcane fields, the Indian population in Durban is now the largest in sub-Saharan Africa. The most famous Indian immigrant to Durban was the young lawyer Mahatma Gandhi who arrived in 1893 and worked for 21 years in Natal. Grey Street exists today as the old Indian business and residential area of Durban and the cultural heart of the KwaZulu-Natal Indian community.

And what of future literary trails? Other areas in KwaZulu-Natal with literary trail potential, in that they are linked to writers and/or their writing, include Inanda, which already has an existing cultural heritage trail for tourists but could make more of the writing of John Dube, Credo Mutwa, and Mewa Ramgobin, and even of Mahatma Gandhi, given the heritage site of Gandhi's original printing press en route; Pietermaritzburg, which, besides the Paton trail, could feature Bessie Head's birthplace, places linked to Tom Sharpe, James McClure and the Dhlomo brothers, HIE and RRR, born nearby; whilst similar links could be made in 'Cato Manor' area for writers like Ronnie Govender, Mi Hlatswayo and Kessie Govender – again a museum of Cato Manor has been established in the area which provides a general historical background for the tourist; if not specifically literary pilgrim.

But this is all in a future which may or may not come to pass. It is readers with enough enthusiasm for writers whose works they enjoy who remain the driving force, the potential literary pilgrims. The work of the Literary Tourism in KwaZulu-Natal project, with its linked writer/ place website, documentary films, student projects and now its first trails might be seen as a step in the direction of such a 'new' literacy with its next generation of literary consumers who might wish one day to visit places because of what someone once wrote about them. In an effort, therefore, to encourage a broad awareness of this province's plethora of writers amongst the reading population, the project offers – as William Kent wrote in his early *London for the Literary Pilgrim* (1949) – 'material for incense at many shrines.'[10]

Notes

1. Mike Robinson and Hans Christian Andersen, eds., *Literature and Tourism: Essays in the Reading and Writing of Tourism* (London: Thomson, 2003), 73.
2. David Herbert, ed., *Heritage, Tourism and Society* (London: Picador, 1995), 13. Authenticity is vital in making the tourist experience worthwhile – the reason people leave their homes to tour is, according to Fawcett and Cormack, to find recreation and leisure, but also to search for 'authenticity…something

that is not adequately provided in the experiences of everyday life.' Clare Fawcett and Patricia Cormack, 'Guarding Authenticity at Literary Tourism Sites,' *Annals of Tourism Research* 28 (3) 2001: 687–8.

3. Lindy Stiebel, 'Hitting the Hotspots: Literary Tourism as a Research Field with Particular Reference to KZN, South Africa,' *Critical Arts* 18 (2) 2004.

4. See Stephen Coan, ed., *Diary of an African Journey: the Return of Rider Haggard* (Scottsville: University of Natal Press, 2000); and Lindy Stiebel, *Imagining Africa: Landscape in the African Romances of H Rider Haggard* (Westport, CT: Greenwood Press, 2001).

5. Steven Robins, 'City Sites,' in Sarah Nuttall and Cheryl-Ann Michael, eds., *Senses of Culture: South African Culture Studies* (Oxford University Press, 2000), 405.

6. Rider Haggard, *Jess* (London: Smith, Elder and Co., [1887] 1900), 22.

7. Rider Haggard, *Diary of an African Journey*, 203.

8. Ibid., 230.

9. *Gateway to KwaZulu-Natal*, April 2006, 8.

10. William Kent, *London for the Literary Pilgrim* (London: Rockliff, 1949), 10.

Index

Abbotsford, *see* Scott, Sir Walter
Ackroyd, Peter, 165
Adamson, Archibald, *Rambles through the Land of Burns*, 38, 39, 41, 42, 45
Addison, Joseph, 185
Ainslie, Hew, *A Pilgrimage to the land of Burns, and Poems*, 39
Alcott, Bronson, 70
   grave (Concord, Mass.), 193
Alcott, Louisa May
   grave (Concord, Mass.), 193
   Little Women, 146
Allbutt, Robert, *London Rambles 'en Zig-Zag' with Charles Dickens*, 141–3, 148
Alloway, *see* Burns, Robert
American tourists, 146–8, 175–83, 184–94
   see also Brown, Cooper, Emerson, Greenwood, Hawthorne (Nathaniel), Hawthorne (Sophia), Irving, James, Sedgwick, Stowe, Twain
Andersen, Hans Christian, 217
Andersen, J.A., *A Dane's Excursions in Britain*, 65
Anderson, Alexander, *In Rome. A Poem in Sonnets*, 31
Anderson, Benedict, 134
Angellier, Auguste, 37
Aretino, Pietro, 18
Ariosto, Lodovico, 18, 112
Arnold, Matthew, 134, 199
Atkinson, William, 64
Austen, Jane
   house (Chawton), 11n
   Mansfield Park, 146, 147
Austin, Alfred, 'At Shelley's Grave', 32–3
Avery, Simon, 98

Bachelard, Gaston, *The Poetics of Space*, 87
Baedeker, Karl, 107, 108, 109, 116
Bann, Stephen, 4, 71n
Barnes, Julian, 24n
Barnes, William, 164–5
Barrie, J.M., 120, 165
   home (Kirriemuir), 124, 125
Barry, Charles, 75, 81
Barry, Edward, 75–6, 78, 79, 81
Barthes, Roland, 4
Bartram, William, 198, 206
Bate, Jonathan, 101
Baudrillard, Jean, 4
Baumgarten, Murray, 11n
Beecher, Charles, 200, 203
Beecher, Henry Ward, 203
Beecher, James, 200
Bender, Barbara, 26
Benjamin, Walter, 4, 88, 210
Besant, Walter
   house (Frognal End), 124
Bettey, J.H., 167
Black, Adam and Charles
   guidebooks, 107–8
Blanchard, Leman, *Life and Literary Remains of L.E.L.*, 53, 57–8
Blatchford, Robert, *Merrie England*, 99
Blessington, Lady, 53, 59
Blore, Edward, 64
Blind, Karl, 98
Blind, Mathilde, 9, 96, 121–2
   'The Avon', 97
   'Evensong (Holy Trinity Church)', 97
   'Shakespeare', 97
   'Shakespeare Sonnets', 96–9
Blunden, Edmund, 164, 165, 166, 167, 170, 171, 172
Blyton, Emma, *To the Memory of Keats*, 30–1
Boccaccio, Giovanni, 18
Bookman, The, 9, 119–26

221